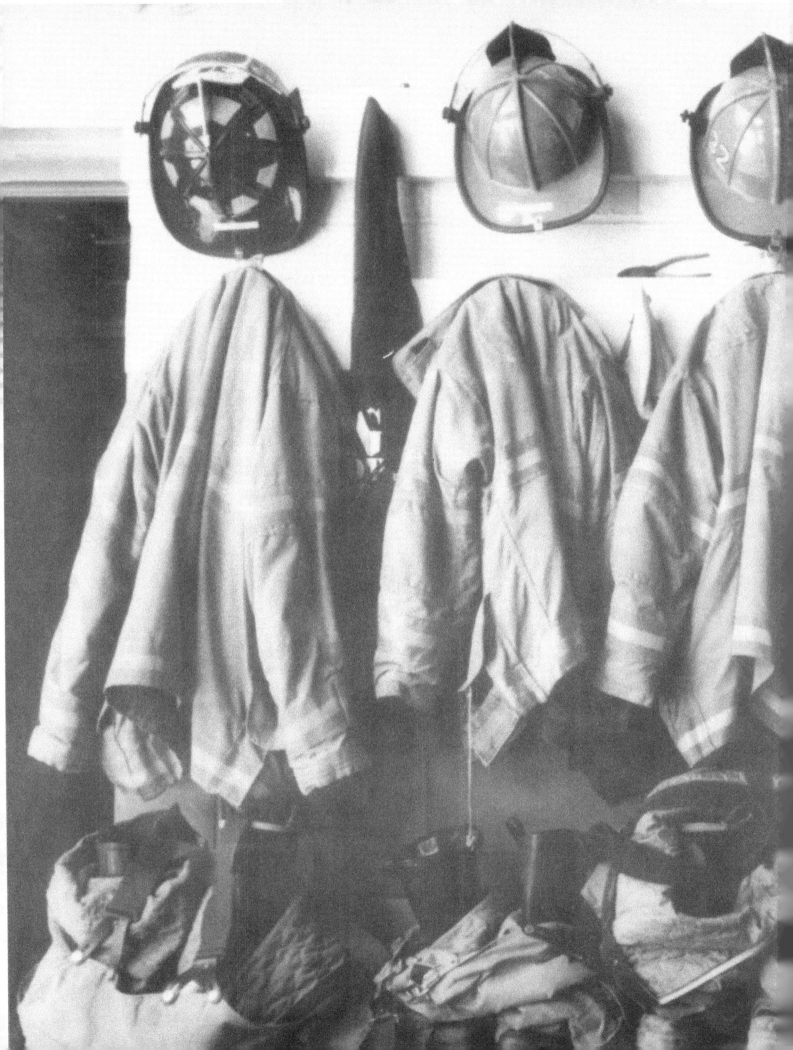

BALTIMORE COUNTY FIRE SERVICE

Millennium Edition

TURNER PUBLISHING COMPANY

TURNER PUBLISHING COMPANY

Turner Publishing Company Staff:
Publishing Consultant: Keith R. Steele
Designer: Peter Zuniga

Library of Congress Control No.
2001091495

ISBN: 978-1-68162-427-3

Additional copies may be purchased directly from the
publisher. Limited Edition.

Special thanks to Bernie Salgonik, *Pro Tech Images*
and Jay Sonntag

TABLE of CONTENTS

C.A. Dutch Ruppersberger
Baltimore County Executive

Executive Office
400 Washington Avenue
Towson, Maryland 21204
410-887-2450
Fax: 410-887-4049

A MESSAGE ...
FROM THE COUNTY EXECUTIVE

It is a distinct pleasure to offer my sincere and wholehearted congratulations to the dedicated and loyal members of the Baltimore County Fire Service. You are frontline providers of one of county government's most critical services and you perform your challenging duties with utmost dignity and professionalism.

You have chosen a noble task that demands exceptional courage, integrity and dedication, and you have chosen to serve with one of the finest fire services in the country. The Baltimore County Fire Service has earned a national reputation for excellence because of the relationship between career and volunteer members, and for the superior work you do everyday in striving to protect the lives and property of area citizens.

Under the capable leadership of John Hohman, Fire Chief, and Craig Coleman, President of the Baltimore County Volunteer Firemen's Association, the Baltimore County Fire Service has made great strides to move into a new century with updated equipment and personnel changes that reflect the demographics of the county. In making these changes, you have held strong to the mission of serving county citizens to the best of your ability.

As you turn the pages of this "Millennium Yearbook," you can reflect upon your past accomplishments and be proud of your contributions as a team in improving the quality of life in our county. I wish you the best for continued success in the years to come.

Sincerely,

C.A. Dutch Ruppersberger

C.A. Dutch Ruppersberger
County Executive

Baltimore County
Fire Department

700 East Joppa Road
Towson, Maryland 21286-5500
410-887-4500

A MESSAGE...
FROM JOHN J. HOHMAN, CHIEF

It is an extreme honor to serve as Chief of the Baltimore County Fire Service. This department, which has both career and volunteer members working together as a team, is one of the most unique fire services in the country.

As we move into the new millennium, the men and women in this department have an opportunity to use some of the most advanced fire technology available. The training each of you receives qualifies the Baltimore County Fire Service as one of the best in the nation, and we can all take pride in the work we do for the citizens of the county.

I am most proud of the fact that this agency does more than just "put out fires." Our Emergency Medical Services Division is an intergal part of our Department. Our proactive efforts in the areas of safety education help the citizens of this community, young and old, learn the techniques to prevent fire in their home and on the job. The safety inspections we conduct for businesses provide a safe atmosphere for people on the job, and in places such as in day care centers, restaurants, and shopping malls.

This yearbook takes a look at our past, our present, and the men and women who devote their lives to the fire service. I look forward to our continued work toward community safety.

John J. Hohman, Chief
Baltimore County Fire Service

 Census 2000 For You, For Baltimore County Census 2000

 Printed with Soybean Ink on Recycled Paper

Come visit the County's Website at **www.co.ba.md.us**

6

**THE
BALTIMORE COUNTY
VOLUNTEER
FIREMEN'S ASSOCIATION**
Public Safety Building
700 East Joppa Road
Towson, MD 21286-5500
Phone: (410) 887-4885
Fax: (410) 887-4852
www.bcvfa.org

MEMBER COMPANIES

*Arbutus Volunteer Fire Co.
Arcadia Volunteer Fire Co.
Boring Volunteer Fire Co.
Bowley's Quarters Vol. Fire Co.
Box 234 Association
Butler Volunteer Fire Co.
Central Alarmers Association
Chestnut Ridge Volunteer. Fire Co.
Cockeysville Volunteer Fire Co.
Cowenton Volunteer Fire Co.
English Consul Volunteer Fire Co.
Glyndon Volunteer Fire Co.
Hereford Volunteer EMS/Rescue Co.
Hereford Volunteer Fire Co.
Hyde Park Volunteer Fire Co.
Jacksonville Volunteer Fire Co.
Kingsville Volunteer Fire Co.
Lansdowne Volunteer Fire Co.
Liberty Road Volunteer Fire Co.
Long Green Volunteer Fire Co.
Lutherville Volunteer Fire Co.
Maryland Line Volunteer Fire Co.
Middleborough Volunteer Fire Co.
Middle River Volunteer Fire Co.
Middle River Vol. Res. Ambulance Co.
North Point-Edgemere Vol. Fire Co.
Owings Mills Volunteer Fire Co.
Pikesville Volunteer Fire Co.
Providence Volunteer Fire Co.
Reisterstown Volunteer Fire Co.
Rockaway Beach Volunteer Fire Co.
Rosedale Volunteer Fire Co.
Violetville Volunteer Fire Co.
Wise Avenue Volunteer Fire Co.
Woodlawn Volunteer Fire Co.*

AFFILIATIONS

MEMBER

L to R: Vice President-Administration Elwood Banister, Retired Fire Chief of Baltimore County; Vice President Finance John W. McClean, Vice President, Patapsco Bank; Joel C. McCrea, relationship Manager, Maryland Department of Business and Economic Development: President Craig E. Coleman, Educational Specialist, Maryland Institute for Emergency Medical Services Systems Vice President-Operations, Garrett D. Zour,Supervisor, Baltimore County Department of Public Works; Robert Frank, Field Engineer, Kodak Polychrome Graphics; Susan Coroneos, Comptroller, Townsend Capitol, Inc.

The three thousand men and women who staff our thirty-five volunteer fire, rescue, emergency medical service and rehabilitation service companies are as diverse as the population of Baltimore County, coming from all walks in life. We have doctors, lawyers, teachers, bankers, craftsmen and laborers. A suprising number earn their living in the emergency services, as career firefighters or EMS providers, in Baltimore County as well as in surrounding jurisdictions. The officers of our Association reflect this diversity. Without pay we give the citizens of Baltimore County the benefit of our time, energy and skill, for all are truly volunteers. I am proud to serve as their president.

Craig E. Coleman
President

Guardian Knights

P.O. Box 26553
Baltimore, MD 21207

e-mail: gkiabpff@yahoo.com

January 9, 2001

To members, former members, and friends of the Baltimore County Fire Department:

The Guardian Knights are pleased to participate in the production of this yearbook. Not since *Hands, Horses and Engines,* Baltimore County Fire Service Centennial Committee 1982, has there been a published documentation of Baltimore County's Bravest. We are encouraged by the contrast in content between the Centennial document and this "Millennial" document. It is our hope that when future generations of firefighters look at this book, they will draw inspiration and pride from the melange of race and gender documented in these pages.

Sincerely,

James Artis Jr.
President

Photographed left to right: Zachary Stith, Patrick Taylor, Lorryn Clayton, Dana Camak and James Artis Jr.

Baltimore County Maryland Chapter of the International Association of Black Professional Firefighters
Visit us on the web at www.geocities.com/gkiabpff

BALTIMORE COUNTY PROFESSIONAL FIRE FIGHTERS ASSOCIATION
LOCAL 1311
BY & FOR PROFESSIONAL FIRE FIGHTERS

AFFILIATIONS:
International Association of Fire Fighters, AFL-CIO
Metropolitan Baltimore Council of Unions
Maryland State & DC AFL-CIO
Maryland State & DC Professional Fire Fighters

CHARTERED SEPTEMBER 10, 1958

MICHAEL K. DAY, SR., President
JAMES L. KINARD, Secretary-Treasurer
MICHAEL D. CROSBY, 1st Vice President
JOHN F. QUIRK, 2nd Vice President
STEPHEN T. GISRIEL, 3rd Vice President

The Baltimore County Professional Fire Fighters Association, established in 1958, is an affiliate of the **International Association of Fire Fighters**. With over 960 Active Members, and over 350 Active-Retired members, Local 1311 stands proud over its tradition of working on behalf of the men and women who serve the citizens of Baltimore County as Career Fire Fighters, Paramedics, Officers, and Emergency Medical Providers.

Our motto is, **"We're There Because We Care**." Throughout the years we have consistently proven that fact by supporting the Fire Department in its public relations endeavors, and further by organizing and funding our own outreach programs to the residents and employees of this fine County.

Local 1311's **Victims Assistance Committee** provides 24/7 support from a team of individuals who, while off duty, respond to domestic fires and disaster scenes to offer assistance. To help the victims handle the next 24-48 hours, the VAC team provides direction, guidance, and certificates for clothes, food, and even toys for the children.

Did you know that 75% of fire-related deaths are due to fire gases? Since 1990 Local 1311 has distributed thousands of **smoke detectors** free of charge to Baltimore County residents in need.

Local 1311 initiated the **Fire Prevention Poster Contest** held annually in Baltimore County, and remains a primary sponsor of this well-received educational program for children.

Also for children, Local 1311 provides educational materials throughout Baltimore County's Elementary Schools for **Fire Prevention Week** in the Fall, and **EMS Week** in the Spring. We encourage children and their families to establish EDITH (**Exit Drills In The Home**), and teach them about fire safety and prevention techniques.

Traditionally, Local 1311 is the largest single sponsor of the **After-the-Prom** program which keeps High School graduates safe while still providing a memorable and fun activity to celebrate this milestone in their lives and education.

And not just Baltimore County! In response to the tragic events of September 11, 2001, our membership and the community we serve joined forces to raise over $350,000 for the IAFF's **New York Fire Fighters 9-11 Disaster Relief Fund**.

Further, we support many charities of special interest to those serving in the fire prevention and medical services fields. Over the past ten years, our Association and its members have contributed well over $600,000 to **Muscular Dystrophy**, and over $200,000 to **Burn Research and Care**. We have also made very generous donations to **Big Brothers**, the **American Heart Association, Shock Trauma of Maryland**, the **American Cancer Society, Cerebral Palsy**, and an array of other worthwhile charities.

Shown in the **picture**, from left to right, are members of the Baltimore County Professional Fire Fighters Association Executive Board: 1st Sgt Chuck Evans, Sec-Treasurer Jim Kinard, 1st Trustee Ross Mickle, 2nd Rec. Secretary Dan Brinkley, 1st Rec. Secretary Ted Moffitt, 1st Vice President Mike Crosby, 2nd Trustee Jack Freeland, 3rd Vice President Steve Gisriel, 2nd Sergeant Al Euler, and President Michael K. Day, Sr. Not photographed: 2nd Vice President John Quirk, Trustee Pat Henderson

Baltimore County Professional Fire Fighters Association • 52 Scott Adam Road, Cockeysville, MD 21030-3282 • 410-683-1311 • Fax 410-666-0156 •32

John J. Hohman
Fire Chief

Mark E. Weir Sr.
Assistant Chief

Harold C. Cohen
Division Chief

A. Danelle England-Dansicker
Division Chief

Mark F. Hubbard
Division Chief

Jonathan G. Kuruc
Division Chief

David J. Murphy
Division Chief

Lawrence N. D'Elia III
Battalion Chief

James E. Devers
Battalion Chief

Mark J. Ewers
Battalion Chief

Joseph J. Fannon Jr.
Battalion Chief

Bruce C. Kesting
Battalion Chief

Stephen G. Lancaster
Battalion Chief

Paul S. Leverton
Battalion Chief

Steven R. Miller
Battalion Chief

William D. Purcell
Battalion Chief

Michael Robinson
Battalion Chief

Charles E. Watkins
Battalion Chief

Ameen I. Ramzy, M.D.
Medical Director

Janet T. Johnson
Executive Officer

John C. Parham
Fair Practices Administrator

Craig E. Coleman
President

James Doran
Administrator

V. LaVern Pearce
Office Coordinator

VOLUNTEER STAFF

Joel C. McCrea
Sr. Vice President

Elwood H. Banister
Vice President, Administration

John W. McClean
Vice President, Finance

Gary Zour
Vice President, Operations

Robert L. Frank
Secretary

Susan Coroneos
Treasurer

BALTIMORE COUNTY FIRE DEPARTMENT
MOTTO STATEMENT

PRIDE
PROFESSIONALISM
RESOURCEFULNESS
INTEGRITY
DEDICATION
EDUCATION

MISSION STATEMENT

"THE MISSION OF THE BALTIMORE COUNTY FIRE DEPARTMENT IS TO PROVIDE THE HIGHEST QUALITY PROTECTION, EMERGENCY MEDICAL SERVICES, FIRE PREVENTION, SAFETY EDUCATION, COMMUNITY SERVICE, AND MITIGATION OF EMERGENCY AND NON-EMERGENCY INCIDENTS TO THE CITIZENS OF AND VISITORS TO BALTIMORE COUNTY.

OUR SERVICE DELIVERY IS ENHANCED THROUGH TRAINING, EDUCATION, PLANNING, AND TEAMWORK. WE WILL SAFELY ACHIEVE OUR MISSION WHILE REMAINING ECONOMICALLY RESPONSIBLE THROUGH THE EFFECTIVE AND EFFICIENT USE OF ALL RESOURCES."

Anthony P. Orban
1935-1939, 1951-1959

Winfield H. Wineholt
1959-1968

J. Austin Deitz
1968-1975

Paul H. Reincke
1975-1990, 1996-1997

Elwood H.Banister
1990-1994

James H. Barnes
1994-1995 (Interim)

Allen A. Thomason
1995-1996

John F. O'Neill
1997-2000

John J. Hohman
2000-present

Fire Investigation Division

Fire Dispatch

Fire Marshal's Office

L to R- Sarah Fosbrink, Field operation office coordinator; John Parham, Fair practices administration; V. LaVern Pearce, Volunteer Association office coordinator; Michele Wilkinson, Records custodian; 3rd floor.

Fire Rescue Academy Staff

Fire Specialist, Don Adams Community Awareness and Safety Education

Captain Jerry Pfeifer, Field Operation

Emergency Medical Services

Management Information Services

Community Awareness and Safety Education. FF/EMT Wendall C. Whittle, Donna Welsh, FS Donald Adams, Capt. Glenn A. Blackwell.

Jim Doran, Volunter Association Management Assistant

A.V. Services, Tricia Mudd and Kathy Bowman

Field Operations Administration

Administrative Services-Budget

Executive Staff. Standing L to R; Jennifer Werry Stewart, Sally Lysakoski, Lt. Charles Rogers, Janet Johnson. Seated L to R; Ellen O'Donnell, Charnetta Holman, Carole Muller.

Office of Emergency Preparedness

Payroll/Administrative Services

Volunteer Association

Fire Department Choir

First group of EMS Field Coordinators "In Service"

Gov. Parris Glendening and Capt. Bruce Conrad

Tom Rice, Truck 1 and Couth Carter, Truck 16

Demolition of the burn tower in Towson

Fire Safety House at the State Fair

Demolition of burn building in Towson

Fire Prevention Poster contest 2001

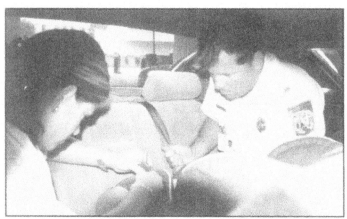

Child car seat installation

State Fair

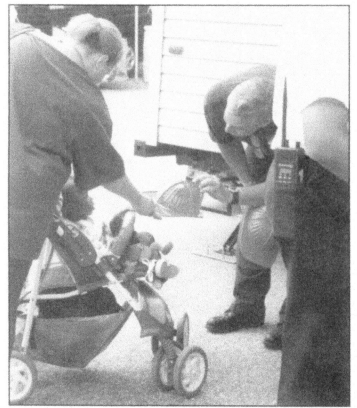

State Fair

Pulling the line

Putting a new medic into service, ribbon cutting

Hookup

Ground breaking for new Fire and Rescue Academy

L to R; FADO Michael Ruppert, T.C. Priester III, Steven Priester, Capt. T.C. Priester, Jr. at Dulaney Valley Fallen Heroes, May 99. Picture from Sun Paper.

Members of the Baltimore County Fire Service Who Died in the Line of Duty

Year of Death	Name	Affiliation
1928	Monroe Seitz	BCVFA
1933	John D. Kane	BCVFA
1933	Clarence Almony	BCVFA
1933	Ellwood Hicks	BCVFA
1940	S. Howard Miller	BCVFA
1941	Linwood P. Brookhart	BCFD
1951	Clyde Hedrick	BCVFA
1955	Carl S. Dill	BCFD
1955	William J.H. Miller	BCFD
1961	Clarence W. Belt	BCFD
1964	Joseph Smith	BCVFA
1965	Robert E. Thomas	BCVFA
1968	Raymond E. Otto	BCVFA
1970	Phillip E. Watts	BCVFA
1971	Milton R. DeSombre	BCVFA
1971	Charles E. Hopwood	BCVFA
1971	Douglas Mueller	BCVFA
1971	Warren E. Schaffer	BCVFA
1971	Glenn S. Meekins	BCFD
1973	Richard W. Ocheltree	BCFD
1974	Douglas L. Green	BCFD
1978	Ray W. Smith	BCFD
1979	Ira D. Jollymore	BCFD
1979	Charles T. Friedel	BCFD
1979	Joseph K. Ludwig	BCFD
1981	John W. Burch	BCVFA
1981	Thomas J. Levy	BCFD
1984	Walter J. Barowski	BCFD
1984	James A. Kimbel	BCFD
1984	Henry J. Rayner	BCFD
1988	Albert C. Howard	BCVFA
1990	Daniel J. Raskin	BCVFA
1992	Herbert B. Campbell	BCVFA
1997	Charles E. Weber Sr.	BCVFA
2000	Robert W. Humphrey	BCVFA

THE HISTORY OF THE

BALTIMORE COUNTY
FIRE SERVICE

Baltimore County is located in Central Maryland. It almost completely surrounds Baltimore City, borders Pennsylvania to the north and has 178 miles of shoreline on the Chesapeake Bay. Philadelphia is less than 100 miles northeast and Washington, DC is 35 miles southwest. Easy access to important national and world markets is provided as a result of good transportation networks, which include four interstate highways, a high-speed beltway, national roads, rail service, airports, and shipping facilities. Many businesses are attracted to the County because of this and the availability of a multi-skilled, flexible, stable work force with a strong work ethic. Many colleges, universities, and technical schools in the area provide a high concentration of professional/technical graduates for employment, and there is a large percentage of two-income households, which provides a thriving consumer market, attracting many large retail centers. Its proximity to Washington, DC makes it an ideal location for federal agencies, such as the Social Security Administration. Scattered throughout the county are high technology companies, industry and other research and development firms, like those in the Hunt Valley corridor.

Nearby cultural facilities, tourism centers, and recreational facilities (golf courses, tennis courts, horse racing tracks, state parks, camping, hiking and sailing facilities) are available to the more than 750,000 citizens who reside in urban and suburban communities or in rural farmland settings. There are no incorporated subdivisions in the 610 square miles of the county which is a charter-type government.

An elected County Executive and seven elected County Council members govern from offices in Towson, the county seat. Various county agencies are run by Department Heads appointed by the County Executive and confirmed by the County Council.

The Fire Department, founded in 1882, employs a Career service of uniformed and civilian personnel, two of whom are assigned to the administrative office of the Baltimore County Volunteer Firemen's Association. The Fire Service enjoys a symbiotic relationship with approximately 3,000 volunteer members who operate out of 33 separately incorporated stations and whose two rehab units render assistance at large scale incidents and at special ceremonies.

Quality emergency service is provided through the Career and Volunteer partnership, which has earned national acclaim for its effective cooperation and coordination. Excellence within the Department is achieved through proactive management in which training, prevention, education, and professional qualifications are emphasized.

Engine 1-1951 Mack, 750 GPM

1900: Volunteer fire companies are established at Sparrows Point with support from the Maryland Steel Company.

1901: A strong movement toward volunteer firefighters—reminiscent of the firefighters' clubs of Baltimore City in the 1830s—sweeps the county. A citizens' resolution that the paid department be abolished is considered by the Baltimore County commissioners, but ultimately dies.
The total budget of the Baltimore County Fire Department is $30,000, a figure that will be repeated in 1902 and 1903.

1902: The Landsdowne Volunteer Fire Association No. 1 is formed with twenty-five members. The Hamilton Volunteer Fire Department is established on Hamilton Avenue east of Harford Road. The latter will exist until 1919, when its location will be annexed by Baltimore City.

1903: The volunteers of the Pikesville fire company est. in 1897 pull their wagon to the Sudbrook Station, mount it on a flatcar, and take it to the fire that destroys the Glyndon Station.

1904: The Glyndon Volunteer Fire Department is formed.
Alert Volunteer Fire Company is incorporated at Belair Road and Spring Avenue.
A fire of undetermined origin destroys most of Baltimore City's business district. More than 1,500 buildings on forty acres are lost. A total of 771 firemen and thirty-three steam engines, from Howard, Harford, and Anne Arundel counties respond along with departments from as far away as Wilmington, York, Harrisburg, Atlantic City. Washington, D. C., and Philadelphia. Five Baltimore County fire companies are involved: Roland Park, Highlandtown, Sparrows Point, Relay, and St. Denis. The last company reaches the conflagration via the Baltimore & Ohio Railroad; the Sparrows Point company uses the trolley system.

1905: The Lauraville Volunteer Fire Company is formed by Samuel Imwold and his six sons, who constitute the entire original company. It will be absorbed into the Baltimore City Fire Department in 1919.
The county fire budget grows to $33,000.

1907: The Boring Volunteer Fire Company is organized. The Baltimore County Volunteer Firemen's Association is founded, with members from thirteen companies. John J. Lindsay is elected the association's first president.
A major fire seriously damages Baltimore Clay Company in Westport. A handsome hand-drawn hook and ladder truck is housed in the fire hall at 4th and E streets. In bad weather Maryland Steel Company stations a team of horses and driver to haul the hook and ladder in response to alarms.

1908: A fire causes a million dollars in damage at the Standard Oil Works in Canton.

1909: The Pikesville volunteer company established in 1897 votes to buy a chemical engine instead of "an automobile truck."
Violetville Volunteer Fire Company No. 1 is organized in

response to many fires in the area. Its very existence seems to quell fires: at one point its fire apparatus will not leave the firehouse for seventeen months.
The Parkville Volunteer Fire Department is started with a membership of seventeen.
The Lutherville Volunteer Fire Company is formed and purchases a horse-drawn hose and ladder truck from the Roland Park Fire Department.
The Baltimore County fire budget grows to $60,000 in part because of a firemens' pay raise from $50 to $55 a month.

1910: The Baltimore County Fire Department enters the motorized age with the purchase of a Webb-Thomas motorized pumping engine, painted bright green with gold-leaf decorations, for the Roland Park department.

1911: The county buys its second motorized pumper, an American LaFrance, and assigns it to Catonsville.
The new position of mechanician is created, first held by Philip G. Priester, who will go on to become fire marshal.

1912: After a misguided purchase of a commercial truck that was converted into a fire engine, Pikesville replaces it quickly with an American LaFrance engine. That engine will remain in service for twenty-five years and make a thousand calls.
The Arcadia Volunteer Fire Department is launched after the gift from the county commissioners of a horse-drawn engine. Local citizens take turns supplying horses for the Arcadia company.
A fierce fire destroys the Atlantic Transport and Storage Company at the foot of Clinton Street.
The Baltimore County Fire Department creates the position of district chief with special responsibility for the industrial section of the county east of the Baltimore City line. Industrial fires have become a large problem.
Gardenville and Arlington receive American LaFrance pumpers.
Roland Park is assigned a White Auto Company ladder truck.
A car is purchased for the use of the fire marshal.

1913: Reisterstown Volunteer Fire Company is started in reaction to several disastrous fires. Its first apparatus is a Challenge hand-pump equipped 280 feet of hose, ladders, axes, and eighteen rubber buckets, to be replaced a year later by a Packard truck with chemical tanks.
The county fire budget is $105,000.
A fire all but destroys the Union Abattoir Company of Claremont in the stockyards area southwest of the Baltimore City limit. The city department joins in fighting the fire and bills the county for $1,500 in costs. The county at first refuses to pay, then settles on $1,300. This results in a formal mutual aid pact between the city and county.
A decision is made to build a repair shop for motorized fire apparatus, to be located in Catonsville.
In what probably is the first medical call in the county. Ladder 12 of Roland Park responds to an alarm to find, not a fire, but a man who has fallen out of a tree. The

injured man is placed on the truck and taken to a physician's office.

1914: Lutherville buys, after elaborate fund-raising activity, a Federal motorized truck with ladders, a hose reel, and Howe fire pump.

1915: Vigilant Volunteer Fire Company of Essex is organized. Its first firehouse is a two-story frame building with a bell tower, erected at a cost of $2,500. Three years later the company will purchase a 1914 Bessemer motorized chassis and mount on it a hose wagon body, chemical tanks, a pump, fore hose, and a forty-foot ladder.

A contract is awarded to the Ahrens-Fox Engine Company for a triple-combination pumper. In a test it throws a one-and-three-quarter-inch stream of water two hundred feet vertically and three hundred feet horizontally at seven hundred gallons per minute. The engine is delivered to Mt. Winans.

1913: Cockeysville est. in 1896 acquires its first motor-driven engine, a 40-horsepower White with a 500-gallon pump and space for 500 feet of hose.

1916: The Baltimore County Volunteer Firemen's Association is incorporated under state law. The association has al-

ready been influential in legislative efforts, particularly in working for a volunteer firemen's pension law, in which Maryland leads the nation.

For unknown reasons (perhaps in part due to accounting changes), the county department's budget drops to $87,000.

1918: During World War I a proposal is made (according to historical records of the Glyndon department) to mount gun racks on fire engines.

The matter is dropped, doubtless for the good of all, considering the rivalries among companies.

1919: Despite fierce opposition from the county, Governor Emerson C. Harrington signs legislation by which Baltimore City annexes forty-six square miles of Baltimore County. The county fire department loses seventy-five percent of its manpower and apparatus. The fire companies of Mt. Washington, Arlington, Mt. Winans, Highlandtown, Gardenville, Govanstown, and Roland Park are lost in the annexation. The county's apparatus is reduced from eleven engines and one truck to three engines. The *Union News* denounces the "Prussians" of the city.

The county department begins to rebuild immediately. Two 750-gpm American LaFrance pumpers are purchased at a cost of $23,000 and assigned to the Towson and Catonsville stations.

The department's budget drops to $52,000.

1920: Stopgap operations are implemented, including adding paid firemen to operate the apparatus of the Pikesville Volunteer Fire Company, moving equipment from Towson to the fast-growing Essex area, and using a temporary fire station in Dundalk.

A contract is awarded for a separate fire alarm system for Baltimore County.

The county commissioners allocate $150,000 for construction of joint fire and police stations in Halethorpe, Dundalk, Fullerton, Pikesville, and Essex.

1921: The fire alarm system is completed and located in the Towson station.

The Pikesville station moves to Reisterstown Road.

Halethorpe occupies a new two-story brick station at Washington Boulevard and Halethorpe Farms Road. The St. Denis Volunteer Fire Company disbands.

Owings Mills establishes a volunteer company but, despite purchasing an American LaFrance Type 38, triple-combination 500-gpm pumper, is at first overshadowed by Pikesville and other nearby companies because the alarm system bypasses the station. The members frequently learn of fires when they see the engines of competing companies rushing by their firehouse.

1922: A major fire ravages the J. L, Wilson Lumber Yard at Frederick Road and Egges Lane in Catonsville. Practically all of Baltimore County's fire apparatus is brought to bear on the fire.

1923: An American LaFrance pumper and hose truck with a chemical tank is purchased for $11,500 and assigned to Essex.

The county department's budget is $112,000.

The J. S. Wilson Lumber Yard is hit by fire again. The fire goes to three alarms.

1924: Fire Marshal Priester dismisses a captain, a lieutenant, and a number of firemen from different companies for such charges as "leaving quarters without permission, refusing to obey orders, being under the influence of liquor and being late for duty."

The work schedule for firemen at this time is twenty-four hours per day with an hour off for each meal (with the requirement that firemen live close by the firehouses) The firemen have one day off each week.

A group of young men organize the Hereford Volunteer Fire Company.

The repair shop in Catonsville, manned by Wilbur Kelly and Basil Sollers, is unusually busy this year with equipment breakdowns. Examples: Engine 8 (Fullerton) participates in a Defense Day Parade in Towson. The right front spindle of the reserve engine breaks off at the wheel—resulting in "a mashed radiator, frame bent on left side, broken on the right, both front springs broken, right side pan torn, both front fenders mashed beyond repair, steering gear shaft broken off, upper and lower crank case broken and hood damaged." Engine 1 (Towson) snaps a rear axle in Cockeysville while returning from a house fire in Phoenix; out of service for three weeks. Engine 2 (Pikesville) collides with a one-ton truck, which dents the three-gallon tank and breaks the chemical holder. Engine

7 (Essex) responds to a fire and loses a snow chain, which becomes entangled with the engine's drive chain.

A major fire at the H. C. Williamson Veneer Factory on York Road in Texas causes $100,000 in damages.

1925: The Baltimore County Fire Department receives its first notice in a National Board of Fire Underwriters report. The department is described as consisting "of seven full-paid companies located so as to effectively cover a belt [izronic term!] averaging about 4-1/2 miles in width extending around the limits of Baltimore City. Several volunteer companies also are provided in this district." The report goes into considerable detail about the department's Gamewell fire alarm telegraph system, housed at the Towson station.

1926: The department (Engine 6, Dundalk) responds to its first "aeroplane" fire, one of them involving the Maryland National Guard, at Logan Flying Field.

A case of arson appears in Reisterstown, responded to by Pikesville and Reisterstown volunteers, when a stable burns, leaving evidence of deliberately scattered coal tar.

1928: A county volunteer fireman is killed in line of duty, the county's first death of a firefighter. Fireman Monroe Seitz from the Reisterstown company approaches a burning car just as the gas tank explodes and sprays him with burning gasoline.

"The Great Reisterstown Fire," starts in Sander's Meat Market, burns for eleven hours, destroys eight stores, and causes $250,000 in damages.

The McDonough School near Pikesville suffers damage of over $300,000 in a fire that brings fire companies from Pikesville, Owings Mills, Glyndon, Catonsville, Towson, and Fullerton.

The county commissioners allocate $75,000 for construction of a new fire station in Catonsville. This results in transfer of the department's repair shop from Catonsville to Texas, Maryland.

Marshall Priester orders the replacement of solid tires with pneumatic tires and installation of windshields on apparatus with open cabs.

Conversion of chemical tanks to plain water tanks begins.

1929: Fire completely destroys the Glyndon Methodist Church. Eyewitnesses describe the interior of the church as "like a blast furnace."

The Cockeysville Volunteer Fire Department purchases a Nash ambulance and offers the first free ambulance service in Maryland.

1930: Much of Baltimore County is still in farmland. The first call of the newly-formed Long Green Volunteer Fire Company is a barn fire on Sweet Air Road. The company uses the bell of nearby Wilson United Methodist Church as its alarm device.

Rosedale Volunteer Fire Company is organized as the first volunteer company in the eastern part of the county, which previously was served by Fullerton and Essex stations. Rosedale's organization is marked by a dispute between proponents of volunteer fire service and advocates of paid service. The fire marshal, attending a parade of Rosedale

Entertaining the crowd

1955 Mack B-85, Engine8. Owner Leroy and Nancy Badders

volunteers intended to show off their new Mack Model BG, a 500-gpm pumper, is pelted with stale fish. Rosedale's first apparatus is a Mack Model BG, 500-gpm rotary pumper with a 300-gallon tank.

1931: The budget of the Baltimore County Fire Department is $231,000.

Pikesville starts the department's second medical service with a Packard ambulance. In the next ten years the vehicle will log 3,100 responses.

1932: The first all-new fire company since the 1919 annexation, Fire Station No. 9 is established at Woodlawn. Its initial equipment is a 1919 American LaFrance 760-gpm pumper. The Volunteer Fire Department of Hyde Park is formed as a civil defense unit in an old barn on Spring Lane near Back River. Its first equipment is a Chevrolet truck with a civil defense pump behind the cab and a hose bed behind the pump.

1933: The county commissioners direct the fire department to inspect "all public buildings in Baltimore County in which the public gathers for entertainment, such as moving picture parlors, dance halls, etc., for the purpose of eliminating fire hazards.

The department purchases two American LaFrance 750-gpm, rotary gear "Scout" model pumpers. They are assigned to Towson and Essex.

The effects of the Great Depression are all around. All members of the county fire department take a voluntary pay cut of 10 percent, which is based on money that previously was paid into the firemen's pension fund. This continues for three years.

Responding to a false alarm, two firefighters from Hereford Volunteer Fire Company, Elwood Hicks and Clarence Anthony, die when their engine's front axle spring breaks, throwing the pumper out of control on Weisburg Road.

1934: The Baltimore County Fire Department reaches agreement with the Maryland Department of Forestry, whereby the fire department will be reimbursed half the cost of fighting fires in the county's woodlands.

The Owings Mills company moves into its first permanent station house.

1935: Philip G. Priester, known to the public variously as chief engineer, fire chief, fire marshal, and chief engineer, dies after leading the department for eighteen years. He will be remembered for a number of inventions, particularly a device for ringing the large bell on fire engines automatically by means of a connection to the engine's motor. Anthony P. Orban, a resident of Catonsville, is chosen to succeed Priester.

1936: The North Point-Edgemere Volunteer Fire Company is chartered. The company's firehouse is on North Point Road.

1937: A two-platoon system is introduced, significantly changing the work lives of county firemen. There are now two shifts, "A" and "B," with ten-hour days and fourteen-hour nights. The men work eight-day periods that consist of three fourteen-hour nights and three ten-hour days linked by a twenty-four hour tour of duty. Thirty firemen are added to the department to implement the plan.

New uniforms are designated for the department. Members, who provide their own uniforms, are directed to consult their "tailors" and order "New York City"-style overcoats.

Two-man, enclosed, coupe-type cab engines are introduced to the department. The first two of these are American LaFrance Invader models, equipped with 600-gpm rotary gear pumps. They are assigned to Halethorpe and Dundalk. The Cockeysville company purchases the county's first water-hauling apparatus, a Diamond-T tractor-trailer tank truck. Cockeysville also introduces a three-wheeled motorcycle equipped with small tools and extinguishers for fighting field fires.

1938: Special nozzles known as "Bresnan Distributors," are introduced for the special purpose of fighting cellar fires.

Two more American LaFrance Invaders are purchased and assigned to Catonsville and Towson.

The Arbutus Volunteer Fire Department is formed. A used danced floor from the Arbutus Community Association is cut up to provide walls for the firehouse,

Chief Orban works with the telephone company to place

fire district maps in every telephone exchange.

Fire department inspections are expanded to include garages, stores, halls, schools, and apartment houses with three or more apartments.

1939: A ladies' auxiliary of the Baltimore County Volunteer Firemen's Association is formed at a meeting in Pikesville. Eight ladies' auxiliaries of individual companies attend and agree to set up the county organization. Charter members are Arbutus, Landsdowne, Pikesville, Reisterstown, Rosedale, and Sparrows Point. Mrs. Bessie Marshall is elected the first president.

A tank truck is purchased for Woodlawn.

Anthony P. Orban resigns as Chief and is succeeded by Frederick C. "Fritz" Maisel.

1940: The Maryland Line Fire Protective Association is formed.

1941: Two of Towson's engines collide while responding to a fire at Aigburth and York Roads

Fire companies from Baltimore County assist at a forest fire in the Fort Smallwood area of Anne Arundel County. Twenty-five homes are destroyed. The Arbutus Company alone fights sixteen house fires in thirteen hours.

Baltimore County companies help battle a major fire at the Mill Building of the Donut Corporation of America in Ellicott City in Howard County. The loss in the fire is more than $3.5 million.

The Hereford Company loses S. Howard Miller, who has a heart attack and dies en route to a fire.

1942: Bells on engines give way to sirens because of the war effort. Many citizens, trained to think sirens mean air raids, are confused at first.

The Arbutus volunteer company purchases the local community hall, a 500-gallon Ward-LaFrance fire truck, and a Buick Limited sedan, which is converted into an ambulance.

The county commissioners order a $15 pay increase for firemen.

Ambulance service, previously provided only by volunteer fire companies, is extended to paid companies. Three Buick ambulances are purchased and assigned to Towson (Ambulance 1), Catonsville (Ambulance 2), and Essex (Ambulance 3).

County firemen use gas masks while battling a blaze on York Road in Towson for two hours. Streetcar traffic is held up for over three hours, as a fire that Fire Chief Frederick Maisel calls the "most contrary thing" he has ever seen.

Wise Avenue Volunteer Fire Company is formed. Its first equipment is a civil defense trailer pump pulled by hand or by car. The company mounts the pump on a used Studebaker trash truck minus the trash body. For eleven years the company relies on a neighbor, Mrs. Frances Dove, who activates a siren when she receives a telephone alarm.

The Volunteer Fire Department of Hyde Park begins in an old barn on Spring Lane near Back River, with a 1932 Chevrolet truck.

Middle River Volunteer Fire Company, formerly Wilson Point Civil Defense Fire Unit, opens in a wooden shed on Cypress Drive near Wilson Point Road.

1943: The *Woodlawn Ledger* reports (March 4) Air Raid Signals received and observed: Yellow 8:31 p. m.; blue 8:50 p. m.; red 9:10 p. m.; blue 9::20 p. m.; white 9:31 p. m.; and the reporting of John Schultz, Tracey Lauder, Carl Volp, and Ted Roher to duty.

The Maryland Line company digs a 57,000-gallon cistern with the assistance of fire companies from Hereford and New Freedom and Stewartstown in Pennsylvania.

Engine Company No. 9 (Edgemere) is placed in service on North Point Road. The company uses a Seagrave 750-gpm pumper with a canopy-style cab.

Cowenton Volunteer Fire Company grows out of a civil defense unit. At its inception its fourteen members, seven men and seven women, operate a civil defense fire trailer which is housed at Gambrill's Coal and Lumber Yard.

1944: The Red Cross offers firemen training in basic first-aid techniques.

1945: The year opens with three especially difficult fires. In January fire strikes a large building in Sparrows Point that houses a meat market, a department store, the Sparrows Point Post Office, a telephone exchange, and the Masonic Hall. Paid companies from Dundalk, Edgemere, Essex, Fullerton, and Towson respond, along with volunteers from Sparrows Point, North Point-Edgemere, and Rosedale. The second, at McDonogh School for Boys, causes $15,000 in damages and destroys 200 tons of hay. Seven county departments respond. Shortly after, firefighters are ferried to Sue's Island to fight a blaze at the Baltimore Yacht Club. They drag hose through the water behind the Coast Guard vessel that takes them to the island. They save a cottage and the clubhouse but lose three buildings.

Middleborough Volunteer Fire Company is founded as World War II nears its end, growing out of a civil defense unit. A firehouse is built at the intersection of Sassafras and Middleborough Roads.

Woodlawn Volunteer Fire Company, also a civil defense unit, is organized out of citizens' concerns that an existing company, Engine Company No. 3, has too large an area to cover. The new company starts with a 1918 U. S. Army fire engine from Fort Holabird.

English Consul Volunteer Firemen's Association is given permission by the Presbyterian Church of the same name to build a small garage on church property. The company, originally a civil defense group uses a skid pump mounted on a trailer. Donations from community residents enable the company to buy a vintage Diamond-T truck for conversion to a fire truck.

Yet another civil defense unit converted to firefighting is Community Volunteer Fire Department of Bowleys Quarters and Vicinity. The first firehouse of the new company is in a wooden building behind a bar at Chestnut and Bowleys Quarters Roads.

1946: Rockaway Beach Volunteer Fire Company begins operations with a Mack pumper

A special unit staffed by the Rosedale Ladies' Auxiliary (after taking firefighting courses at the University of Maryland and first-aid courses conducted by the Red Cross).during World War II now goes out of service.

1947: The Volunteer Company of Hyde Park leaves its barn for a two-story firehouse on Sussex Road.

The Fire Prevention Bureau is created. It will operate separately from the Baltimore County Fire Department.

The department adds the position of assistant chief and divides the county into two battalions, each with a battalion chief. Edward Gail of Engine No. 6 (Dundalk) supervises the district east of York Road; William Hunt of Engine 1 (Towson) supervises the district to the west of York

The county fire service responds to 2, 273 fire alarms, the three county ambulances to 2,930 emergency calls. Essex is the busiest station, with 533 responses.

The National Board of Fire Underwriters report finds the department "fairly well manned and equipped to protect the built-up sections of the county." Recommended improvements include more ladder protection, elimination of the practice of selecting a new chief with each change of administration, and adequate civil service protection for members of the department.

Liberty Road Volunteer Fire Company is formed for the Harrisonville/Randallstown area of the county.

1948: A new pay scale is introduced. Firemen move from $219 to $235 per month, captains from $241 to $275, battalion chiefs from $274 to $315; the chief engineer, annually, from $4,800 to $5,220.

Before these pay raises are granted, the firefighters' first union is dissolved, a demand of the county commissioners.

The Fire Investigation Division is created under the direction of Captain Nelson S. Williams.

The Firemen's Training School is established. It operates at various sites, among them Old Bay Shore Park, and then moves to the Civil Defense School in Texas, Maryland.

In reaction to the death of a little boy, hit by a car while bike riding, Middle River Volunteer Ambulance Rescue Company is formed by concerned citizens. The company's first ambulance is a Chevrolet, soon replaced by a Packard.

Providence Volunteer Fire Company is founded, operating with a civil defense trailer pump pulled by car. The equipment is primitive, but the company manages to contain a fire at a church until Towson engines arrive.

1949: Ambulance 4 is placed in service at Dundalk, a Buick purchased for $6,200.

A " long-day" elimination plan goes into effect. Firemen will work an eleven-day cycle of five days (ten hours), a 24-hour period off duty, five nights (14 hours), and another 24-hour tour. The plan requires the hiring of twenty-one new firefighters.

A new fire station opens at Sollers Point Road and Dunmanway in Dundalk. Engine 6 and Ambulance 4 are assigned there.

The department buys the first ladder truck to be purchased since Roland Park Ladder 12, a 65' Seagrave Ladder, was lost in the 1919 annexation.

1951: The Fire Prevention Bureau, created in 1947 as an independent entity, is brought under control of the fire department.

Towson, Station 1, 1954 Dedication, York Rd and Bosley Ave

1952: The annual National Board of Fire Underwriters report recommends yearly testing of pumpers, publication of up-to-date rules and regulations, daily station drills, the response of battalion chiefs to all box and telephone alarms for building fires, in-service company inspections, and the testing of fire alarms at proper intervals. On the fire insurance industry's rating scale (one to ten), the Baltimore County receives a class five rating.

A two-way radio communications system is started.

1953: Hereford Volunteer Ambulance Association is formed. It operates in the beginning on dispatches from the Cockeysville police station.

Jacksonville Volunteer Fire Company is organized with the purchase of an American LaFrance pumper that had been standing idle at Cockeysville.

The National Association of Fire Underwriters recommends ladder companies in Towson, Catonsville, Dundalk, Pikesville, Halethorpe, and Fullerton "as soon as practicable."

Butler Volunteer Fire Company is organized. Its remodeled 1934 Seagrave pumper operates from a firehouse on Falls Road.

1954: Providence Volunteer Fire Company builds its first permanent fire station on Providence Road.

A third battalion is created. Battalion chiefs are ordered by Chief Anthony Orban to respond to all building fires in their districts.

Additional lieutenant positions are created to allow for an officer always to be on duty in each engine house

The work week is reduced to 67.2 hours.

A hundred 60-watt mobile radio transmitters and receivers are installed in fire apparatus and chiefs' cars.

The department buys its first Jeep, equipped for field and brush fires.

Two paid ambulance companies go into service, one stationed at Edgemere, the other at Fullerton.

1955: The year begins with a massive fire in the Westgate Shopping Center on Edmondson Avenue. The fire claims the lives of Captain William Miller and Fireman Carl Dill. These deaths are the first in the history of Baltimore County's paid department where firemen actually were fighting a fire.

The Baltimore County Fire Department occupies a new headquarters and training facility approximately half a mile from the center of Towson. The headquarters facility, headed by Chief Anthony P. Orban, is designed to serve fifteen paid companies and twenty-seven volunteer companies, in a county with a population of 325,000 and an area of 610 square miles. The facility is described in the November issue of *Firemen* magazine.

Butler Volunteer Fire Company wins the Baltimore County pumping contest with its 1934 Seagrave pumper.

Central Alarmers and the Box 234 Association, fire buff organizations, are formed.

1956: Chestnut Ridge Volunteer Fire Company is chartered,

Four lives are lost in department operations during the year. There are 5,501 fires reported. Dundalk 6, with 549, has the most responses. Rosedale Volunteer Fire Company leads the volunteer response with 189.

1957: The Baltimore County Fire Department becomes the Baltimore County Fire Bureau, a result of the county's adoption of the charter form of government and the combining of fire, police, jail, traffic, and civil defense agencies in a Department of Public Safety.

A general fire sweeps through the Essex business district, destroying five businesses, a bank, and an office of the Chesapeake & Potomac Telephone Company. Losses are estimated at $1 million.

Middle River Volunteer Ambulance Company builds its first heavy-duty rescue truck, nicknamed "Leaping Lena."

1958: This year opens with simultaneous three-alarm fires at Thorn Motor Company in Catonsville and the Spring Grove State Hospital on Walker Avenue. .

A severe late winter storm causes all twenty of the fire alarm box circuits to go inoperable.

Middle River, Bowleys Quarters, Lutherville, Pikesville, and Arbutus dispatch floodlight and rescue squads to the search for victims of a commercial airliner crash over Middle River.

Local 1311, International Association of Firefighters (Baltimore County Firefighters Association is founded. The initial membership is 21.

Governor Spiro T. Agnew cancels the purchase of a three-acre fire station site at Old North Point Road and Willow Avenue because $67,000 would be needed to make the site feasible for construction.

Seven racehorses die in a barn fire at Oak Ridge Farm (property owned by cousins of a battalion chief) near Catonsville,

caused by three boys smoking straw cigarettes.

Kingsville Volunteer Fire Company, sponsored by the Kingsville Lions Club, opens in a firehouse on Bellvue Avenue off Bradshaw Road after planning since 1954. The company purchases its first equipment and builds its firehouse after a highly successful door-to-door fund-raising campaign.

The Baltimore County Fire Bureau is reorganized. There are now three divisions: suppression, service, and prevention. Deputy Chief Louis C. Maisel is placed in charge of the fire prevention division with the title of Fire Marshal. There are now four battalions

1959: Citing ill health, Chief Anthony Orban retires . He has served as head of the department twice, 1935-1938 and 1951-1959. He is succeeded by Winfield Wineholt.

The National Board of Fire Underwriters issues a supplementary report reiterating its earlier recommendations for more ladder companies.

1960: County officials approve a new pay scale. Firefighters get an increase of $200 annually. Starting salary for firefighters is raised from $4,000 to $4,185.

Baltimore County firefighters get new uniforms. The "pillbox" uniform hat is replaced by a wide-crown military-style cap.

A three-alarm fire rages out of control for nearly three hours in a shopping center on Harford Road. Ten companies fight the blaze.

1961: Halethorpe Fire Station is completed, and Truck 5 is placed in service.

The county commissioners approve the purchase of 1.5 acres of land the Middle River Fire Station at a cost of $40,000.

A new Station No. 5 is dedicated in Halethorpe. One of the ladder companies recommended by the National Board of Fire Underwriters is placed there.

1962: A new station, 11, is opened on Loch Raven Boulevard near Glendale Road.

At year's end firemen fight a three-alarm fire at Aircraft Equipment Testing Company on Graves Court off Stansbury Road. The blaze is fought in sub-zero temperatures and high winds.

1960 Mack, Engine 12. Owner Leroy and Nancy Badders

The county fire department responds to 16,722 emergency alarms.

1963: In one month alone the county department handles 1,161 fire calls and 731 ambulance calls. A very dry period causes the number of fires to average forty per day compared to fifteen for a normal period.

Middle River Station No. 12 is placed in service.

James Devereux, county director of public safety, announces "moonlighting" rules, with a 20-hours-a-week restriction on certain jobs.

Additional personnel are added to the fire prevention and arson divisions. F. Lee Cockey will command the two divisions.

The Baltimore County Firefighters Union charges that top officials of the county are waging a "concerted anti-union" campaign to frighten its members from joining the Independent Baltimore County Classified Employees Association. An "immediate" halt to anti-union activity in the higher echelons of the fire department is ordered by County Executive Dale Anderson.

A new aspirator, based on a test model built by Arbutus fireman Ed Kelly, is put in service.

1964: The department renumbers some of its equipment. Engine 10 at Station 1 in Towson becomes Engine 101; Engine 13 at Station 6 in Dundalk becomes Engine 61; Engine 12 at Station 7 in Essex becomes Engine 71; Engine 14 at Station 10 in Parkville becomes Engine 10; Engine 16 at Station 12 in Middle River becomes Engine 12; and Tank Truck 1 at Station 3 in Woodlawn becomes Tank Truck 3.

1965: Robert E. Thomas of Hereford Volunteer Fire Company is killed in a Jeep accident while fighting a woods fire. Roll-over bars are installed on both volunteer and career Jeeps.

Fire Station 13 moves into a new building in Westview.

1966: County police and fire personnel vote ten to one against entering the federal Social Security system.

The fire department will pay overtime instead of compensatory time.

Fire Station 14 is opened on Falls Road in Brooklandville.

Station No. 15 in Eastview moves into its new building.

Fire Station 16 occupies a new building on Golden Ring Road.

Construction bid for Texas Station No. 17 is approved.

1967: Station 17 added in a new firehouse at York and Galloway Roads in Texas.

Chief Frederick "Fritz" Maisel , a former major league baseball star, head of the county fire department from 1938 to 1951, dies.

1968: County fire companies go to Baltimore City to assist during racial riots.

Rumors circulate about retirees being cut out of future pay increases. The county administrator reiterates that police and fire retirees who joined the department before 1959 will on retirement receive half of all general raises granted their active duty counterparts.

Seventeen fire stations are equipped with shotguns and

fifty rounds of ammunition for protection of the stations in future riots.

The career companies respond to 28,000 emergency calls, the volunteer companies, over 13,000.

Chief Winfield H. Wineholt retires as Fire Chief. County Executive Dale Anderson appoints a special nominating committee, which recommends Deputy Chief Austin Dietz for chief. Dietz began his firefighting career with the Woodlawn station in 1937.

1969: Fire Station 18 added in a new station house in Randallstown.

There are now six battalions.

Control of hazardous materials and inspections of hazardous processes become priorities for the department.

1970: Deputy Chief F. Lee Cockey retires after 41 years with the department.

Ambulance responses total 23,898.

1971: A bid for new Fullerton Station 8 is awarded.

An Intravenous Therapy program is inaugurated, Training is given at Greater Baltimore Medical Center.

1972: Severe thunderstorms and torrential rains cause widespread flooding in eastern Baltimore County. Both volunteers and career companies are overwhelmed by calls for assistance. Four volunteer firefighters are swept to their deaths by a raging Bean Creek. They are Charles Hopwood and Douglas Mueller of Cowenton Volunteer Fire Department, and Warren Schaffer and Milton DeSombre of Bowleys Quarters Volunteer Fire Company.

The Mobile E. K. g. Telemetry System is introduced,

The county's ambulance service begins cooperation with the Maryland State Police Medivac helicopter and Shock Trauma Unit.

Two truck companies are added: Truck Company 8, located first in Golden Ring, then in Fullerton, and Truck Company 17 in Texas.

1973: The first CRT certificates are presented to ambulance personnel from the Essex, Dundalk, and the Emergency Medical Services instructor cadre.

1974: Ambulance responses for the year are 30,742.

Fire Station No. 19 opens on Reisterstown Road.

The department begins a minority recruitment program. At the inception of the program the department has only two blacks among its 721 firefighters.

1975: J. Austin Deitz, Fire Chief since 1968, retires after 38 years of service. County Executive Theodore Venetoulis appoints Deputy Chief Paul Reincke to succeed Deitz.

1976: A supervisor car for Emergency Medical Services 4 is placed in service.

Phantom boxes are introduced.

A system of professional qualification begins.

The 24-hour clock is introduced in the fire department.

Advanced Life Support equipment is added to half of the volunteer ambulances during the year.

Engine 19, Garrison

1977: Carroll J. Huffines, president of Local 1311, is defeated in an election by Ralph J. Wolfe of the Dundalk station.

The Baltimore County Fire Department signs a mutual aid pact with Anne Arundel, Carroll, Howard, and Harford counties, and Baltimore City.

The department's first Medals of Honor are awarded to Captain Bradford Thomas and Cardiac Rescue Technician Gilbert Swann, both of English Consul Volunteer Fire Company's Medic 375, and James Yost of the Arbutus Volunteer Fire Company.

1978: County Executive Theodore Venetoulis delivers on his promise to introduce collective bargaining for county employees. The County Council passes legislation. Supported by the Firefighter union Donald Hutchinson is elected County Executive and promises a 42 hour workweek.

North Point and Battle Grove Road will be the site of a new Edgemere Station.

1979: Local 1311 becomes negotiating agent for wages, benefits, and working conditions for Baltimore County firefighters. One hundred firefighters and 25 pieces of apparatus fight a three-alarm fire at the Maryland Job Corps Center.

Mrs. Ruth Alban becomes the first woman to serve as president of a volunteer company in the county.

A four-alarm fire begins with a series of explosions at Suburban Propane Company at Hanover and Old Hanover Roads near Woodensburg.

A firefighter on the scene describes it "the equivalent of a 15-alarmer."

The Baltimore County Firefighters Association, Local 1311 of the International Association of Firefighters becomes the recognized bargaining agent for firefighters in Baltimore County up to and including the rank of Captain. Bargaining agreement includes additional days off in first step toward a 42-hour workweek.

1980: A new "911" reporting and computer-assisted dispatching system is adopted by the fire department.

Carroll J. Huffines gets elected as President of the Baltimore County Firefighters Association.

1981: Hydraulic rescue tools are placed in all truck companies. The era of fire alarm boxes ends.

Carroll J. Huffines steps down as President of Baltimore County Firefighters Association and James H. Boyd is selected by the Executive Board to fill out the term.

1982: Baltimore County firemen observe the centennial year of the career department and the Baltimore County Volunteer Firemen's Association observes its 75th anniversary. The county government stops funding the municipal fire alarm system, which had been leased from the telephone company. Now citizens rely totally on telephones and private alarm agencies.

Baltimore County Firefighters Association gathers over 14,000 signatures to change the County Charter to provide Binding Arbitration as a settlement mechanism for disputes with the county. The voters overwhelming vote in favor of Arbitration for Firefighters. James H. Boyd is re-elected as President of the Baltimore County Firefighters Association.

Membership of Local 1311 is 712,

1983: (January) Baltimore County Circuit Court Judge James S. Siekas upholds a referendum approved by county voters the previous November, allowing binding arbitration for county firefighters.

Chase, Station #54 opens March 10, 1983

Paramedic Unit 7 is placed in service to provide Emergency Medical Service for the northern portion of the county.

(March) Contract negotiations reach an impasse and an arbitration panel is formed. Local President James H. Boyd says the issues include a multi-year contract to replace the current one-year contract, improved working conditions for radio dispatchers, and reduction of the workweek from 50.7 hours to 42 hours. The union also seeks a 5.5 percent pay increase for 1984.

(April) A four-year contract, granting the highest public employee wages in the state, is ratified by the union. There is to be a 3 percent raise, a 42-hour work week, and a guarantee that firefighters will receive the highest wage benefits negotiated by any county employee group.

Station Officer Barry Short of the London Fire Brigade visits the Police-Fire Arson Investigation Unit to examine the unit's methods of fire investigation.

The county fire department requests $180,000 to repair the leaky roofs.

A six-alarm fire at B & B Auto Glass on Harford Road in Parkville rips through the basement and causes $2 million in damages.

Emergency advice is now authorized for the time when the ambulance is on the way. Civilian operators can give medical instructions to callers over the telephone during emergencies.

March Contract negotiations between the Baltimore County Firefighters Association and the County Administration reach an impasse and both sides agree to submit their proposals to an arbitration panel. Prior to the convening of the panel the County Administration proposes a four year contract that includes a reduction in the workweek from 50 hours per week to 42, and a guarantee to give Firefighters the highest raise granted to any other county employees over the life of the agreement. County Executive Hutchinson delivers on his campaign promise to reduce hours per week to 42.

1984: Parkton, Began Service as EMS 7
Mercantile Inspection Program
Job classification of Fire Apparatus Drive/Operator is created. James H. Boyd steps down as President of the Baltimore County Firefighters Association. John J. Hohman is elected to fill out his term.
Insurance Services Office begins review of Baltimore County, Quick Access Pre-fire plans start
Fire-Rescue Academy, Fire Prevention move to Lutherville Elementary School offices.

1985: Perry Hall, Station #55 opens July 1
John J. Hohman is unopposed and re-elected as President of Baltimore County Firefighters Association. Emergency Medical Technician position created, originally called Medic Unit Driver Attendant.

1986: A fire at the Baltimore Yacht Club, in the Essex area, destroys four boats, damages three others.
Fire Specialist position created and all employees reclassified to a higher grade (resulting in 5 to 10% increase) plus a 5% cost of living increase. Dennis F. Rasmussen elected County Executive supported by the Firefighters Association.

1987: Sparrows Point, Station #57 opens September 1, 1987
Firefighters Association and Administration agree to terms of new four-year agreement that includes over 70 changes to current Memorandum of Understanding. Included in the agreement is parity between police officers and firefighters as promised in County Executive Rasmussen's campaign a year earlier. Also significant increased leave hours to employees and guaranteed number of employees granted leave per shift. Baltimore County takes over fire protection at Sparrows Point. Fire Department begins a fourth shift and 42 hour average work week.

1988: The fire department buys 2,000 one-way breathing devices to protect firefighters and paramedics who try to save lives by mouth-to- mouth resuscitation.
Watch groups are formed in response to eight barn fires over the past two months in the northern part of the county and southern Pennsylvania.
January 1988—Professional Qualifications system used for promotions
Hannah More, Station #56 opens May 1988
Dundalk Station 6 dedicates its new firehouse, renovated and expanded from the 1949 original.
A fire destroys the Residence Inn on Beaver Dam Road, under construction.
Baltimore County Firefighters Association agrees to modify labor agreement resulting in reclassification (phased in 5%) increase, plus 4% cost of living increase. John J. Hohman is unopposed and re-elected as President of Baltimore County Firefighters Association.

1989: 800 Megahertz radio system, August 1989
BCFFA agree to contract with 4% cost of living increase. Number of uniform positions peaks at 1,150.

1990: John Quirk is named plaintiff in Fair Labor Standards Act suit filed on behalf of EMS personnel Baltimore County Firefighters agree to contract including $340,000 in incentive pay for all ranks below rank of Lieutenant. Roger Hayden elected County Executive. After 16 years as Chief Paul H. Reincke retires. Elwood H. Banister appointed Fire Chief

1991: Emergency Medical Workers sue the county for overtime pay, claiming that the Fair Labor Standards Act entitles them to overtime for hours worked per week beyond forty. Local car dealers donate child safety seats for distribution by the fire department.
Assistant Chief Position, added
Ground is broken for Edgemere Station 9.
Field vehicle designations "Paramedic 1" through "Paramedic 8" are changed to "EMS-1" through "EMS-8."
Budget cuts eliminate proposed fire station and fire training academy at Sparrows Point.
Administration and BCFFA reach impasse; employees do not receive any cost of living increase. Kevin B. O'Connor is elected as President of Baltimore County Firefighters Association.

1992: Back River Neck, Station #58 opens April 28, 1992
County offers retirement incentive and 90 uniform positions are eliminated. Administration and BCFFA remain at impasse no cost of living increase for second year.

1993: Hundreds of layoffs face Baltimore County workers. Leaders of the union scramble to keep colleagues off layoff lists.
County Executive Roger B. Hayden proposes ending accident leave and placing county employees under workman's compensation.
Administration and BCFFA remain at impasse no cost of living increase for third year.
Canadian and Russian firefighters visit the Baltimore County Fire Department for two weeks.

1994: Two-hundred-year-old Groff's Mill, the only intact structure from the Owings mills that gave the town its name, is struck by arson. The Baltimore County Sign Shop is also hit by arson. The blaze destroys the carpentry and paint shops, specialized tools, two county trucks, and a car. Damages are estimated at $1.4 million.
"Chiefo the Clown," new member of the Public Safety Education Division, is introduced by Fire Specialist Donald Adams.
After three years of impasse the BCFFA agree to a contract with Hayden administration. Highlights include, union proposed straight time overtime, significant pension change paid by employees, 4% cola, and guaranteed staffing levels. Number of uniformed positions reduced to 1,000. Chief Elwood H. Banister retires, James H. Barnes appointed interim Fire Chief. Charles A. "Dutch" Ruppersberger elected County Executive supported by the BCFFA. Kevin B. O'Connor is unopposed and re-elected as President of Baltimore County Firefighters Association.

1995: The county council consider the problem of retroactive overtime to paramedics.

BCFFA agrees to contract including reduction in pension contribution and changes in longevity system.

Allen A. Thomason appointed Fire Chief

1996: The County Council approves spending $213, 151 to buy seven-tenths of an acre on Walker Avenue near Old Court Road for a new Pikesville station.

Semi-automatic external defibrillators, for use by first-response teams, are placed on some engines

The county plans to move the fire department repair shop to the Grumman facility in Glen Arm.

Fire Chief Allen A. Thomason resigns as of May 28.

Retired Chief Paul H. Reincke is reappointed chief.

A ribbon-cutting ceremony at Carroll Manor Elementary School officially dedicates one of five 30,000-gallon undertanks that will be used in areas without hydrants.

Eight new medic units (Type I—all-aluminum First Responder body mounted on a 1995 Super Duty Ford chassis) are placed in service, at Towson, Woodlawn, Essex, Edgemere, Middle River, Golden Ring, Sparrows Point, and Back River.

1997: Groundbreaking ceremony is held for new Pikesville Station No. 2. A $1.6 million fire station will be built by BCI Contractors.

Medic No. 2 is placed in service at Pikesville.

Engine 60 places in service in July 1997.

A first-response Emergency Medical Services team, made up of paid and volunteer personnel, will function at events where there are dense crowds and limited egress.

The fire department's paramedics claim time-and-a-half pay for work over forty hours, though firefighters are exempt from federal law.

Eight new medic units are placed in service—at Towson, Woodlawn, Essex, Edgemere, Middle River, Golden Ring, Sparrows Point, and Back River.

At this point all career stations have medic units.

A high school program for firefighters is introduced, including emergency medical training.

Ruppersberger administration reaches agreement with over 200 EMS employees on FLSA class action suit resulting in over 1.7 million in back pay and all EMS employees in the future will receive 1-1/2 time for all hours over 40. BCFFA agrees to contract including 3% bonus and increase in day differential. Also included in contract is a 3% cost of living in 1998. Paul H. Reincke retires, John F. O'Neill appointed Fire Chief. Kevin B. O'Connor is unopposed and re-elected as President of Baltimore County Firefighters Association.

1998: Scott Self Contained Breathing Apparatus replaces MSA masks

Automatic External Defibrillators put in Battalion Chief vehicle.

1999: BCFFA agrees to a four-year contract including colas of 6% in 1999 and 4.5% in the following three years.

2000: Retirement incentive offered to Deputy Chiefs and Battalion Chiefs, command staff reduced, funds used to add four medic units. John F. O'Neill retires, John J. Hohman appointed Fire Chief. Michael K. Day is elected as President of Baltimore County Firefighters Association.

2001: Division Chief position created. BCFFA negotiates Deferred Retirement Option Program.

The preceding history draws substantially from
Horse, Hands, and Engines (© 1982 Baltimore
County Fire Service Centennial Committee).

Special thanks to
Joseph (Jay) Sonntag,
Battalion Chief (ret.)
Emergency Medical Services

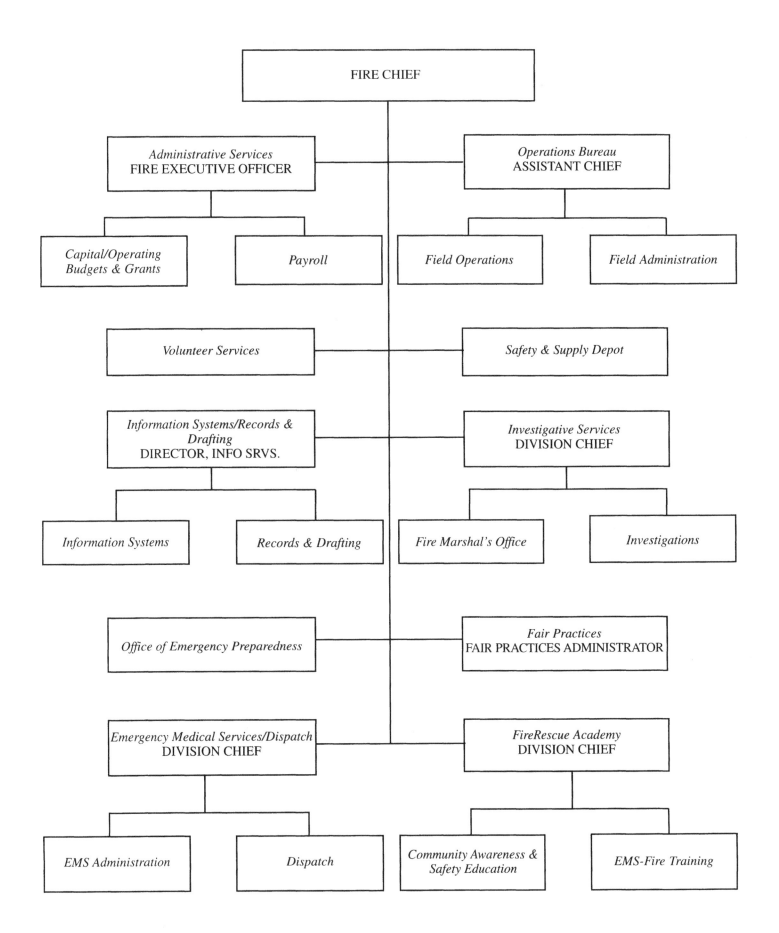

FIRE CHIEF

Administrative Services
FIRE EXECUTIVE OFFICER

Operations Bureau
ASSISTANT CHIEF

Capital/Operating Budgets & Grants

Payroll

Field Operations

Field Administration

Volunteer Services

Safety & Supply Depot

Information Systems/Records & Drafting
DIRECTOR, INFO SRVS.

Investigative Services
DIVISION CHIEF

Information Systems

Records & Drafting

Fire Marshal's Office

Investigations

Office of Emergency Preparedness

Fair Practices
FAIR PRACTICES ADMINISTRATOR

Emergency Medical Services/Dispatch
DIVISION CHIEF

FireRescue Academy
DIVISION CHIEF

EMS Administration

Dispatch

Community Awareness & Safety Education

EMS-Fire Training

Fire and Medic Unit Locations

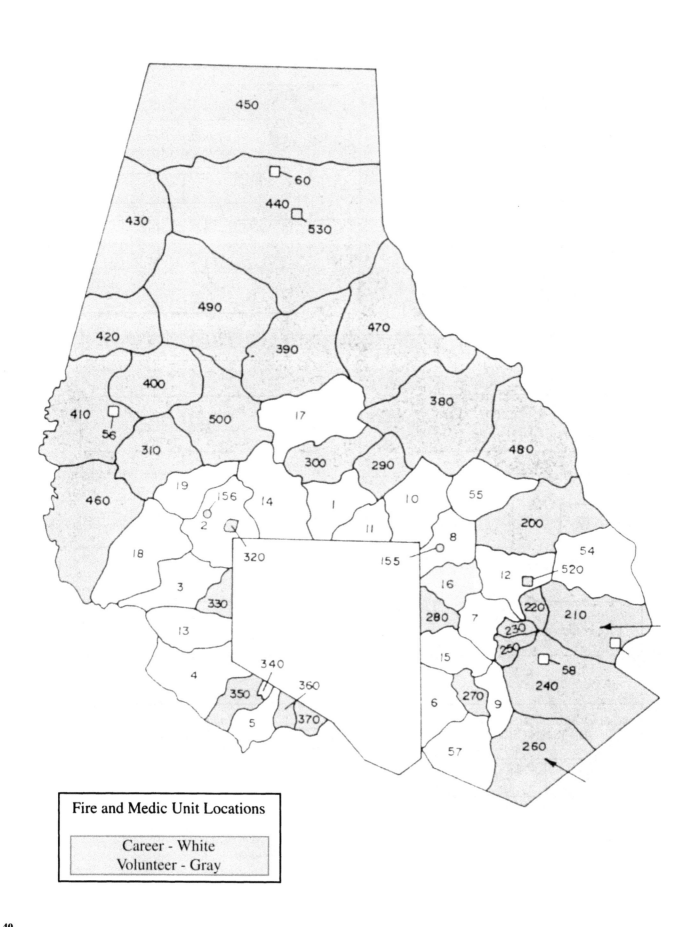

Fire and Medic Unit Locations

| Career - White |
| Volunteer - Gray |

THE HISTORY OF THE

VOLUNTEER FIRE SERVICE

In 1878, two Baltimore County communities, Towsontown and Waverly, decided that they needed organized fire protection and formed Volunteer Fire Companies. Over each of the 116 years that followed, dedicated men and women have continued the tradition of neighbors helping neighbors in their time of need.

Some of the earlier companies have disappeared, while others have arisen where population shifts have made their presence needed. Today, 33 volunteer fire, rescue, and emergency medical services companies, with nearly 3,000 skilled and dedicated men and women work side-by-side with their colleagues in career stations, protect Baltimore Countians. Two associate members provide canteen service throughout the county.

In 1907 the volunteer companies joined together to create the Baltimore County Volunteer Firemen's Association. From its beginnings as a largely social organization, the association has grown into a strong union of companies, whose elected officers are assisted by two full-time staff members, in spacious, modern offices. The association provides the mechanism for the companies to govern their collective selves; establishing and enforcing standards on manning, training, apparatus construction and equipment. It is the mechanism for the companies to interface with the Fire Department and with the county and state governments.

Officers of the association are elected at each annual convention in September, serving for terms of one year, to which they may be re-elected.

1942 Ford/Ward LaFrance sold to Liberty Road Vol. Fire Dept., Harrisonville, MD. Shown refurbished by LRVFD, ca. 1993

Adapted by Danny Coolahan, 1998-1999

The following represents the origins, evolution and progress of the Arbutus Volunteer Fire Department, Station 35, of Arbutus, Maryland. The first part (1938 to early 1960s) has been adapted from an earlier history written by unknown author(s) which was originally printed in the 1963 Silver Jubilee program. Most of what is written is believed to be fact and is derived from old newspaper articles, minutes of meetings, log books and memories. Some of what is written has been orally passed down throughout the years and can not necessarily be proven, but is worthy of mentioning. Be it fact, rumor, or legend, this is the story of the neighborhood fire house in the town of Arbutus.

THE BREAK-UP AND NEW BEGINNING

The year was 1938 and the surrounding towns just southwest of Baltimore City were mostly rural villages still feeling the effects of the Great Depression like the rest of the country. The streetcar ran out of Baltimore, through Arbutus, and into Halethorpe. The many family farms of the area were still producing crops and dairy products. The interstate system and townhouse developments had not yet split the rolling hills. The terms metropolitan," "suburbs" and "shopping centers" were meaningless to the tight knit communities.

At the Violeteville Volunteer Fire Dept. in November 1937, a bitter disagreement over the leadership of the company climaxed with the departure of 17 members. Led by Robert D. Lycett, the newly formed Community Volunteer Fire Company of Violetteville seized an American La France Pumper, ambulance, player piano, and a few other items. The two factions of the small town fire department both elected officers on Friday, February 4, 1938 and battled for dominance over one another in the following months.

The matter was finally settled by Judge C. Gus Grason in the Circuit Court of Baltimore County on Thursday, October 20, 1938. He awarded control of all equipment and assets to the original group and ruled that the others must surrender the apparatus that had been seized earlier. Rather than concede, the men decided to form a new department. Chief Engineer Anthony P. Orban of the Baltimore County Fire Dept. advised the men to locate west of the railroad tracks in Arbutus and he would help them in any way that he could.

The Arbutus Volunteer Fire Department of Baltimore County (AVFD) was incorporated at ll:55 a.m. on November 21, 1938. Sixteen original member's names were recorded on the Articles of Incorporation: Robert D. Lycett, Oliver C. Kendrick, Fred P. Gick, David Harmening, Clarence W. Joh, Everett Nash, James Forder, Joseph F. Marks Sr., Joseph F. Marks Jr., William Marks, Howard E. Ittner, Paul M. Rock, Edward S. MacNabb, Fred Suresch, Ernest Cavey and Maurice W. Scholing. Other sources indicate a seventeenth person, James R. Grimm, as being a charter member but his name does not appear on the articles of incorporation.

The Arbutus Community Association leased a portion of their land on the north side of Linden Avenue to the new firemen and

donated their carnival dance floor as lumber for construction of a building. On November 26, 1938 the men met on their new grounds to begin construction of a firehouse. They cut the dance floor up into three parts, which were then used for the first floor walls. They went into debt to buy the necessary materials to complete the building. The finished product was nothing more than a two story garage with two doors on the first floor for the fire engine and ambulance, and sleeping quarters upstairs.

With the huge debt facing them and the need for operating expenses, they started holding "Country Store Bingo" to raise funds. Bingo would continue to be one of the major sources of income for AVFD even after 60 years.

In 1939, application was made to the Baltimore County Commissioners for an appropriation to maintain a volunteer fire department. An appropriation of $500 was made for the following two years and after that, $1,000 per year. The Baltimore County

1927 American LaFrance 500 GPM pumper, ca. 1938-42

1927 American LaFrance 500 GPM pumper, ca. 1938-42

Engine 351, 1966 Mack C-85FD, 750gpm

1957 Scaling Boat, 1960 Pontiac-Ambulance, 1954 Dodge-Rescue Squad 354, 1947 Seagrave-Eng 351, 1962 Chevy Apache-Ambo, 1947 Willy's Jeep Forest Firefighter-Brush 352

Fire Department also donated some used 2-1/2 inch fire hose which was greatly needed and appreciated. Later that year, AVFD members Oliver Kendrick, Maurice Scholing, and David Harmening formed a by-laws committee. Soon thereafter, a Constitution and bylaws were adopted.

Rapid Growth In The Early Years

In 1942 the Arbutus Community Association relocated across Linden Avenue to a new building at their present location (Town Hall). The AVFD bought the old community hall which was next door to their small firehouse. The upstairs of the old hall was converted into a recreation room and sleeping quarters for those who would spend the night on duty. The firemen continued to use both buildings for the next 22 years.

During this year the Department replaced their apparatus. They bought a new 1942 Ford/Ward LaFrance, 500 GPM pumper and a Buick Limited Sedan which was converted into an ambulance. These were also the war years and the Civil Defense Headquarters for the 13th District of Baltimore County was set up in the sleeping/meeting room on the second floor of the original firehouse.

In 1945, an addition was built onto the back of the old community hall building. The basement level of the addition had room for the parking of two more pieces of apparatus behind one large garage door. About the same time, a Chrysler station wagon was bought for use as an "emergency vehicle."

In 1947, the Department went into the rescue business. A 1947 International Panel Track was purchased for use as a floodlight/rescue squad and was later designated Rescue Squad 353. This vehicle transported a floodlight system, boat and grapple hooks, portable cellar pump, and an acetylene torch. Also that year, a 1947 Seagrave-750 GPM pumper (later Engine 351) replaced the 1942 Ford/Ward LaFrance. The old Ford/Ward LaFrance was sold to the newly formed Liberty Road Volunteer Fire Department as their first engine.

A new 1948 Buick Roadmaster ambulance was acquired the following year. This ambulance was outfitted to carry up to four patients at one time. This was known as the "swoop and scoop" era. Ambulance personnel were instructed to a minimal of first aid skills as compared to the standards of today. Ambulance attendants would "swoop" down on patients and "scoop" them up to be rushed to the hospital with little or no medical treatment. The ambulance carried a two-body Emerson Resuscitator, one oxygen inhalator, first aid equipment, and a two-way police radio operated under the direction of the Baltimore County Police Department.

Although growing, the community was still largely rural. Much of the surrounding area was still wooded and many of the original farms were still in existence. A brush vehicle was added to the department in 1951. The four-wheel drive, 1947 Willy's Jeep Forest Firefighter was bought to aid the firemen in fighting brush fires.

In 1955, a 1954 Dodge Floodlight/Rescue Squad was bought to replace the old rescue squad. This bigger truck was much better suited to handle more technical rescues. It was equipped with an acetylene torch, power saws and drills, railroad jacks, grapple hooks, asbestos suits, smoke ejector fans, portable generator, floodlights, and many other rescue tools. The new Dodge became Rescue Squad 354 and the old International was retained by AVFD until 1960 when it was sold to member Harley Bush.

One year later, a 1956 Cadillac Ambulance (Ambulance 356) was added to accommodate the growing number of medical calls. This may have been when AVFD became a "double ambulance" company. This Department had become largely responsible for ambulance service in most of the southwest corner of Baltimore County as well as parts of Howard and Anne Arundel counties.

In 1958, a 1957 Seaking-14 foot flat-bottom aluminum boat (Boat 350) and trailer were purchased to replace the old boat. This boat, after more than 40 years, is still in service for appropriate uses such as ice rescues.

Changes and New Ideas

At AVFD, the year 1961 brought about what probably seemed to be a radical change. In an attempt to lure new members, the age requirement was lowered from 21 to 18. This change came, but not without a fight. There was probably a great deal of resistance to letting in young members. The 18 to 21-year-old members still needed parental consent and were not considered full members until their 21st birthday.

The Arbutus Volunteer Fire Department Ladies Auxiliary was "reorganized" in 1963. This group of ladies were the spouses of

1940's Chrysler Emerg. Vehicle, 1947 International Rescue Squad, 1947 Seagrave 750 gpm, 1948 Brick Roadmaster

Stu Langford in Engine 351, 1987 Hahn in July 4, 1993 Parade

members and were a supporting unit of the department. Not only did they help in fund raising for vital equipment and expenses, but offered moral support as well.

1963 was also a year of an invention which contributed greatly to the work of ambulance personnel but has been, for the most part, forgotten about. The design of the suction units found on ambulances for many years was the idea of AVFD member Ed Kelly.

Several Arbutus firemen, including Mr. Kelly, were attending ambulance school at City Hospital. Their instructor, Dr. Wilder, suggested a more efficient means of operating a suction unit by means of the ambulance's engine intake manifold. Used to suction fluids out of a patient's mouth, the old suction devices were run off of an oxygen cylinder and were wasteful and unreliable. Mr. Kelly made a prototype system on his own car and then applied it to the two ambulances at AVFD.

One of the newly equipped ambulances was taken back to Dr. Wilder for a demonstration. Dr. Wilder photographed the device and showed it to the Baltimore City Fire Department's Chief of Ambulances. Soon afterward all of Baltimore City's ambulances were outfitted with the system.

This was a true advancement and became widely accepted as a standard in ambulances for many years. Unfortunately, Mr. Kelly's design wasn't patented and he was never credited with his invention outside of AVFD.

MODERNIZATION OF THE DEPARTMENT

Once more AVFD felt the growing pains of a department growing as rapidly as the community around it. The original little firehouse and the "old hall" were just not big enough for the two ambulances, fire engine, rescue squad and jeep. Once again a major change was just around the corner.

A bid was sealed with Ira Rigger Construction Company for the erection of a new modern fire station with an adjoining banquet hall at a cost of $147,272. On Sunday, May 4, 1964, a groundbreaking ceremony took place on the site of the new station. BcoFB Chief Winfield Wineholt and AVFD President Robert Brittingham officially turned over the first shovel of dirt that day.

AVFD moved to its new home at 5200 Southwestern Blvd. on Tuesday evening, October 20, 1964 after more than 25 years at 1330 Linden Ave. The modern building had four apparatus bays, hose tower, sleeping quarters, office space and a large banquet hall for rental and departmental affairs.

After the transition was complete, the two old buildings were razed for parking space. The public was invited to an official dedication ceremony and open house on Sunday, October 10, 1965.

During the next several years AVFD continued its growth with the acquisition of more modern apparatus to replace the aging equipment. In December 1966, a new 1966 Mack C85-FD-750 GPM pumper (Engine 351) was delivered; in 1968, a new 1967 Jeep brush unit (Brush 352); in 1971, a 1969 Brockway/Providence Heavy Rescue Squad (Rescue Squad 354). Between the early 1960s and the late 1970s, the ambulances were being replaced at a rate of about one every two years.

POWER BOAT? NEW COLORS? WOMEN?

By the time Hurricane Agnes hit Maryland in August 1972 it had been downgraded to a tropical storm but it still managed to devastate much of the east coast. AVFD, along with every emergency department in Baltimore County and surrounding jurisdictions, was overwhelmed with a massive overload of calls. Death and destruction were the end results of the catastrophic flooding which caught most by surprise.

After the waters had subsided, it was decided that AVFD would not be caught off guard again as it was during the torrential storm. A 1973 Boston Whaler power boat and a 1973 Chevrolet Custom 20, 4x4 pick-up truck (Utility 358) were bought in preparedness for the next "big one." In a short time it was realized that the power boat would not be around to see the next "100 years flood." So after very few emergency responses and many "training" (fishing?) trips, the Boston Whaler was sold in 1974.

In 1978, AVFD purchased a 1978 Seagrave 1250 GPM pumper, although this one was not a replacement. This fire engine/pumper, designated as Engine 352, was in addition to the compliment of apparatus. But this engine was noticeably different than the others; the color was lime-green/yellow instead of fire engine red. The color choice was a new visibility safety standard being adopted by fire departments all over the country and had already started being used on AVFD medic units.

It had been decided to become a "double engine company" much like some of the other surrounding departments. This gave the department the dubious distinction of being the only "double engine" and "double medic" company in Baltimore County.

Once again in the late 1970s, AVFD was stirring with a very hot and controversial topic; women as active riding members. For years the women who wished to help the department became members of the Ladies Auxiliary. But by this time, many women were wanting to do more than help raise money and work at department events. Women were fast becoming part of the American workforce and competing in male dominated jobs. Many career and volunteer fire departments nationwide had already, incorporated women into their workplace with much success.

It was 1980 when the first women were accepted as full members of AVFD. Unfortunately, for many years some still insisted that the women did not belong in the firehouse and were not physically or mentally capable of being a firefighter. But for nearly 20 years, women have competently filled nearly every rank within the department. Not only have they served as firefighters and paramedics but also as Operations officers, Administrative Officers, including president, and served on the Board of Directors. To this day, AVFD is well known for having a higher than average percentage of female members.

A Changing Society Reflected Within The Department

Throughout the 1980s, AVFD continued with the modernization and upgrading of apparatus in a highly technological time. The ambulances were state of the art Advanced Life Support (ALS) equipped units. The Rescue Squad and "Old Mack" engine were both professionally refurbished but when they came back to AVFD they were no longer fire engine red. They had been given the new lime-green/yellow paint scheme.

The aging brush jeep was severely damaged at the scene of a woods fire near present day Giant shopping center on Wilkins Avenue. In the 80s the Arbutus area was nearly saturated with development. The farms were all gone and very few fields or wooded areas remained. Since brush units were being maintained at nearby Catonsville #4 and Halethorpe #5 career stations, it was decided that after more than 30 years a brush jeep was no longer needed at AVFD.

On August 6, 1987, a 1987 Hahn 1250 GPM pumper (Engine 351) arrived at AVFD to take the place of the 1966 Mack. The "Old Mack" was a reliable and favorite piece of many, but it was far too outdated to compete with the modern fire engines of the day. Many members still reminisce about responding to fires on cold winter nights while standing on the back step of the old rig. In July 1987 the engine pulled out of AVFD for the last time with the firehouse siren blowing in tribute to "Old Mack."

For several years, the Ladies Auxiliary had difficulty recruiting new members and retaining the old members. A lack of support from AVFD had also been a very discouraging factor for the ladies who were trying to help the department. In 1990, after many years of dedication, the remaining ladies of the auxiliary voted to dissolve their organization.

Towards the 21st Century

In the early hours of a June morning in 1993, a much anticipated addition to the family arrived. A 1993 Spartan Gladiator/ American Fire & Rescue, Heavy Rescue Squad (Rescue Squad 354) finally rolled into Arbutus after years of planning and waiting. The old 1969 Brockway had been showing its age for some time. The squad had difficulty making the climb up the beltway

towards US Rt. 40 since being weighed down over the years with heavier and more advanced equipment. The old squad found new paint and a new life as Reserve Rescue #1 with the Baltimore City Fire Department. Very often, the Brockway can still be seen responding to emergency incidents through the busy streets of down-

1947 Seagrave 750 gpm, c. 1947-64

1947 Seagrave, c. 1947-64

Fire Drill Sunday (1st Sunday of Month), 1947 or 48

1993 First Line Apparatus. L-R: Medic 356, 1988 Ford E-350/Medtec; Medic-355, 1986 Ford E-350; Eng. 352, 1978 Seagrave 1250gpm; Eng. 351, 1987 Hahn 1250gpm; Squad 354, 1969 Brockway/70 Providence; Utility 358, 1986 Chevy Suburban.

Lt. Theresa Drayer and FF Stu Langford

Hollywood Theater, Nov. 15, 1995, Lt. John McDowell, FF Tony Shockney, Capt. Todd Robbins

From left: Lt. Donald Schatt, Joe Bockman Jr., Lt. Joe Tebo, Jim "Slim" Stanley, Stu Langford, Stacey Enfield, Pat Carlton, John Simone

Rescue Box 5-6, Nov. 1, 1999 - Halloween partier in jeep going wrong way on I-695 - head on impact with car killing driver of car.

town Baltimore or sitting "in quarters" at the John Steadman Station on Lombard and Eutaw Streets.

The new squad had more than enough pulling power and room for all necessary tools, but something else was also very different.

Red was back! After about a 10 year absence, AVFD decided to start returning their apparatus to a more traditional white over red paint scheme. Nobody really liked the lime-green/yellow anyway and if they did, they wouldn't admit it.

It was noticed that there was an increasing amount of potential members being turned away due to the fact that they were not yet 18 years old. These young adults would simply seek membership at the other surrounding volunteer companies who had been accepting members at 16 years old for many years. Another hot debate at AVFD was brewing! Tempers flared at the thought of letting "children" become riding members. The initial attempt to allow the young members failed approval by the membership but the fight wasn't over. In 1995 the by-laws were once again amended to allow members between the ages of 16 and 18. The young members had to have guardian consent and were strictly limited to certain hours of departmental participation during the school year. In addition, the young members had to present their report card quarterly and could be suspended from department activities for failure to maintain "C's" in all classes.

During a time of litigation, strict training standards, and insurance considerations, the 40 year old aluminum boat was brought into question. There was no real training or certification to use the boat for water rescues and it became a liability concern. The membership decided to commit to the development of a properly trained water rescue team within the department instead of getting rid of the boat all together. This was also AVFD's way of specializing in a rescue field to comply with Baltimore County's Rescue - 2000 plan.

In 1996, under the instruction of Rescue 3 International, training began for swift water rescue technicians and the beginning of AVFD's Swift Water Rescue Team (SRT-35). A Nuway, 12 foot inflatable raft was donated and proper water rescue equipment such as helmets, wet suits, ropes and personal flotation devices were purchased. AVFD and Kingsville Vol. Fire Dept. (St. 48) together became the Swift Water Task Force for Baltimore County.

In 1997, AVFD had a remarkable amount of changes. Half of the parking lot was crumbling and full of pot holes. The other half was a little bit of stone and a lot of mud. During large hall events, parking was what you made of it. After an enormous amount of work and cutting through red tape, the lot was finally paved with asphalt and striped with dedicated parking for loading handicapped and department members.

Also that year, a dedicated group of ladies reorganized the Auxiliary. Membership was now open to both male and female members who did not want to ride the apparatus but were interested in helping with department events. Bingo and dances were just a couple of the Auxiliary sponsored events to raise money for the benefit of AVFD.

One of the most exciting events of 1997 was the replacement of the dilapidated 1978 Seagrave pumper. The old Seagrave was badly rusted, leaking, and wasn't able to pump the 1,250 gallons per minute of water for which it was rated. A 1997 Pierce-Dasch, 1250 GPM pumper found a home at AVFD as the new Engine 352. The Seagrave went to Levels Volunteer Fire Dept. in Levels, West Virginia where it was truly welcomed as a "modern" fire engine.

In September 1998, the AVFD Auxiliary made a gracious presentation to the department. A new set of Holmatro rescue tools for Squad 354 replaced the 1970's era Hurst rescue tools. The new

Lansdowne VFC Carnival Parade, Hollins Ferry Road and Kessler Road, July 1996. Back Row: Jim "Slim" Stanley, Lew Harvey, Don Gutberley, Lt. John Simone, Lt. Tony "Rocco" Shockney, Lt. Glen Peacock, Capt. Doug Simpkins. Bottom: Jennifer Mosner, Scott Miller, Wayne Wagner, Will Simister.

Firebox 4, Maiden Choice Lane, Catonsville, MD

tools were smaller, lighter, faster, stronger, and more technologically advanced than the old Hurst system.

Also in 1998, a decision was made to replace Engine-351 instead of refurbish it. The 11 year old Hahn 1250 GPM pumper was still in good condition but was showing signs of its age. Engine 352 was less than a year old and was met with great success in design and performance. Since the blueprints were still fresh and the price was still relatively current, Pierce would become the builder of the new Engine 351. The 1999 Pierce Dasch 2000-1250 GPM pumper was nearly a twin to the 1997 model and arrived during the summer of 1999. The Hahn and 57 sections of extra hose were sold shortly after being put up for sale and months before the new engine would arrive. S&L Fire Equipment of Andalusia, Alabama purchased it in order to refurbish for the local volunteer fire company in the town of Andalusia.

The 1988 Ford/Medtec ambulance (Medic-356) had also served diligently for longer than anyone had expected but was in dire need of replacement. The committee reviewed many different design plans and companies and came to a decision on a 1999 Ford F-350/ Horton-Type I ambulance. The new ambulance arrived in May and put into service in June 1999. The 1988 Ford was retained by the department and converted into a Swift Water Rescue response unit and redesignated as Special Unit 359.

In May of that same year, a special meeting was held and a decision agreed upon to open a substation at the University of Maryland Baltimore County (UMBC) campus. Medic 355 would be housed on campus and "University Members" would staff the unit during the school year. The "University Members" would be given the same training and responsibilities as regular members but would have no voting rights and would be held accountable to the fire line officers and Board of Directors of the department.

TODAY

AVFD recently celebrated an achievement of 60 years of commitment to their community and hopes to continue providing professional protection to the citizens of Baltimore County for many more years. All the services of the equipment, and the members, are completely volunteer. Expenses of the department are met by fundraising events such as the annual carnival, fund drive, bingo, photo drive, and hall rental to name just a few.

Pedestrian bridge collapse, 1999, one fatality

As the 20th century came to a close in 1999, the department had responded to 1,019 fire/rescue calls and 1,615 ambulance calls for the year. Through the efforts of the men and women of the Arbutus Volunteer Fire Department, who have worked long and faithfully for the advancement of their organization, this department has reached an enviable position among the volunteer fire companies of Baltimore County.

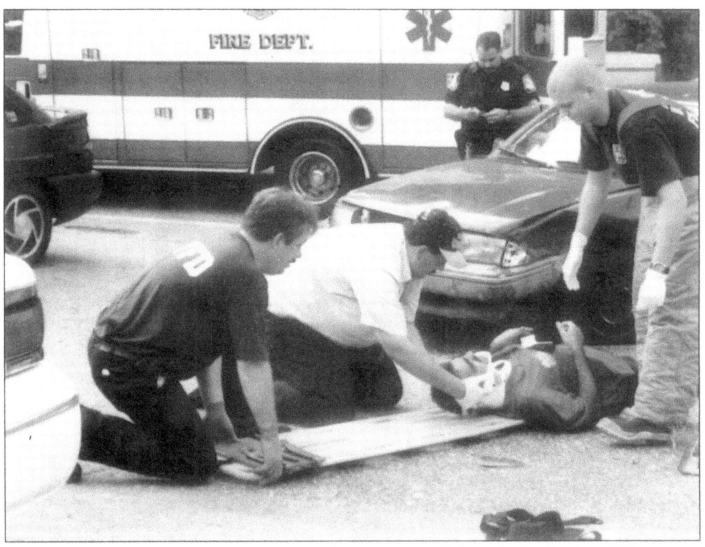

1050 PI, Wilkens Ave and Maiden Choice Lane. Charlie Deavers, Jim McCewen, B.J. Simpkins Jr., ca. 1998

49

THE HEREFORD VOLUNTEER FIRE COMPANY

The Hereford Volunteer Fire Company was founded in 1924. In 1999 we celebrated our 75th anniversary. There have been many changes in northern Baltimore County over the last three quarters of a century. Our district has grown, changing from a rural agricultural area to more of a residential community. Through the years, Hereford's Officers have pioneered many improvements to better protect out community and our firefighters. Some of these have been: One of the first 5-man enclosed cab fire engines. Our 1948 International. One of the first Brush Units, #443, arrived in 1954, and one of the first Special/Tanker Support Units, #444, was put in service in 1982.

To further meet the changing times, we are now planning a one and a half million dollar building project which will include a new hall and a new 6-bay engine room. Our chief is Kenneth C. Bollinger III and our president is Wayne G. Smith.

During a recent interview, Chief Bollinger talked about one of our most memorable calls. A rescue box for Station 44 was dispatched on April 8, 1997 at 18:23 hours. The call was for the report a child who had fallen into a well shaft. The units responding were Engine 442, Medic 535, Medic 60, Squad 533, Truck 17, Truck 58 (from New Freedom, PA). and Battalion Chief 1. Hereford's policy is to run both engines, 441 & 442, the Special Unit 448, and the Utility Truck, 449 on all Station 44 Rescue assignments. This brought the second engine and the other two units to the scene for additional manpower.

Engine 442 with Lt. Mike Hood was first on the scene. Lt. Hood along with driver Jay Huber, and firefighters Kenneth Thompson, Chris Lang and Charlie Badders discovered that the child,

Roderick, was trapped 40 feet down in the well. Engine 442's crew immediately set up a command site and established a fresh air supply to the child. Engine 441 arrived shortly with Lt. Roger Simmons. His crew consisted of driver, Wayne Smith, and firefighters Deborah Hood, David Flemming and Timothy Hann. They quickly began to dismantle the structure above the well. This was done to make room for the rescuers to work safely above the shaft.

Chief Bollinger arrived in Special Unit 444 with a crew of Phil Kearney (driver) and firefighter Jeff Adams. This crew, along with the crew from Utility 449 with Asst. Chief Louis F. Stiffler Jr., driver Robert Warns and firefighters, Kurt Holloway and Chad Heaps, set up the system of ladders to be used as anchor points for the rope lift. They also established a landing site for the state police Med-evac unit. Throughout the ordeal, constant communication was maintained with Roderick. In addition, an information officer was constantly talking with the child's family. The child was extricated by firefighter Mark E. Gardner of Truck 17 who is also a member of Hereford Volunteers.

Mark descended to the bottom of the shaft where he comforted and stabilized Roderick for his trip to the surface. Both were then lifted out by the rope system. Roderick was met by medics and his family. He was given a field exam and then transported to the hospital for further tests. Fortunately he was found to have only minor injuries.

The HVFC crews received a special award for their handling of the call and the local and national media ran special reports on the incident.

Compiled and submitted by C. Stewart Rhine, HVFC Company Historian.

Hereford Volunteer Fire Company Crew from Well Rescue of 4/8/97. Standing L to R - Fred Stiffler, Wayne Smith, Bob Warns, Roger Simmons, Tim Hann (in back), Kurt Holloway, Chuck Bollinger, Chris Lang (in back), Charlie Badders, Jeff Adams, Kenny Thompson, Debbie Hood, David Fleming, and Mike Hood. In Front: Roderick Aguillard, the child who was rescued, with Mark Gardner his resuer.

Celebrating 100 Years Of Service Pikesville Volunteer Fire Company

Members of the Pikesville Volunteer Fire Company are celebrating! After marking 100 years of protection for Pikesville and the surrounding communities, the Pikesville Volunteer Fire Company has grown to become one of the busiest volunteer companies in the nation, averaging almost 11 calls per day. The medic unit, rescue squad, fire engine, ladder truck and special unit responded to a total of 4,181 calls in 1996.

Known as the company of firsts, the Pikesville Volunteer Fire Company is a leader in volunteer fire protection. Pikesville was the first volunteer company in Baltimore County to reach 3,500 calls in a year; the first in Baltimore County to implement floodlight service (1939), the county's first heavy duty rescue

truck (1956); the county's first air compressor truck (1962); the first female firefighter to continue her career with the paid department now a division chief, the first couple to continue to the paid department - now they're married; and the first company to have a snorkel (1974).

A Look Back: A group of local citizens met for the first time to discuss the need for organized fire protection on February 4, 1897 at the Odd Fellow's Hall.

The group nominated names for the fire company. Pikesville Salvage Corps, Pikesville Hook and Ladder Company, Pikesville Truck Company, and Pikesville Volunteer Fire Company were the nominated names. Pikesville Volunteer Fire Company won the election by an overwhelming margin of 23 votes to 4 for Pikesville Hook and Ladder, and 2 for Pikesville Salvage Corps.

The following year, a fire hall was built on Old Foley Lane and a community dedication celebrated its opening. The company purchased a Holloway ladder wagon for $500. Volunteer members pulled this wagon to fires.

In April 1898, the Holloway truck made its first run. The blaze at Dunbarton caused an estimated $200 in damage.

In 1899, the Pikesville Volunteer Fire Company purchased its second piece of equipment, a Gould hand pump for $35. It was mounted on a flat spring wagon with fire hose and other hand fire fighting equipment. When needed, horses were borrowed from merchants and farmers.

This unique piece of equipment is still owned by the fire company and has been restored to its original condition. Without the use of a public water supply, the, pump drew from wells, cisterns and streams.

Sometimes a well would run dry just as the fire was brought under control.

In 1900, a new fire house was built at a cost of $475 to the company. A new truck was donated by Davis Blacksmith Shop owner Henry Davis. The new unit was built for the Gould hand pump and was equipped with steps, seats and rails.

The first piece of motorized equipment, an Atterbury Pumper, was purchased in 1912. Another pumper was added in 1915.

And in 1921, a new two-story brick fire house was built, combining a police station on one side and the county career and Pikesville Volunteer firefighters on the other. At first, the county did not have a fire engine, so the volunteers shared their 1915 LaFrance with the career men.

Ambulance service was added to the operation in 1930. With the community's help, a Packard ambulance was purchased. Upon its retirement 10 years later, the Packard had logged 76,892 miles in transporting 3,508 accident and sick patients to and from the hospitals.

The first floodlight service in Baltimore County was introduced by the Pikesville Volunteer Fire Company in 1939. It was used to overcome hazards created by poor lighting during evening fires. The unit was self contained, manufactured its own current and carried two 1,000 watt floodlights, one 500 watt floodlight and four 150 watt lights.

During wartime, manpower was greatly diminished. A few of the more seasoned members of the company maintained volunteer fire service until the others returned from duty. The community dedicated a plaque in honor of the volunteer firemen who served in the armed forces. The plaque was displayed on the base of the flag pole in front of the elementary school. It is now displayed in front of the firehouse with the original bell from the tower. Each year, a memorial service honors members of the Pikesville Volunteer Fire Company who served their country as well as their community.

In the late 40s and 50s, the town of Pikesville was busy expanding. The Pikesville Volunteer Fire Company was involved in that growth, as it sponsored many activities for fund raisers as well as fun events. Door-to-door projects, parades, carnivals, Little League sports, tree lightings, train gardens, hospital visits, fire prevention, civil defense or Red Cross training helped raise funds to enable the purchase of new equipment.

By 1960, the company was growing too large for its shared quarters with the career men. After a successful fundraising drive, groundbreaking took place for the new firehouse on Sudbrook Lane with the dedication of the building in September 1963. Bands, marching groups and a community wide celebration marked the occasion.

During the late 1960s and early 1970s, the company again updated its equipment and technology. Firefighters underwent training to become emergency medical technicians. In 1974, the Pikesville Volunteer Fire Company became the first in Baltimore County to add a snorkel.

During the 1980s and 90s, the company committed to more intensified training and more advanced equipment. Training on confined space rescue and hazmat incidents and the addition of a 100 foot aerial truck in 1988 reflected a commitment to the changing needs of the community.

Over this period, the membership greatly expanded.

Today, a membership roll of over 150, one third of them in active service, provides enough manpower to keep the Pikesville Volunteer Fire Company responsive to the thousands of calls each year from the community. And the community itself has willingly and generously supported those who keep it safe. The Save-A-Heart Foundation, the Covenant Guild and many individual residents and community groups of Pikesville acknowledge and support the Pikesville Volunteer Fire Company as an essential part of the community. Their contributions not only fund the purchase of essential equipment, but help to finance needed training sessions and drills for the volunteers.

No matter where the volunteers may be—part of a parade in Ocean City providing emergency medical treatment, serving as backup to a fire in another district, or saving a little boy's puppy the community can be sure that the Pikesville Volunteer Fire Company will always provide unparalleled medical, fire and rescue protection for the citizens of this and the surrounding communities.

They have depended on it for the last 100 years and they can count on for 100 more.

The Pikesville Volunteer Fire Company has survived because of dedicated individuals, entire families, generations of unselfish, caring people.

One reason for the success of the Pikesville Volunteer Fire Company is the dedication of the Ladies Auxiliary, which has provided constant support for 64 of the company's 100 years. Assistance with fund raising, working elbow-to-elbow, and also administrative functions has enabled the active members to be where they need to be - on the trucks fighting fires and helping the community. And their own fund raising endeavors have funded countless items essential to the operation of the company and educating the public about fire prevention.

The Ladies Auxiliary and members of the company have been there both county and state wide. The two groups helped organize the county association and auxiliary. The fire company has had nine members serve as County President and four as State Association President. Likewise, the Ladies Auxiliary has had five state and seven county past presidents to their credit, with two more on the way.

History Of The Ladies Auxiliary To The Pikesville Volunteer Fire Company

ANNUAL REPORT - 1997

On the first Monday in July 1933, a group of Pikesville ladies met in the school house with a representative from the Pikesville Volunteer Fire Company and Mrs. Bessie Marshall, State Auxiliary Organizer, to discuss plans for organizing a Ladies Auxiliary to the Pikesville Volunteer Firemen's Company. It was decided to hold quarterly meetings on the first Monday of each month. Annual dues was $.25. Mrs. Nina Shipley was appointed acting president to service until election of officers at the October meeting. The following ladies were present, forming the charter membership:

Maude Chenoweth
Elizabeth Berryman
Rachel Hamelt
Virginia Chenoweth
Nina Shipley
Ella Eichom
Katherine Keyes
Ellen Bosley
Kate McKim
Nellie Johnson
Lillian Shipley
Mamie Purcell
Kate Salter
Rita Simmons
Evelyn Whitcomb
Nanie Bowersox

At the first regular meeting in October 1933, the following officers were elected to serve: President, Mrs. Elizabeth Berryman

1st Vice President, Mrs. Nina Shipley
2nd Vice President, Mrs. Kate McKim
Secretary, Mrs. Rita Simmons
Treasurer, Mrs. Lillian Shipley

The officers were installed by Mrs. Bessie Marshall. Special meetings were called throughout the year to discuss the goals of the auxiliary and plan methods to raise funds to aid the firemen. Some of the methods used were card parties, coupon redemption from various articles sold at the American Store Company, magazine subscription sales and nominal fees for the purchase of Constitution Books. A Dunlopello Mattress - $23.45, and cover - $125.00, were given to the firemen for the ambulance.

The Ladies Auxiliary to the Pikesville Volunteer Fire Company joined the Ladies Auxiliary to the Maryland State Firemen's Association in June 1934 with yearly dues being $5.00. Three delegates were sent to Convention held in Cambridge, Maryland. At the meeting on June 4, 1934, it was agreed that a collection be taken for flowers at each meeting which would be cared for by the Sunshine Committee. Mrs. Virginia Chenoweth was elected treasurer of the Ladies Auxiliary to the Maryland State Firemen's Association. The bank balance at the end of 1934 was $73.02, with the beginning of an auxiliary that produced fire presidents of the Ladies Auxiliary to the Maryland State Firemen's Association and nine Presidents of the Ladies Auxiliary to the Baltimore County Volunteer Firemen's Association.

On January 6, 1936, the following members were elected:
President, Mrs. Nina Shipley
1st Vice President, Mrs. Elizabeth Berryman
2nd Vice President, Mrs. Kate McKim
Secretary, Mrs. Grace Zimmer
Treasurer, Mrs. Webster Shipley

In 1937, Mrs. Virginia Chenoweth asked everyone to support the Hospital Fund Ball of the LAMSFA to be held on April 3rd at the Rennert Hotel in Baltimore. At this event, she presented a small gold helmet pin in memory of her father to be worn by the Presidents of the State Auxiliary. From 1937, it has been the pleasure of the following presidents to wear the pin: Virginia Chenoweth (1938), Jennie Schneider (1943), Helen Mitchell (1956 and 1969), and Mary J. Berryman (1978).

The turn of the century (1950) brought innovations and additions, such as visits to Veteran hospitals, baskets for the needy and the dream of having a hall and kitchen. A kitchen fund was set up. By 1952, we had acquired 62 members who were active on various committees. Many of our special affairs were held in Ames Church Fellowship Hall.

In 1958, the ladies volunteered time assuming responsibility of calling ambulance drivers during the day. "Although confining, it was another way we managed to help our firemen." For several years, the firemen raffled a car on the last night of the carnival. Since the firemen were responding to fires, members of the Ladies Auxiliary spent several evenings walking through the neighborhoods selling chances.

By 1961, our kitchen fund had grown to $7,036.00 and we began getting prices and meeting with the firemen.

On January 6, 1963, our dream had come true and we were buying new utensils, china and other kitchen needs, including drapes for the hall and hangers for the coat room. Reservations for dinners, testimonials, banquets, Lions Club, weddings and dances were being taken. On September 22, we dedicated our new "Fire House." Governor Millard Tawes was the speaker. Other notables were present from the State Association, Baltimore County Association, other club representatives from the area and friends, all contributing to a delightful affair. Refreshments were served by the Ladies Auxiliary.

President, was present, along with President Smith N. Stathem.

In 1966, our Treasurer, Margaret Reitemeyer, was severely injured in a hit and run accident and spent many months in the hospital recuperating. On November 7, Helen M. Kellar was installed as Treasurer.

In 1968, President Dorothy Daughton led us through a busy year. We continued to purchase kitchen articles.

1969 gave us our fourth president of the Ladies Auxiliary to the Maryland State Firemen's Association, Helen Kellar. She named Mary Berryman as her executive chairman. With another busy year, we managed to present our firemen with $4,779.09.

1971 gave us our ninth president of the Ladies Auxiliary to the Baltimore County Volunteer Firemen's Association, Mary Berryman, and a first for the County Association with Mary's husband, John (Elizabeth Berryman's grandson), serving as President of the Men's Association.

As the years passed we not only grew in membership, but also in accomplishments. Realizing the need for an ambulance, we earmarked our money to this committee giving the firemen $5,500.00. We purchased a new ceiling for the community hall, helped with the roasts and worked hard to bring to the firemen a total financial commitment of $6,482.04.

As the years passed, our work continued but became harder due to limited membership. The firemen informed us that changes would take place after the first of the year.

In 1974, the firemen leased the community hall to an outside concern. The $1,029.00 donation from the Ladies Auxiliary for the purchase of the chairs and tables was placed in the ambulance fund. Our President, Dorothy Daughton, felt that she needed to step down. Another Berryman assumed the presidential role, Mary (granddaughter-in-law of our first president).

1976 and 1977 brought another Berryman to the position of President, Sharon Berryman Bull. We hosted the January 1977 meeting of the Ladies Auxiliary to the Baltimore County Volunteer Firemen's Association at the Liberty Road Fire House, held three bake sales, two raffles and other activities.

On February 4, 1978 at a joint installation, Sharon Bull was again installed as our president for two years. We presented our firemen with a check in the amount of $2,000.00 and offered our help whenever needed. At the June Convention in Ocean City, Maryland, Berryman was elected president of the Ladies Auxiliary to the Maryland State Firemen's Association. Our annual Christmas party was held at the Kiwanis building adjacent to the fire house.

In 1979, we were fortunate to have four of our charter members still with us. To the others and members for whom the bells have tolled, we will always remember their assistance, guidance and devotion to the Auxiliary and wish them a restful sleep of peace.

January, 1980 found us preparing for installation of officers to be held on February 2, 1980. The Ladies Auxiliary motioned to start a Preservation Fund for the old pumper.

In May 1980, CPR classes were started for members of the Ladies Auxiliary.

In August 1980, blankets were purchased for the firefighters. As we progressed, by-law changes were submitted, voted in and implemented.

In early 1981, the Ladies Auxiliary motioned and passed to buy Bay Masks (adult and child) and other equipment.

February 1981 saw the loss of Nina Shipley.

By mid-June, we were planning for our flea market.

February 1982 brought us news that Past President, Mary Berryman, and her husband were planning to move to Florida.

In December 1982, our recording secretary resigned and the position was temporarily filled.

April 1983 saw the members busy participating in the envelope stuffing party for Honorary Membership.

Illness hit several members in November 1983. Sarah Rhoades became ill and Margaret Reitemeyer fell and broke her hip.

1984 saw several members becoming ill. The Ladies Auxiliary voted in several new members.

1985 saw the Ladies Auxiliary presenting funds toward new bay doors. Our membership kept growing with the presentation of four new members. Our Past President, Sarah Rhoades, died and a memorial service was held on February 13, 1985.

In late 1985, the Ladies Auxiliary purchased new blankets and pillows for the firefighters. We lost another vital member of our auxiliary, Helen Kellar. Several babies were born to our younger members.

By 1987, the Ladies Auxiliary purchased mattresses, pillows, pillow cases and bedspreads for the firefighters.

1992 found us preparing fire prevention projects for children. We were awarded the Helen Little Memorial Award for entering Freddye the Firetruck.

June 1995 saw us heavily involved with our cookbook project. The Auxiliary participated with the Firefighter Ball.

April 1996 found us reaching out to the community after a condo fire. The Ladies Auxiliary donated funds toward food vouchers for those people displaced on the fire.

1997 brought us into providing refreshments for fire safety training on three different occasions. Pillows were purchased for the firefighters. The Ladies Auxiliary to the Pikesville Volunteer Fire Company was awarded the Silver Spring Trophy, the Community Outreach Award and the Jane Toad Award at Convention.

As we look back on our history, the Ladies Auxiliary to the Pikesville Volunteer Fire Company has reached both juniors and seniors in an effort to teach them fire safety. As we continue on this path, we will strive to continue our projects and educate those in need.

Past Presidents

Ladies Auxiliary

Elizabeth Berryman	1933-34
Nina Shipley	1935-37
Elsie Adams	1938-40
Mary Henley	1941
Jennie Schneider	1942-44
Helen Kellar	1945-46
Charlotte Purcell	1947
Helen Mitchell	1948-49
Katherine Mullen	1950-1951
Cora Schaffer	1952-53
Helen Mitchell	1954-55
Sarah Rhoades	1956-57
Sally Bosley	1958-59
Helen Keller	1960-61
Sarah Rhoades	1962-63
Dorothy Daughton	1964-73
Mary Berryman	1974-75

Sharon Bull	1976-79
Rose Burnham	1980-83
Sharon Bull	1984-87
Angela Schaller	1988-89
Brenda Burgan	1990-93
Karen Magness	1944
Sharon Bull	1995-96
Norma Levin	1997-99
Cathy Koch	2000

PVFC Timeline

1897: PVFC founded by a group of local citizens, as the second-oldest volunteer fire company in Baltimore County.

1898: Fire hall dedicated near Reisterstown Road and Sudbrook Lane.

1898: The Company's $500 Holloway truck makes its first run.

1899: PVFC purchased a Gould hand pump and mounted it on a flat spring wagon.

1900: New fire house built by Philip Watts for $475. Henry Davis donated a new horse-drawn fire truck specially built for the Gould Pump.

1912: Atterbury truck purchased, the company's first piece of motorized apparatus and county's second.

1915: American LaFrance pumper placed into service.

1921: New, two-story brick fire house built to house police, career and volunteer fire fighters.

1930: Volunteer ambulance service added with the purchase of Packard ambulance, the second such service in Baltimore County.

1939: County's first floodlight service begun at Pikesville. Old "Number 21" retired and a Seagrave engine with a 300-gallon tank is added.

1956: New Seagrave pumper, new ambulance, and floodlight unit added. PVFC scores another county first by adding a heavy-duty rescue truck for automobile accidents.

1960: New building committee formed.

1962: Another county first company purchases air compressor truck to refill breathing equipment. Groundbreaking for new fire hall, fund raising drive accelerates.

1963: New fire hall dedicated with marching bands, parade, speeches.

1965: PVFC begins decade-long upgrades of equipment and technology to meet the increasing community need for emergency medical services.

1968: First high-rise air filling station in the nation.

1974: Twin Mack pumpers purchased, including the first pumper snorkel in the county.

1976: First volunteer fire company with a paramedic in the county. First female firefighters: Danelle England and Jane Rosen.

1981: Peterbilt/Swab Heavy Rescue Squad added. PVFC begins using 4" diameter hoses. Special unit purchased from Grasonville VFC.

1986: New air unit added and new medic unit ordered. Building is modified inside and out. Truck service restarted after 88 years.

1989: *Fire House* magazine ranks PVFC as the 8th busiest volunteer company in the nation.

1991: *Fire House* magazine ranks PVFC 4th busiest volunteer company in the nation.

1997: PVFC celebrates Centennial Year with wide range of gala events.

The Year Was 1897...

...the Orioles' Hughie Jennings was hit by a pitch 49 times that season, a record that stood for 75 years.

...the first country day school in the United States opened at the Gilman School.

...the world's first, true submarine with a combustion engine, "The Argonaut," was invented by Simon Lake and constructed in Baltimore.

...composer John Philip Sousa wrote *The Stars and Stripes Forever.*

...Aspirin was invented.

...Baltimore City celebrated its Centennial Anniversary of incorporation.

...a gallon of gasoline cost 19 cents.

...and a three-bedroom home cost $2,200.

Awaiting Medic Unit

LIBERTY ROAD VOLUNTEER FIRE COMPANY

On the night of July 16, 1947, 13 men sat in a small garage in Harrisonville to discuss the possibility of establishing a volunteer fire company to serve the Harrisonville-Randallstown area of Baltimore County. Among the men was the President of Woodlawn Volunteer Fire Company. He shared his experience with the men and the problems and hardships of forming a volunteer company. A second meeting was held at the Mt. Paran Lecture Hall in Harrisonville, which was opened to anyone interested in forming a volunteer organization. On this night the association was formed and incorporated under the name of Liberty Road Volunteer Fire Company, Inc.

It was decided that beginning the first Wednesday in October 1947, that every Wednesday the members would sponsor a bingo at the Holy Family Church Hall in an effort to raise money for a building and equipment. Two very public-spirited men, Gerard Glos and Dick Smith, donated property to the fire company on Liberty Road near Deer Park Road. Following this donation, the members became highly concerned with purchasing equipment. In April 1948, Liberty Road Volunteer Fire Company borrowed $3,500 from the Randallstown Bank to purchase a fully equipped 1942 Ford Pumper and a 1940 Buick Ambulance from the Arbutus Volunteers. The equipment was kept in the John Deere garage of member Wm. J. Hanley, until the building was completed in September 1948. As of today the company still has the original 1942 Ford Pumper, which is referred to as "the antique."

The company held its first carnival on September 17th and 18th with a great assistance from the Ladies Auxiliary, which raised money to help complete the building. The new 20' x 50' building was dedicated on October 24, 1948 and the first equipment was officially placed in service on this date. The original alarm system consisted of a siren control button at the Randallstown State Police Barrack. To summons the ambulance, several numbers were listed which during the day were received by Miss Mary Blair at the John Deere Garage. Duty men took over between 7 and 11 p.m. at the firehouse. Liberty Road responded to their first fire call on January 2, 1949. In the spring of 1950 the members of the Fire Company built a 1,000 gallon tank truck from an old fuel truck.

With the financial support from the community, Liberty Road was able to buy a new fully equipped ambulance in 1950. In this same year Baltimore County installed the first two-way radio and the unit came to be identified as Ambulance 85. In 1951, plans were drawn for a new addition, which would include two engine bays on the ground floor and a hall and a kitchen on the second floor. The building was completed in 1952. In 1952 we were also connected to the new central alarm dispatch center in Towson. In the mid 1950s each station was assigned a three digit Station number 460 in accordance with the new radio systems. From then on all of the equipment was numbered according to the type of equipment and our station number. In 1960 the new addition was finally dedicated. It included space for an office, a radio watch room, a recreation room, a recreation hall and a modern kitchen, which was fully equipped by our Ladies Auxiliary. The Ladies Auxiliary consisted mostly of the wives and girlfriends of the members and was established on November 20, 1947 in the Wards Chapel Sunday school room.

During 1972, in an effort to get the youth of the community involved with the fire department, Explorer Post 847 was organized. The program started with five charter members, and two years later was changed to the Liberty Road Volunteer Cadet Program.

In May 1975, Baltimore County Fire Department placed a new ambulance at Station 18. Because Ambulance 18 was now helping serve the community, it was decided that Liberty Road would take Ambulance 466 out of service permanently and only operate with one ambulance. In 1976 the company purchased a Mack Engine which they painted red, white and blue, and was named "The Spirit of '76." In 1977, Baltimore County Fire Department and C&P Telephone Company installed Teletype equipment in each station which provided for more efficient communications between fire dispatch and each station,

In May 1981 the company voted in its first female member, Rosemary Jordan. In September 1981 the company decided to have the engine converted to new Detroit diesel engine. Throughout the years much of the equipment has been repaired and replaced. In May 1982 the company purchased a new Seagrave 1,000 GMP Pumper with 1,000-gallon buster tank, Detroit diesel engine, and five-speed transmission. The Seagrave was placed in service August 15, 1982 and is still in service today. In October 1987 the company purchased a new 1988 Ford Crew Cab Pickup truck to serve as Utility 467, which is also still in service today.

In 1991, Liberty Road Volunteer Fire Company was issued a permit to begin constructing a new addition, which included a double engine bay, a captain's office, two storage rooms and restrooms on the first floor and separate men and women's bunkrooms on the second floor. This was a dream come true for the company.

In 1995 the company purchased a 1995 Wheeled Coach ambulance, now in service as Ambulance 465. In 1996 the station experienced a sad loss when, the upstairs banquet hall caught on fire. Fortunately the fire was contained in one corner and quickly extinguished by the firefighters. Unfortunately the hall was a total loss and had to be completely gutted and reconstructed. The reconstruction was completed later in the year.

In 1992, the Seagrave was involved in an accident at the intersection of Liberty and Marriottsville Roads on the way to responding to a call. Luckily there were no serious injuries, but the Seagrave had to be sent to Del-Mar-Va for the necessary repairs.

In 1997 Liberty Road had their first Junior from Liberty Road to complete the program sponsored by Baltimore County Public Schools and the Baltimore County Volunteer Fireman's Association. Robert Kemp was the first junior to completed the program which certified him in firefighter I, EMT and Rescue courses.

In 1998 the station was remodeled, placing a kitchen and committee room in the existing building, and the entire center area of the building was redesigned to give it a more modern look.

In 1999 a 1985 Chevrolet Pick-up was purchased from the military and was put in to service as Utility 467. In addition, in 1999 Melody Wayne was elected the first woman president of Liberty Road Volunteer Fire Department. As of today the company remains very active in serving the community and in the last several years has established a heavy youth involvement.

On the night of July 16, 1947, 13 enthusiastic men sat intently listening to the hardships of forming a volunteer organization, and whoever would have imagined that their dreams would turn into something as wonderful as this. *Respectfully submitted by Krista L. Meyers, Liberty Road Volunteer Fire Department*

PROFILE OF A FIRE CHIEF:

ELWOOD H. BANISTER

Elwood H. Banister, retired Fire Chief of Baltimore County Fire Department. He was employed by the department in 1956 and advanced through the ranks of lieutenant, captain, battalion chief, deputy chief and chief deputy; being appointed fire chief in 1990 and retired in 1994. In addition he has been a member of the Cockeysville Volunteer Fire Company since 1954 and currently serves as president. During his career he commanded the Fire Academy and Emergency Medical Services from 1971 to 1979, during which time Medical Service advanced from basic American Red Cross to Advanced Life Support. He played a major role in the department's acceptance of the National Professional Qualification Standards and assisted in advancing the program to a Maryland State Certification System, which serves as a national model, Chief Banister is a graduate of the National Fire Academy Executive Fire Officer Program, and holds professional qualification certificates as a Firefighter 3, Fire Officer 6 and Instructor 4. He served on the Maryland Fire Rescue Education and Training Commission for 18 years, also the Governors Emergency Management Advisory Council, Region III Fire Chiefs Council, the Maryland Fire and Emergency Medical Services Coalition, the Local Emergency Planning Committee, the State Fire Prevention Commission, the International Association of Fire Chiefs, the International Society of Executive Fire Officers and for years was a member of the International Society of Fire Service Instructors.

Elwood H. Banister

HISTORY OF THE PATCH

The current arm patch insignia worn by all FD personnel was designed by Nancy L. Wagner, and submitted in 1980 by her brother, L. Wayne Oursler as a possible design for the new patch.

This patch was selected from many ideas submitted and has been the shoulder patch worn by all personnel since 1980. It is identifies both Fire and Medical Services and the year the department was established.

In 1980 L. Wayne Oursler was a firefighter at the Towson Fire Station #1 C-Shift. He is currently a lieutenant with Engine Co. #2 in Pikesville.

L-R from back: J. Piker, A. Davies, J. Zulke, P. Rice, B. Clark, T. Clark, M. Davies, Rev. J. Lizor, V. Rice, S. Piker, R. Piffier. Seated left to right: T. Priester, B. Davies, J. Riegel, G. Morgan, J. Cook, B. Harvey, M. Morgan

Citizens in Edgemere met in 1935 to address the urgent need for fire protection for their community. The Edgemere Civic League was formed and met with the county commissioner to obtain a paid fire station. However, after many meetings, the commissioner informed the Civic League there were no funds available and suggested they form a volunteer fire company. Not to be deterred, the Edgemere Civic League's efforts paid off and the North Point-Edgemere Volunteer Fire Department was organized. The first Board of Directors for the new fire company was elected consisting of seven members on Nov. 5, 1936 and the company was chartered on November 10 of the same year.

The first piece of firefighting equipment purchased by the fledging fire company was a 1914 American LaFrance four cylinder 65 gallon engine. With only one fire hydrant at the corner of North Point Road and Sparrows Point Road, firefighters would have to draft water from the Back River or homeowners' wells. Now, of course, fire hydrants permeate the area.

There was no fire house at the time. The engine was parked in an old garage at Snyder and Sparrows Point Rds. In 1945, the fire company was able to purchase property at 7100 North Point Rd. from the Fradkin Brothers for $1,000. In 1952, the fire company purchased property at 7500 North Point Rd. and in 1958, constructed a two bay fire station. Two more bays were added in 1964 to house the additional fire equipment of the growing company. Today, North Point-Edgemere Volunteer Fire Department runs an average of 600 calls annually in its first alarm area.

L to R: Howard Glauber, Unit 155, Chief Donald Warren and Elwood H. Banister. Towson, York Rd and Shealy Ave, 1960's 4 alarm fire.

THE CHESTNUT RIDGE VOLUNTEER FIRE COMPANY
A BRIEF HISTORY

In the the 100+ years of the Baltimore County Fire Service, it stands to reason that the Chestnut Ridge Volunteer Fire Company's history can be considered brief. Brief, meaning since 1954, with the actual Fire Company's establishment of October 2, 1956. This would make "The Ridge" the youngest of the 31 Baltimore County Volunteer Fire companies. Obviously, these 44 years were not without hard work, triumphs and tragedies.

The groundwork for the Fire Company began in 1954 with various community groups raising money, originally for fire extinguishers in homes. In 1956, what was the Chestnut Ridge Fire Protective Association wrote and requested a meeting with the Baltimore County Volunteer Firemen's Association for the purpose of establishing the Chestnut Ridge Volunteer Fire Company. Since fund raising was going on since 1954, the company was ready to proceed with a station and an engine. The station was built in 1957, on the Price property, located on Greenspring Avenue, north of Caves Road. A Ladies Auxiliary was also formed this year.

In 1959, Mr. W.A. Chenoweth, a citizen of the community, donated a Dodge truck. This unit would be designated as "Brush 502." The pump was actually purchased by the efforts of members collecting newspapers from the community. In 1960, 15 fireman completed MFRI basic firefighting. In addition, money was available to purchase the necessary turnout gear, hose, house siren and most of all the first fire engine. The contract for the 1961 Ford/John Bean, 750 GPM pumper was actually signed in March 13, 1961, with the delivery in June. It was officially placed in service on August 18, 1961. The CRVFC was also accepted into the BCVFA on October 19 of the same year.

It was the community's efforts and continuous fund raising by the members, which put the Company on its feet financially throughout these years. The engine would be paid for on April 1, 1965.

Throughout the years, CRVFC responded to several fires, dwellings, barns, and brush. Whether the fire was major or minor, one factor was always prevalent. This was the lack of water. In 1969, the company placed in service Engine 503. This engine would carry 1,000 gallons on-board, which would give 1,750 gallons of water available on the two engines for "the Ridge." This was quite an accomplishment for these times, but

New Engine-Tanker 503 Picture taken before the dedication ceremony. Company members L-R, 1st row: Secretary Cheryl Noetzel, Treasurer Harry Kakel, Vice President Gene Reynolds, President Richard Yaffe, Captain Daniel Uddeme, 1st Lieutenant Stephen Simmers, 2nd Lieutenant Frank Corasaniti, 3rd Lieutenant Jamie Lloyd, Engineer Gilbert Edwards. 2nd Row: Janice Coroneos, Nick Coroneos, Ruth Edwards, Fred Cross, Tim Edwards, Albert McCausland, Marti Fox, Michael Lunnen, Allen Roody, Chastity Lloyd, Martin Listwan, Josh Kakel, Julie Green, Member-at-Large Steve Kinsey, Michael Fox, Charles Cohen, Matthew Glace, Jack Crystal, Reginald Robinson

sometimes still not enough. In 1975, Engine 501 was repainted with a black roof and pillars. This color configuration still exists and is the only such color scheme in the Baltimore metro area.

When it came time to replace Engine 503, it was decided to build an engine-tanker, which could move large quantities of water from the water source to the fire. In 1986, Engine-Tanker 503 was born. This engine was designed with a 2,500-gallon tank and a "jet-dump" which could discharge the water in less than 90 seconds. It also carried a 3,000-gallon folding tank, to hold water closer to the attack pumpers of a fire. The 3rd generation Engine 501 also was built with 1,000 gallons and a "jet dump." A tanker-support unit, Special Unit 504, was also built for the primary purpose of gaining access to ponds and streams and setting up a draft to fill the tankers and provide water at the fires. A medical support unit, Utility 507, was placed in service in 1999, equipped with an automatic external defibrillator, to respond on the increasing number of medical responses on "the Ridge." The 3rd generation Engine-Tanker 503 was placed in service on September 9, 2000.

This engine was a major improvement over the current 503 with state-of-the-art features such as three jet dumps, remote controls for these from the cab, and a hydraulic descending fold-a-tank. The enclosed picture is from the dedication of the new Engine-Tanker 503. Chestnut Ridge had answered its primary need for their community, water supply. Chestnut Ridge still plays a vital part in the BCVFA's rural water committee.

Many members have come and gone. Unfortunately, three members left way before their time. On March 30, 1982, Frank Fenwick, a long time member, and frequent Line Officer was killed in plane crash in Westminster. On July 9, 1990, Engine 501 responded to a fire at Gwynnbrook and Bonita Avenues. This would turn out to be the last alarm for 1st Lieutenant Daniel J. Raskin. He sustained massive injuries and would succumb to his injuries on July 16. He remains and hopefully will remain the only CRVFC member to be killed in the line of duty.

On September 2, 1999, the Chestnut Ridge family would have to hold another Fire Department funeral for one more of their own. Life Member, current 1st Lieutenant and past Captain Bill Newberry passed away suddenly at age 54.

In the 44 years of the Chestnut Ridge Volunteer Fire Company, a lot of sweat and tears have been shed to provide Chestnut Ridge and surrounding communities fire and EMS protection, and rural water supply.

Sources: *Chestnut Ridge Volunteer Fire Company, An Interpretive Chronology,* by Andrea Simmers
Baltimore Sun, July 18, 1990
Community Times, April 1, 1982

Engine Tanker 503, 2000 Seagrave, 1750 gpm pump, 2500 Tank, 50 gal. foam

BOWLEY'S QUARTERS

P.O. Box 4910

BALTIMORE, MD 21220-0910

Bowley's Quarters Volunteer Fire and Rescue Company, Station 21, has a proud heritage dating back to 1945. Over the past 56 years, the company has grown tremendously. Our humble beginning was handful of men using a car to pull a trailer full of basic fire equipment. They operated out of a single bay wooden garage. In the year 2001, our company is proud to operate out of two buildings, the oldest of the two housing fire equipment, as well as our banquet hall. The hall has grown to be one of the largest and most popular halls in the county for weddings, bull roasts and social events.

Seating 400 people, the banquet hall is the primary source of our fundraising efforts. The newer of the two buildings, started in 1997 and dedicated on May 17, 1998, is the main home of the fire suppression, rescue, marine and medical support equipment. An addition is already being discussed to upgrade our facility to better accommodate our firefighters. This will include a training classroom, bunk room, kitchen area and locker room facilities.

The Bowley's Quarters Community is a unique area, comprised of about 2,000 middle and upper income level homes, as well as several apartment and town-home developments. The area is on a peninsula, surrounded by the Chesapeake Bay, Middle River and Seneca Creek. Over the many years, the community has seen its share of floods, hurricanes and tropical storms. Because of this proximity to water, the company has chosen to operate a marine rescue division in addition to regular fire suppression and heavy rescue duties. Comprised of four boats and the supporting trucks and equipment needed to operate, the Bowley's Quarters Volunteer Fire and Rescue Company has become known also as Marine Emergency Team 21. As of 2001, the boats include a 25 foot Parker, a 17 foot Boston Whaler, an inflatable Zodiac kept on Squad 213 and a 23 foot Jones Brothers center console, placed in service on November 14, 2001. That's a long way from the wooden rowboat our early members used!

In addition to the marine equipment, "Bowley's" operates two Class A pumpers, Engines 211 and 212, one heavy rescue/floodlight unit known as Squad 213, one special unit numbered 214, and one utility truck 218. On the same date the new boat was placed in service, November 14, 2001, a new Chevy Suburban utility truck to be known as 215 was also placed in service. This unit will serve as the primary medical support unit. Committees are already in place to look into replacing Engine 211 with a new pumper and the addition of a Basic Life Support Unit. That unit will be an ambulance to meet the growing demand for emergency medical services in our community due to the ever expanding population. We are also very proud to have recovered our first pumper known then as Engine 214. This piece is a 1947 Mack open cab engine that served the community well in its prime years. Minimal restoration has returned it to operational condition. It has been decided by the membership that the unit will be preserved in a "history bay" to be constructed in the future and that the unit will never leave Bowley's Quarters again. It was sold many years ago in order to purchase a newer engine. It was located in a garage in Carroll County and re-purchased by our company.

Our membership consists of about 135 dedicated men and women, many of whom are former active firefighters. About 40 people are currently active, answering around 650 calls per year. We are also proud to say that we have a Ladies Auxiliary second to none and a Junior Fire Brigade that has been operating for several years. We try to encourage the volunteer spirit in the younger people of our community and attempt to gain their interest in the Fire Department at an early age. Our members have seen their share of memorable incidents. Many of our older members refer to Bowley's Quarters as "the disaster capital of Baltimore County," an unjust title for our quiet little waterfront community! In addition to the hurricanes and floods mentioned above, one of which cost two of our members their lives during a rescue effort in 1971, our members have answered the call for many well known incidents.

One of our most memorable calls in recent years was the crash of the Stealth Fighter jet during an air show at Martin State Airport on September 14, 1997. The plane crashed on Chester Road off Susquehanna Avenue as many horrified residents watched the wing break off and the plane crash to the ground. The pilot parachuted to the ground, landing only a few feet from the inferno. That resulting fire burned several structures as well as the jet itself. Our firefighters were first on the scene and put out the heaviest of the fire. Because of the top secret nature of the jet, our community was "taken over" by many Federal agencies for about a week. The Bowley's Quarters station became the command post for this operation, that brought worldwide media attention to our company. The Stealth crash was one of six different plane crashes that our members recall over the history of our department.

And, of course, anyone familiar with the history of Baltimore County will remember the Amtrak Train derailment on January 4, 1987. Squad 213 was the initial rescue company called to the scene and upon arrival, the crew was overwhelmed with several hundred injured passengers and many people still trapped inside the wreckage. The accident occurred when a northbound passenger train slammed into a slower freight train in the Harewood Park Community, just before crossing the bridge over the Gunpowder River. Crews fought extreme cold and other conditions for many days. Ultimately, 16 people lost their lives in the incident. Again, world-wide attention was focused on all the communities in the area, including Bowley's Quarters. Our station was used as a center to house passengers and conduct other command duties.

With the arrival of apartment complexes in the area, came many memorable incidents. Several fires over the years caused firefighters from Bowley's Quarters to request a "second alarm." The apartments also brought sad memories to the community when, in the year 2000, a man named Joseph Palzinski, armed with several guns, began a shooting spree in the Bowley's Community. That incident went on for a week with the gunman moving around our neighborhood in the wooded areas. He was ultimately shot and killed by police during a hostage situation after somehow making his way to Dundalk. Engine 212 and Squad 213 were on the initial call to provide medical assistance to the shooting victims, as well as a landing sight for the State Police Medivac helicopter and floodlight service to the Police Department during their investigation. Media coverage showed the world again that this incident was "unusual" for Bowley's Quarters and that it really is one of the best places to live in Baltimore County.

So come down and look at our community, dock your boat at one of the many marinas in the area, enjoy a meal at one of several restaurants, or spend the day at Miami Beach Park. Our members are sure you will enjoy your visit. And don't forget to stop in Station 21 and see what we are so proud of..

Like other rural communities of the time, neighbors were relied upon in the event of fire. The effectiveness of this practice can be questioned. From newspaper accounts of the time, it is evident that several structures in the Cockeysville area were destroyed by fire. One structure was the residence of Mr. George Jessop Sr., a prominent man in the community.

Mention is made in the April 11, 1896, edition of *The Maryland Journal* that Mr. Jessop has hired carpenters to rebuild his home, which was destroyed by fire on Palm Sunday. The extent of damage the estate suffered is unknown, but the events that follow are an indication that Mr. Jessop did not want a similar fate to befall his neighbors.

In the following months, Mr. Jessop met with several other men in the community to discuss the lack of fire protection in the area. The nearest fire station was located seven miles away in Towson, and could offer no assistance to the tiny village. The residents of Cockeysville were solely responsible for protecting their own community from the devastation of fire, and it was now time to accept that responsibility.

George Jessop Sr. and nine other men from the community took this responsibility seriously. In October 1896, they formed the Marble Hill Fire Department, the oldest volunteer fire company in existence in Baltimore County, Maryland.

The company consisted of ten charter members: George Jessop Sr., who served as the company's first president, George Duncan, Martin Hyland, Louis P. Kraus, Harry Hess, William Storey, John Tyrie, Charles Noppenberger, Carroll P. Benson, and Max Goldberg. Two other men were also involved in the formation of the volunteer company, though not as charter members: Abram Ensor, who acted as Secretary, and Jacob Fowble, who acted as Captain.

The volunteers of the Marble Hill Fire Department consisted of these twelve men; their only piece of equipment was a 20-gallon tank which was mounted on three wheels and pulled by hand. The company operated out of the carriage house owned by Mr. Abram Ensor, located on the corner of York Road and Shawan Road. The carriage house is still in existence today, and stands as an outbuilding on the property of a local real estate office.

Although no early records exist from the Marble Hill Fire Department, its effectiveness as an established fire company in the early years can be questioned. In the June 5, 1897, edition of *The Maryland Journal,* mention is made of a stable and its contents, including two mules, being destroyed by fire on May 28, 1897. The stable was owned by George Jessop Sr., president of the Marble Hill Fire Department!

The ineffectiveness of a 20-gallon hand-pulled tank in an area of hills and valleys soon became apparent to the volunteers. Records indicate that the company purchased a horse-drawn ladder truck with a hand-operated force pump in 1898. The new apparatus was too large to be housed in Abram Ensor's carriage house, so the company began its search for a more modern facility. Jacob Fowble, the company's Captain, offered to sell his carpenter shop to the department, and they readily accepted. The volunteer fire company moved to its new home located at York Road and Ashland Road a short time later.

The community of Cockeysville experienced a flourishing growth over the next several years. The financial success of local mills and quarries, coupled with the thriving agricultural trade of the area, encouraged people to flock to the still-quiet community, away from the hassles of city life. Residences were constructed along the York Turnpike, and the area experienced an economic boost as a new century began in America.

The population growth in Cockeysville increased the risk of fire and required that the volunteers of the Marble Hill Fire Department look for better ways to protect the community. The Baltimore County Commissioners realized the company's dilemma, and in 1900, loaned the volunteers a chemical engine. The large horse-drawn engine had previously been used by the Canton Station, and was replaced because of its age and weight. The Marble Hill Fire Department graciously accepted the use of the engine, despite newspaper articles which suggested that the Baltimore County Commissioners only offered to loan the volunteers the engine because they did not know what else to do with it.

With the acquisition of the new equipment came another problem, one with which the volunteers were becoming accustomed: the carpenter shop purchased in 1898 was too small to house both the chemical engine and the ladder truck. Once again, the company was forced to look for a new location.

It appears that a second building, owned by the Marble Hill Improvement Association, was located at York and Ashland Roads, in front of the carpenter shop. Certain records mention a building being donated to the volunteers, while others mention that each charter member contributed $100 to purchase a building.

By 1907, other volunteer fire companies had been established throughout Baltimore County. The companies knew little of each other's work and difficulties, and many had complaints of not being appreciated by the communities which they served. The companies received very little financial assistance from members of the community, and virtually no financial assistance from the county commissioners.

One August 31, 1907, two delegates from each of the thirteen established companies, including the Marble Hill Fire Department, met at Towsontown for the purpose of forming a volunteer association. They adjourned after discussion, and met again on September 20, 1907, at the Hotel Junker in Baltimore City. Fourteen companies were now represented, and together they organized the Baltimore County Volunteer Firemen's Association, which is still in existence today.

Further detailed history of the early years of the Marble Hill Fire Department is sketchy, incomplete, and in some instances, nonexistent. The first written documentation of the company does

not begin until 1913, 17 years after the company is established. However, newspaper accounts follow the growth and maturity of the company, as more and more mention is made of both the "good turnout" of the Marble Hill Fire Department, and of the numerous items and property saved by the volunteers.

The Marble Hill Fire Department was launched into a new era beginning in 1913. Membership in the volunteer fire company was limited to those few men who lived in the immediate vicinity. The volunteers recognized the need for newer members in order to provide more efficient service to the growing community, but they were hampered by the self-imposed geographical restriction. At a company meeting on April 7, 1913, the members voted unanimously to change the name of the Marble Hill Fire Department to The Cockeysville Volunteer Fire Company, which enabled men from a wider geographical area to become volunteers with the esteemed company.

This observation is evidenced by the annual report submitted by the company on August 13, 1917. The report indicated that the volunteers attended thirty-two fires, saved property valued at $98,400 and suffered an estimated fire loss of $35,605.

The courageous volunteers of the Cockeysville Volunteers Fire Company did much more than answer the community's cries for help. It seems certain members had a desire to pursue a career in drama, and the Entertainment Committee decided to take advantage by staging a play on safety for the community. The play debuted at the firemen's hall on April 11 and April 12, 1924, and raised $113.27 for the company. The play received so much praise from the community and local newspapers that the members took it on the road, performing at various sites throughout Cockeysville and Sweet Air in Baltimore County, at Hampstead in Carroll County, and Hampden in Baltimore City. The play raised an additional $137.70 for the company while on tour. By 1929 the company had once again out grown their station and moved into a new brick station at York and Ashland Road.

The volunteers continued to look toward the future, and in late 1928, made plans to purchase an ambulance. This unit would provide free emergency medical service to the citizens of Cockeysville and the surrounding area. The unit arrived at the station on April 8, 1929, and was placed in service. This made the Cockeysville Volunteer Fire Company the first volunteer company in the state of Maryland to provide free ambulance service. The unit responded to 350 calls in the first year, many of which were outside the Cockeysville area.

In 1937 the company would accomplish another first, with the purchase of a tractor and trailer tanker-pumper unit.

The unit was designed so that it could respond to a fire and leave the trailer section, which contained the water tank, at the building. The tractor would be disconnected, then proceed to the closest water source and pump needed water back to the trailer. This practice eliminated the time that had been wasted in the past searching for an adequate water supply, and resulted in much timelier saves for the company.

The design was exceptional, and very modern for that particular time. The unit remained in service with very few problems through 1962, when it was finally sold because it had simply worn out from the heavy use by the volunteers.

In 1941, the company purchased a three-wheel, 81 cubic inch Harley Davidson motorcycle. The motorcycle had a flat bed area on the rear, and was equipped with Indian tanks, brooms, and rakes. This unit was placed in service shortly after its arrival at the station, and the Cockeysville Volunteer Fire Company had the first unit in Baltimore County specifically designed to fight field fires.

On January 24, 1955, eighteen women met at Cockeysville fire Hall for the purpose of forming a ladies auxiliary. In attendance at the meeting were Ruth Forward, the County Organizer, and Doris Markens, the State Organizer. H. Bayly Johnson, the President of the Cockeysville Volunteer Fire Company, attended the second meeting in February, and officially welcomed the help the ladies would provide.

Details were finalized at the March meeting. Officers were elected to serve for the year, a bank account was opened, bylaws were drafted, dues were established, and committees were organized. The women made applications to, and were accepted in, both the Baltimore County Ladies Auxiliary, and the Maryland State Ladies Auxiliary. The dream that had been pursued for more than 37 years had finally become a reality.

Over the years, the Ladies Auxiliary of the Cockeysville Volunteer Fire Company has been responsible for organizing and running banquets and wedding receptions, bake sales, rummage sales and flea markets, and dances and raffles. They have sold cookbooks and flavorings as a means of raising money. The funds raised by the auxiliary have enabled them to donate money and purchase much needed equipment for the fire company.

Station in 1929

1929 Nash Ambulance

1937 Diamond T. Tanker

Cockeysville Volunteer Fire Company Ladies Auxiliary (1962)
First Row, L-R: Marion Walker, L. Howard, Carol Tracey, Becky Bosley, Jean Roberts, Cathy Price, Elva Baldwin, Ruth Constantine.
Second Row, L-R: Beverly Meinschein, Catherine Roberts, Sadie Smith, Mary Sheeler, Nancy Cole, Ruth Roberts, Margaret Powers.
Third Row, L-R: Mary Smith, Sophie Nash, Ida Goldberg, Julie Philpot, Peggy Johnson, Catherine Bosley, Betty Lee Frederick, Cora Martin, Peggy Shephard, Clarise Arobgast, Helen Banister.

The Cockeysville Volunteer Fire Company continued to grow and flourish in the last part of the eighties. They also experienced the many burdens that accompanied this growth.

The station was in need of major repairs: there were problems with the heating system, problems with the roof and the bunk room, and problems with limited space. The company's annual budget continued to increase, but income had stabilized during the past years. And there was an over-all decline in the general economy.

The Board of Directors met in early 1987 to discuss the company's situation, and concluded that they were not taking full financial advantage of the company's valuable property. A Property Facility Study Committee was appointed by President Elwood Banister, and the real estate consulting firm of Lipman, Frizzell, and Mitchell was hired to investigate the options available to the company. Extensive studies were conducted during the following months, and the available options were presented to the membership.

A motion was then made at the company meeting of November 2, 1987, to lease the front two acres of property, and build a new station on the remaining one acre of ground at the rear of the property. The motion passed by a margin of 41 to 3. The Board of Directors then held a special meeting to review the proposal from the real estate consulting firm, and decided that the company's income could be dramatically increased if the front property was rented.

The company then received an offer from DePaul Limited Partnership. Negotiations took place over the next several months, a deposit was issued to the company, and a lease was signed on October 17, 1988. Foot prints and sketches of the new building were received from architect Gerald Baxter and reviewed by the membership in time to allow for any suggested changes. Some of these changes were submitted and incorporated into the plans by Mr. Baxter. The company was ready to begin the bid process.

A progress report was issued by the Building and Property Committee to the 52 members present at the company meeting on June 26, 1989. Shaeffer and Strohminger, a car dealership, had signed the lease with an option to buy the property after 10 years; approximately $125,000 had been spent to date for the services of the architectural firm and the engineering firm of Daft, McCune and Walker. The committee had approached Baltimore Gas and Electric Company about additional parking on the adjacent property.

They were also ready to approach the Noxel Corporation regarding a rear right-of-way.

The company had received four bids for the construction of the station. The bid opening took place on August 17, 1989, and the contract was awarded to Atlantic Builders for $1,150,000, with construction to be completed in 213 days. The company's loan for $1,164,000 was approved by the Baltimore County Loan Fund on October 16, 1989, and the ground-breaking ceremony was scheduled for the end of the month.

Construction of the new station began in December and was completed at the end of August 1990. Members gathered at the station and began the arduous task of sorting through the memorabilia that had accumulated over the past decades. Things with sentimental importance were saved or distributed to the members; items that did not seem so important at the time were donated to different organizations or disposed of completely. Other items of no use were sold at auctions or flea markets. The entire process took several weeks, and ended when the building was dedicated on October 28, 1990.

The company was in need of other improvements, as well. The 1974 Mack was beginning to show the signs of heavy use,

and a committee was appointed in 1991 to study the feasibility of replacing the engine.

A 1992 Freightliner chassis with a Four Guys body was then ordered in late 1991. The new engine would include a 1,000 gallon tank and a 1,500 gpm pump, and would replace old Engine 399.

Groundbreaking

Construction begins

Near completion

Completed

COWENTON VOLUNTEER FIRE COMPANY

The Cowenton Volunteer Fire Company was originally started in January 1943 as a World War II Civil Defense (CD) Unit. When America entered the war in December 1941, it was recognized that incendiary enemy bombing, particularly of East Coast communities, was a distinct possibility. It was also realized existing fire defenses of that time would be overwhelmed by such a situation. The answer was the Civil Defense Trailer Pump, which had worked so well in England during the Nazi Air Raids of 1940. These units were supplied by the Federal Governments to communities large and small along coastal areas.

The CD pumper consisted of an industrial gasoline engine of about 100 horsepower with a 500 GPM centrifugal pump, all mounted on a trailer suitable for towing by a car or light truck. The unit carried two lengths of hard suction, had an exhaust primer and space for about 500 feet of 2-1/2" hose. It was designed for the most basic form of exterior firefighting.

With such a piece of apparatus, seven men and seven women began serving their community in the embryonic form of what would ultimately be today's Cowenton Volunteer Fire Company. The unit was stored at Gambrill's Coal and Lumberyard. Rudimentary training sessions were held and competitions with other nearby CD units were conducted. Fundraisers were organized and when the receipts were inadequate to meet the needs, members dug down into their own pockets to make up the difference.

Although potential firebombs never materialized, the CD trailer saw use during the war years in the day-to-day protection of the community from other fires. After all, the nearest regular fire companies were at Essex and Fullerton, and anything closer was an improvement.

It became apparent by the beginning of 1945 that the war would be over in the near future. With the need for local fire protection that was demonstrated by the use of the trailer, it was decided to move forward to something more self-contained and possibly with provisions for an apparatus water tank. Plans and fundraisers were devoted to this goal. Thus in 1945, a used 1934 Ford school bus chassis was purchased and converted into Cowenton's first "fire engine" with the addition of the CD pump, a water tank of unknown capacity, and other fire fighting equipment. The unit was housed in Mrs. Jane Bickels

Supply

barn. On July 16, 1945, the company was incorporated. The first Board of Director meeting was held August 13, 1945, with the first company meeting immediately thereafter. The seven "founding fathers" were Clinton DeBaugh Sr., Clinton DeBaugh Jr., Charles Elste, Leroy Eurice, David Foley, John Foley and George Williams.

1946 saw the arrival of the first commercial pumper, a six cylinder Dodge carrying a Hale 500 GPM two-stage pump, a 400-gallon tank, and a standard hose bed. In 1947, a sheet metal building was erected to the right of Jane Bickels home to house both the Ford and the Dodge engines. 1947 also saw the organization of the Ladies Auxiliary. Over the next 35 years, this group of women was a valuable asset to company progress, serving fire ground refreshments, assisting the men in their fund raising efforts, and conducting their own activities to raise money. In addition to their active service, each year the fire company was presented with a check, the amount dependant on the success of auxiliary events. The admission of women to full company membership in 1972 was the death-knell for the auxiliary. They managed to hang on for another decade until October 1982, when they gave the fire company a check for $1,000, put the rest in the Bessie Marshall Fund and disbanded.

1959 saw further progress. Building on land donated by John Carrol and Fred Gambrill, work was begun on the older part of our present day station. This same year saw Cowenton begin community ambulance service using a 1940 unit donated by the Bird River Improvement Association. In 1962, members attended Ambulance School at City Hospital where they learned advanced first aid skills. A few experience members participated in the first CRT programs between 1972 and 1974 and became certified as some of the first ALS providers in the county. The first telemetry unit was placed in service in 1978.

Over the years, training became and integral part of life at Cowenton. Members took part in MFRI training programs and other professional certification course. An in house hydraulics program was developed and a manual written by John Berwick became the standard text endorsed and used by both the Volunteer Association and the paid departments. Mandatory training was instituted in 1971 and continues today. Members would attend or they wouldn't ride; it didn't matter if smoke could be seen from the bay. If there wasn't a currently trained crew, the engine didn't go. This has become the bedrock foundation of the quality, professional service the company provides.

From these humble beginnings, Cowenton Volunteer Fire Company has grown over the years. A building expansion and renovation was completed in 1989. The new drive through three bay station housed two modern KME 1250 GPM pumpers, a fully ALS equipped Ford Medtec ambulance, one of the most versatile Jeep brush units and a four wheel drive utility. In the late 80s, Baltimore County Fire Department conducted a "truck study." Using the rapidly growing community, the planned developments, and zoning requests, it was determined there was a need for an aerial apparatus in the area. After many years of deliberation between Cowenton and the county, and a lot of hard work by the members, a dream became a reality as used 1983 95-foot E-One Stratosphere Ladder Tower equipped with a 1250 GPM Hale pump pulled into the lot. On July 14, 1997 within seconds of being placed in service by Captain Jack Amrhein, it responded on its first call: a 55-14 building fire. On May 12th of that same year, Cowenton became the first volunteer station to provide ALS Support, otherwise know as "Paramedic Engine" service using an SOP created by one of its own members and endorsed by the Volunteer Association. The energetic and innovative members are the only limit of what the future holds. There is a constant effort to improve and expand and with the dedication of the members and the community anything is possible.

Excerpts by John Berwick reprinted with permission

GLYNDON VOLUNTEER FIRE DEPARTMENT

FULFILLING THE NEED — 1904-1994

The Glyndon Volunteer Fire Department was conceived in a meeting of a group of residents called to discuss fire protection on March 4, 1904. It was at this meeting held in Townsend Hall, now known as Redman's Hall, that is was decided to form a volunteer fire company for the Glyndon Community. In accordance with the action taken at that meeting the company was formally organized at a second meeting held on March 25, 1904. The minutes of the second meeting show the following 23 men as active members:

J. Smith Orrick, Chas. R. McNeal, J.J. Dyer, T.R. Arnold, G.H. Taylor, Chas. E. Sentz, Wm. Chineworth, Geo. A. Schull, C.H. Whittle, G.C Dausser, A.A. Rich, W.T. Stringer, C.C. Billmyer, Chas. B. Kelly, Geo. E. Smith, J.H. Lohr, Chas. Switzer, A.M. Ruby, D. Danner, Henry Baublitz, Ernest Benson, Albert Henry and T. Whittle.

The following first officers were elected at this meeting: president, J. Smith Orrick; 1st vice president, Chas. R. McNeal; 2nd vice president, J.J. Dyer; secretary, W.T. Stringer; treasurer, T. Reese Arnold; ass't. secretary, C.C. Billmyer; chief foreman, Geo. H. Taylor; 1st ass't. foreman, Chas. B. Kelly; 2nd ass't. foreman, Chas. E. Sentz; marshal, Wm. Chineworth; ass't. marshal, Geo. A. Schull; librarian, C.H. Whittle; janitor, Grover C. Danner.

In May of 1917 it was decided that the business of the company required weekly meetings and the company elected to meet every Monday night. With the business of organization taken care of, the company turned to the matter of acquiring a piece of fire fighting apparatus. On April 13, 1904, a committee appointed by the President visited the County Commissioners to seek their assistance in the purchase of a piece of apparatus for the fledgling company.

Mr. T. Reese Arnold reported that after thoroughly explaining the needs and objectives of the new fire company, the Commissioners agreed to match whatever money the company could raise up to $300.

With fund raising for the proposed apparatus underway, the secretary of the company was instructed to communicate with Mr. Herrman, then fire marshal of Baltimore County, to ascertain the first steps to be taken towards the purchase of apparatus and what could be purchased for about $600.

The matter of a fire alarm was also considered, and the following article was added to the constitution governing its use of the alarm bell. Article 8 "The Bell."

Section I—The Bell shall be sounded as follows; in case of fire the first member at the house shall strike the bell rapidly a definite number of times which shall constitute an alarm of fire.

Section 2—The sound of a fire alarm being productive of uncalled for fears and excitement on the part of the citizens, the members, therefore, are warned against willingly committing such an offense under the penalty of expulsion.

Section 3—The sounding of the Bell for unusual meetings of the members shall only be done by direction of the majority of the standing committee through the President or in his absence, one of the Vice Presidents respectively.

In the months following the visit to the commissioners, a committee had been investigating the purchase of a piece of apparatus for the company. During this investigation they had visited A.B. Whitlock Company of Baltimore who at the time were making a hook and ladder truck. With their specifications and plans, the approval of the committee, and also the approval of a Mr. Herrman,

the Fire Marshal of Baltimore County, they reported to the company. With the company's approval, they ordered this hook and ladder truck with a gold pump for approximately $600. This truck, was delivered in December 1904. The hook and ladder truck was horse drawn and answered fire alarms with horses supplied by Rutter's Livery Stable.

Considerable discussion was held on the matter of a building to house the apparatus and serve as a fire station for the Glyndon Community. At this time the equipment was being stored at the Glen Morris Supply Building. Later that month the committee reported that Mr. Kelly had bought a piece of property known as the Smith lot and would sell a portion of the property to the company. With the company's approval, a lot with 25 front feet and 87-1/2 feet deep was purchased for $125.

With the business of the company moving ahead rapidly it was decided that the company should incorporate. The original charter of the organization was drawn up by Mr. Rich, free of charge.

Having acquired the lot on Railroad Avenue, a committee was appointed in March 1905 to draw up specifications and plans to erect a building on this property.

On June 15th, the building committee reported to the company that they had sent out plans and received bids on the proposed building. The bids submitted were opened and were as follows: S.G. Marshall, $1,150; G. Walter Tovel, $1,150; John McEwin, $1,486.

Not having sufficient funds to erect a building of the type planned, the building was tabled for the time being.

The first recorded report of a fire alarm was on July 19, 1905, at the Culbreath Farm. The foreman reported that the apparatus was gotten out and hurried to the fire until stopped halfway being informed that it was not necessary to proceed. The fire had been put out by the farm hands. The foreman further reported that in addition to himself, Mr. Rutter and a third man responded with the apparatus. It was estimated that the apparatus could have reached the fire in 15 minutes from the time of alarm.

On October 5, 1905, a new committee was appointed to investigate construction of a building for a fire station. They were authorized to erect a one-story building to cost between $600 and $700.

In November 1905, it was brought to the attention of the committee that the hook and ladder truck then stored in the Glen Morris Supply Building was being eaten up and destroyed by the fertilizer being stored on one side of the truck and the horse stable on the other. The truck was then moved to the Kingsbury Wagon Shed (now State Rds. Garage).

The company elected to join the Maryland State Firemen's Association in May 1906. In August 1907 a letter was received from the Towson Fire Department, then a volunteer company, requesting a delegation from the company to attend a special meeting at Towson on August 20th. The purpose of this meeting was to organize the Baltimore County Volunteer Firemen's Association. A second meeting was held on September 20, 1907, at the Junker Hotel in Baltimore. At this meeting the association was formally organized and officers elected. The Glyndon Volunteer Fire Department was one of the original 14 companies forming the Baltimore County Firemen's Association.

The new fire station was finally completed on the Railroad Avenue property in January 1908. The fire apparatus was moved

1937 Ford Pumper later modified to operate as a ladder truck, and finally modified to serve as a brush unit.

1966 Mack Pumper

from the Kingsbury Shed to its new quarters and on January 30, 1908, the first meeting was held at the new engine house using a stove, desk and chairs donated by the members of the company. This structure was used by the company until the present building was occupied in 1956. The building is still standing and is presently occupied by Northwest Radiator.

In the short space of two years this young fire company had become a fully organized operating fire department with a modern piece of apparatus and a new building to house it. They had helped to organize the County Firemen's Association and had become deeply involved in the affairs of the State Firemen's Association. This remarkable progress is a tribute to the civic interest and energy of the original 23 members and the many who became members in these early years.

Unfortunately, the company records do not contain any record of the early fire alarms that the company responded to and because of this an interesting facet of the history of the fire company has been lost.

In October 1912 it was decided to secure a hand drawn chemical apparatus from W.H. Whiting Company on approval for 30 days. The apparatus was delivered and demonstrated at an oyster supper held on November 8-9, 1912. At the December 26th meeting of the company Mr. Wheeler, Chairman of the committee reported that the apparatus performed as specified and recommended that the company purchase it. The recommendation was accepted by the membership and the equipment purchased for the sum of $275. An air proof box was later constructed at the engine Association, of which GVFD is a member, directing all volunteer companies to remove all "All Service Masks" from service. Only self-contained type masks were to be used such as Cemox or air bottle type. The company procured three Surviair masks for each E401 and E403 and retained two Cemox on each engine.

In October 1974, with the number of alarms rapidly increasing, the company found itself continually short of manpower during the normal workday. To help serve their community better, the company accepted and trained seven female firefighters to help man the equipment. The first seven female firefighters were Maxine D. Warner, Rosemary Stem, Maxine E. Warner, Carol Beimschla, Mary Merriken, Donna Warner and Jill Warner. All passed the University of Maryland Basic Firefighters Course and were allowed to ride the equipment and have proven to be an asset in fire suppression. Of course in the beginning these were not the best dressed women in town in the fire scene. Until the company was able, due to delivery times to purchase firefighting gear, to better fit these new firefighters, they used the available equipment. Another step taken in late 1974 to increase their available manpower was to offer firefighters first option on renting the company's apartments next door.

Individual equipment update took place starting in January 1975 when many members purchased tone alert radios to replace their conventional radios. The tone alert system sounds an alarm similar to an alarm clock when the Glyndon Volunteer Fire Department siren is toned to blow through the county's radio control system. At a cost of $226 per individual, fire call alerts have been modernized, cutting minutes off the response time and furnishing large crews during night time hours.

The Glyndon Volunteer Fire Department was continually studying the needs of their community. As a result, in July 1975, President R. Warner appointed a committee to look into the purchase of an aerial ladder truck, to add to their existing fire suppression units. This committee existed of Chief J. Warner Jr., C.E. Cole, E.R. Brown Sr., R.W. Stem Jr., J. Whiteside, J.E. Warner III and R. Warner. Their investigation disclosed that new aerial ladder trucks were running from $160,000 to $225,000. These prices were far higher than what the company could possibly finance at that time.

The committee then turned to trying to find a clean used piece of equipment to start their truck company. In late March 1976, the committee found a lead on the sale of a 1960 Peter Pirsch 85' ladder truck at the Goodwill Volunteer Fire Co. in New Castle, Delaware. On April 30, 1976, the company placed a deposit of $3000 down for a hold until arrival of a newly ordered aerial at the Goodwill VFD.

On October 2, 1976, the balance of $27,000 was paid to Goodwill VFD and a team of Chief J. Warner Jr., E.R. Brown Sr., J.E. Warner III, J. Whiteside, C.E. Cole and R. Warner, picked up GVFD's new but used aerial ladder truck. This was on a very rainy Saturday afternoon in an open cab unit. Arriving in Glyndon a little damp, the team was now faced with the problem of putting a 42'6" long truck in a 35' fire house.

On February 18, 1977 this new equipment addition was placed in service to be called Truck 404 at a total cost of $40,000. The first run for T404 was to 415 Valley Meadow Circle on February 21, 1977. On February 18, 1978 T404 ran on a 2nd alarm fire to assist Carroll County on a building fire at 838 Main Street in Hampstead and used the ladder pipe for the first time.

Again in mid-April 1975, the company found it advisable to update their equipment. With the increase in the number of times air bottles need to be filled with air, the company decided to install an air cascade reservoir of three 3500 lb. cylinders at a cost of $1086.80. These large cylinders are kept filled by the air unit from Pikesville Volunteer Fire Co. (A328).

In 1976, a committee was appointed to proceed with the Building and Expansion Program. On April 5, 1976, the company voted to hire an architect to draft the plans and specifications for the addition to the building. Later that same month, Frank J. Norwicz, Architect, was contracted for the sum of $2800 to provide the drawings and specifications. These architectural drawings were submitted to the company in September 1976 and bid requests were immediately placed to contractors.

In April 1977, the Zoning Commission approved the complete project. On September 15, 1977, the O'Meara Construction Company was contracted to complete the building expansion as it presently is constructed.

April 1979 saw upgrading of our hose load from 1-1/2" to 1-3/4" hose for better firefighting capabilities.

June 23, 1979 saw a dreaded propane fire at Suburban Propane on Old Hanover Road, Woodensburg, where our Department alone used 960.75 man hours to help extinguish. Apparatus responded from as far away as B.W.I. Airport to assist in extinguishment.

In July 1979, at a cost of $1,630 we replaced our Meushaw appliances with the more modern Humat for a quicker and better operation to supply water from hydrant to fire scene.

Our 75th Anniversary was celebrated in 1979 as we hosted the Baltimore County Firemans Association Convention at our Station.

With the addition of Truck 404 in 1977, our truck company operations were used numerous times in Carroll County, so a Carroll County Radio was installed in the truck on January 28, 1980.

On March 23, 1980 our Department received 20 pagers from Baltimore County, that were distributed to officers, operators and the most active members to help notify members of emergency responses. Later on more pagers were acquired and distributed.

A committee was appointed to look into purchasing a newer ladder truck. After checking on many leads, a motion was made to purchase a 1972 Mack Power Ladder from World Wide Equipment Co., on March 17, 1986.

The 1972 ladder truck, T404 was put in service July 23, 1986. The old Peter Pirsch Ladder Truck was sold to Rock Hall and delivered August 2, 1986 for a price of $25,000.

A loan of $55,000 was made from Baltimore County to put Truck 404 in service.

A Committee consisting of R.W. Stem Jr., R.W. Stem Sr., J.E. Warner Jr., Edward C. Schultz, Russ Lessner and Bill Fowble, with Chairman J.P. Brach were appointed to check into the purchase a new engine and specifications were started on January 18, 1988. After specifications were completed and bids secured, it was decided to purchase a 1250 G.P.M. Pumper with a 750 gallon tank from Emergency One of Ocala, Florida in April 1989 for a price of $204,921.

On March 7, 1989, Truck 404 was designated a Tower Ladder.

In November 1988, some of our members and one engine were involved in the filming of the movie *Her Alibi* starring Tom Selleck.

The new 800 MZ communication system was placed in service during November 1989.

On April 23, 1990, a motion was made to purchase a 5" hose load for new Engine 403 that was delivered and put in service July 2, 1990, at a cost of $6,500.

Dedication of the new Engine 403 was held May 20, 1990.

On June 29, 1990, the original alarm bell that had been on loan to Gill's Church was returned to our Department.

For use in ventilation a new positive pressure fan was purchased for a price of $1,375 and was placed in service on Truck 404 in October 1990.

A tornado struck the area of Chartley in Reisterstown on Thursday, October 18, 1990. The top floors of several apartment complexes were blown off and numerous homes were damaged in the area of Glyndon Drive, Shirley Manor and Northway. The tornado seemed to leap to a complex of apartments near Bond and Glyndon Drive and then to Bond Avenue and the Railroad tracks where more houses were damaged extensively. Our Department spent a total of 960 man hours over two days assisting Reisterstown in evacuation, lighting and search details. It was considered to be a total of three alarms for this emergency. The Baltimore County and State Officials were on hand to survey the damage and the area was pretty well cleaned up of debris and fallen trees in record time. Power was restored to the area by 1700 hours Saturday, October 20, 1990.

The Department purchased a VCR for $249 to assist in our training program on October 22, 1990.

After continually repairing a used generator we had purchased for our original Truck 404, it finally gave out completely and a new Honda 6.5 K.W. unit was purchased for $2,550 in July 1991 and was placed in service on Truck 404.

January 20, 1992, the Department donated $200 toward the Fire Safety House that was a cooperative venture by the Volunteer and Career Departments in Baltimore County. This structure was constructed on wheels so that it could be moved from place to place as a training facility in fire prevention to the general public.

September 21, 1992 approval was given to install a new sign in front of the building for a price of $4,168. The sign was constructed and installed November 16, 1992. by Pearsons Signs. The old alarm bell that was returned from loan was incorporated in construction.

Approval was also given for installation of electric door openers by C&D Doors of Hampstead for $2,765.

An Ankus Rescue tool was purchased for $3,995 to be carried on Engine 403 for use in rescue operations when the squad or truck are not on the scene.

On November 16, 1992, an electric powered diesel pump was installed in place of the hand pump used for many years.

Throughout its 90 years of community service, the members of the Glyndon Volunteer Fire Department have striven to provide the most modern and effective fire protection possible to the residents of the Glyndon Community. This remarkable growth has only been possible through the self-sacrifice of all of the members, past and present, and through the constant and generous support of the residents of Glyndon.

1916 Federal Apparatus and members. L to R-on truck-Walter Snyder, J. Edward Bollinger, John Boylston, Edward Wilson, Grafton C. Wheeler, Charles W. Fishpaw, Charles F. Sentz.On ground-C. Howard Whittle, William Roylston.

The Ladies Auxiliary of the Glyndon Volunteer Fire Department was organized in 1953 by Mrs. Frances Rook, Mrs. Rosemary Stem and Mrs. Susie Reter for the purpose of helping the men. The first meeting was held on March 10, 1953, in the old fire house on Railroad Avenue. The first officers were Mrs. Frances Rook, President; and Mrs. Susie Reter, Vice President. They were installed by Mrs. Zulauf, President of the Baltimore County Association. The men donated a new gavel and a check for $100 to help the ladies get started. There were 94 charter members.

In May 1954, the first fried chicken dinner was held. In March 1957, the first donation to the firemen was in the amount of $1,300: $1,000 for the building fund and $300 for the equipment. Also, a pledge of $450 to the new Carroll County Hospital and $200 to the Maryland State Hospital fund were made.

In March 1959, the men gave their first Appreciation Dinner and Dance for the people that had helped with the carnival. Each year since, they have held the dinner and dance in March. At that time, the ladies presented the firemen with two checks. They were in the amounts of $2,500 for the building fund and $1,000 for the equipment.

When the new fire house was opened in 1956, the ladies furnished the kitchen. The third anniversary celebration of the Auxiliary was held in the new building on Butler Road on March 13, 1956. The Auxiliary serves several public dinners each year on Sunday afternoons. They also cater luncheons, bowling banquets, dances, wedding receptions and private dinners.

Over $75,000 has been donated to the Glyndon Volunteer Fire Department by the Ladies Auxiliary since they were organized 26 years ago. The Brush Unit was furnished through the Ladies Auxiliary. In addition to the $75,000 mentioned above, the Auxiliary gave the men $10,000 in March 1979, as they celebrate their 75th Anniversary. They also, in March, donated furniture to furnish the new recreation room, curtains for the meeting room, recreation room and the hall.

The Ladies Auxiliary has been busy for the past 15 years with catering banquets, weddings, private parties, public dinners, breakfast, sub sales, food stands for craft shows, flea markets, open houses at the fire house, casino nights and Monday night bingo for nine years, plus many other activities.

We have donated since 1980 through 1993, about $73,000 plus a copy machine, computer, printer, renovated the kitchen, a new dishwasher, new supplies for the kitchen and 200 chairs and new tables for the hall.

Two members of the Auxiliary have served as presidents for Baltimore County Ladies Auxiliary. They are Rosemary Stem 1981-82, Judi Stem 1991-92 and at present Joan Wolfenden is serving as treasurer 1993-94.

There are 13 members of the original 94 charter members as follows: Claudia Barnes, LaRue Brown, Ruth Brown, Carrie Heflin, Edith Linthicum, Mary Merriken, Susie Reter, Rosemary Stem, Nancy Stocksdale, Maxine Warner, Ruth Warner, Mrs. Yates Wilson, Mary Zentz.

The Ladies Auxiliary of the Glyndon Volunteer Fire Department consider it an honor and privilege to serve the Glyndon Volunteer Fire Department for the past 40 years.

Ready for transport, trench rescue

REISTERSTOWN VOLUNTEER FIRE COMPANY

BEGINNINGS, GROWTH AND PROGRESS

Fire fighting in this area until 1913 consisted of neighbors voluntarily responding to a blaze armed with their own buckets, forming the legendary bucket brigade.

Today, good neighbors still respond voluntarily to fires, only now they are known as the Reisterstown Volunteer Fire Company and they respond to calls with some of the finest equipment available, acquired through their own hard work and the support of the community they serve so faithfully, a tradition that extends back to the beginning of the Company.

In 1913, after three bad fires, the residents got together and decided to form a volunteer fire company. With this part of the organization work underway, the women of the community got together and set up a picnic supper, a project that cleared $412.29. From those humble beginnings The Reisterstown Volunteer Fire Company started.

First equipment was a Challenger hand pump, 250 feet of 1-1/2 inch hose, 30 feet of two inch hose, 18 rubber buckets, two ladders, two axes, two hooks and a hand operated chemical tank; total cost $285.39. Everything was kept in Arthur Uhler's barn.

At the July 1913 meeting a constitution and by-laws were adopted, patterned after those of the Glyndon Volunteer Fire Company and it was decided the name of the company would be "Reisterstown Fire Company No. 1 of Reisterstown."

Just a year later, in May 1914, with financial help from the county commissioners and by public subscription, two important acquisitions were made. A 1912 used Packard fire truck was purchased for $3,400, of which $2,900 was paid in cash with a note signed for the balance. It was a right hand drive vehicle with carbide headlights. There was no cab or windshield, so in cold weather the driver (Wilbur Kelly was the first) had to wear goggles and gauntlet gloves.

The first fire on record to which the Company responded with the new truck was on September 30, 1914 at the residence of W.M. Harden. The report stated that the Company saved 50 logs, a pile of cordwood and an oak tree.

The other 1914 acquisition was the old Odd Fellows Hall on Main Street, built in 1852 by the Independent Order of Red Men. It was to be the first engine house and served until the present station house was built in 1949. Purchase price was $1500 of which $500 was paid in cash with a mortgage assumed for the balance, the deed being signed July 14, 1914.

In April 1914 the Company joined the Baltimore County Volunteer Firemen's Association and on June 8 of the year, the necessary legal documents were drawn up making the fire company a corporation, an action deemed necessary with the ownership of the fire house and major equipment.

However, in September of that year, the Company found itself in financial straits and demonstrated the initiative and resourcefulness that was to mark its future progress. Funds were needed to meet the note due on the fire truck so members were asked to pay their dues a year in advance, thus avoiding a financial crisis.

During 1915, cement steps were constructed and a coal bin installed at the engine house.

A metal barrel was acquired for drinking water during the annual picnic in 1916 which featured the Baltimore County Boys Brigade who held a sham battle along with two ball games. During this year too, the mortgage on the fire house was completely paid off.

In January 1917, the picnic lots on Chatsworth Avenue were purchased for $450 from Mrs. E.P. Shaffer. Since then additional property has been purchased until the entire Firemen's Grove now belongs to the Company.

It was during 1917 the Red Cross Circle requested a detail of firemen with extinguishers attend their meeting as moving pictures were to be a part of the entertainment and fire protection was desired.

During 1917 the Company voted that all active members who enlisted in the military service of the United States during the war with Germany should be carried on a special Honor Roll and should not be liable for payment of dues. First names to appear on the Honor Roll were W.D. Peregoy and William Uhler.

Insight into the economy of the era was provided in the 1920 minutes which listed: "Paid Gas & Electric bill of .72 and telephone of $1.75; paid janitor $5.00 per month; received $400 as county appropriation; net profit on picnic $1,101.20; served 1,399 suppers at .35 each; invited to Hampstead Fire Company parade; decided to paint the firetruck for the occasion; host to Baltimore County Firemen's Convention."

First fire siren was ordered from Federal Electric Company on March 30, 1925 for $516 less 5% for cash. However, difficulty was encountered mounting the siren on top of the engine house and running a wire to the telephone exchange so it was near the end of the year before it was finally operational.

During October 1925 a Packard chassis was purchased for $700 less a donation of $50 from the C.W. Dorn Company, which was renovated for use as a chemical tank, replacing the antiquated 1914 truck. Most of the conversion work was done by members George H. Stevenson and J. Edwin Eline.

The most disastrous fire in the history of the town occurred February 11, 1928, known as the Great Reisterstown Fire, burning for over 11 hours, destroying eight stores and causing damage of $250,000. The fire was discovered by Marion H. Michael at 3:45 a.m. in Sander's Meat Market. Weather was near freezing with snow covering the entire area. There was no public water supply in Reisterstown at the time so it was necessary to pump water from Johnson's ice pond, located in the woods between Westminster Road and Cockeys Mill Road about two miles west of town. It required a tractor to pull the engine through the mud and snow to get to the pond and then several engines were needed to relay the water to the fire through one 2-1/2 inch hose line.

Eventually 18 fire companies arrived to assist in trying to control the blaze. One of the fire companies coming the farthest was the Lineboro Company who traveled 35 miles over very bad roads, a trip that took them over one hour and 50 minutes one way.

Apparently the firemen were exhausted afterwards because the only report made was a note stating: "4:00 a.m. 6:00 p.m., 130 gallons gas; 11 hours pumping - gallon oil."

Reisterstown suffered the only loss of life in the line of duty during 1928, answering a call for an automobile fire at Reisterstown Road and Gwynnbrook Lane on July 26. On arrival the car was burning and Fireman Monroe Seitz took a hose line and approached the vehicle. At that moment the car's gas tank exploded, spraying him with flaming gasoline. Fireman Seitz died a few days later of these burns in a Baltimore hospital.

Early fire engine

Because of the major fires in the business district, the Company made plans to build a reservoir to provide a ready source of water for fighting fires within the town. The reservoir served its purpose many times until city water arrived in 1937 when the reservoir was drained and filled with dirt.

Baltimore County Fire Bureau converted to what is called Central Alarm in March 1954, whereby all fire calls are channeled through headquarters in Towson and individual companies are alerted and volunteer station sirens are blown by radio control.

Manpower was quite a problem during World War II when most of the younger men were away in the armed forces. Older members came out of retirement to man the fire apparatus during the emergency.

During the 1950s it again became increasingly difficult to secure sufficient manpower for fire and ambulance calls during the day when most active firemen were away at work. Accordingly, the Company employed a full time paid fireman for the day hours starting in April 1958 for which no additional compensation was received from the county but the Company felt the action increased the efficiency and service to the community.

After the close of the war in 1945, the Company started considering plans for a new fire station. On July 23 plans for the new building were approved by the Company by a vote of 67 to 3. A contract was awarded Charles B. Tovell and Company and a $50,000 loan was secured. The new building, still standing at 108 Main Street, was dedicated January 30, 1949.

An ambulance was added to the fire company's equipment through the generosity of the Kiwanis Club in January 1946. Primary function during this time was transport of patients to and from hospitals, a service discontinued in later years. As the population and medical advances were made, more demands were made on the ambulance. Calls made in 1948 were 189, in 1986 they were 1,136. Some of the strain was relieved with the opening of a Baltimore County Fire Department (paid) paramedic unit based at Hannah More Center in 1987, but that year still found 856 calls made by the volunteers at Reisterstown.

Training for the ambulance crews initially was a basic knowledge of first aid and the ability to transport residents or apply bandages and/or splints when necessary. Currently, in order to even ride the ambulance, 110 hours training are necessary, qualifying as an EMT (Emergency Medical Technician). To continue on to become IV Technician, 24 more hours are required and to go still further and become a paramedic, 200 more hours are required as well as certification by the state of Maryland. And, like firefighters training, the ambulance crews must pay for their classes and do it on their own time, so they can volunteer to serve the community.

In May 1967 the Reisterstown Junior Fire Company was established in conjunction with the Explorer Post 410 that was started in October 1964, giving young men the best of both areas.

During the 1983 Post charter night and installation of officers, the then Company assistant Chief Bob Higgs explained the program, "it provides activity for boys 14 through 18 years of age, exists to keep the Company going with at least 50 percent of the Scouts continuing in the Fire Company. Many become Company officers. Right now the Chief, vice president, Captain, five lieutenants, ambulance Captain and lieutenant are all former Post 410 members."

With the dawning of the technological era, responsibilities of the volunteers broadened, equipment became more complex, training more in-depth and techniques more sophisticated. Just as the Company was very much an integral part of the community from its inception, it continued with an ever broadening scope.

A testing of this capability to meet community needs occurred with the arrival of what was officially called a torrential downpour but what was called by the majority of residents, Hurricane Agnes. Many demands were made on the volunteers during this disaster and their tasks were made more difficult because numerous roads were flooded, bridges washed out and other roads blocked by fallen trees. Volunteer firefighters started working to relieve the situation when the heavy rains started doing damage on June 22, 1972 and they worked around the clock, combating the torrents destruction, then dealing with the aftermath. "It was a couple of days I will never forget," was one firefighter's observation.

One of the most unusual demands was the result of two local youngsters who called the fire house in 1976 for help; help in rescuing two canines trapped in a storm sewer on Cherry Hill Road, one being a large German Shepherd and the other a full grown Labrador Retriever. With calm ingenuity they brought the frightened animals out of the small confining sewer one at a time and in rather unorthodox fashion, treating the whole incident as though it were an everyday occurrence. To all the anxious youngsters watching, the volunteer firemen became instant heroes.

Realizing the complexity of demands on the Company were increasing, a Rescue Squad was purchased in 1974, their first which was a used GMC to be used mainly to provide the capability for heavy rescue work such as auto accidents, building collapses, cave-ins and train derailments (and it has been used for every one of those purposes plus more). It was also to be used to provide electrical power for working fires. And over the years, it has been used in numerable times for all these services, used so much that it was replaced with a new Ford built to the Company design, dedicated in May 1980 and which is still in use.

One of the biggest and most threatening fires flared at Suburban Propane Company on Hanover and Old Hanover Roads, starting with

a big boom when a 300,000 gallon storage tank exploded sending flaming bits of metal and debris in all directions and giving the impression of a war zone, a situation repeated all too often during the long day. Although it went to six alarms, fire officials stated there was enough equipment for a 16 alarm fire. It all started about 10:30 a.m. Saturday, June 23, 1979 and was finally extinguished about 5:30 p.m. of that same day although firefighters remained on the scene until after midnight pouring water on undamaged tanks to guard against any heat buildup.

Diversification has become a way of life for the volunteers during the past decade. This was dramatically illustrated when they supplied round-the-clock medical supervision during Franklin High School band's bid for the *Guiness World Book of Records* in April 1980. The band played continuously for over three days and two nights at the Strawberry Patch with constant medical assistance available courtesy of the Company.

Dedication of Company members and community support have been the mainstays throughout the years, building a fire company of which every resident can be proud. In this brief history, that never wavering devotion to service is evident, continuing today as the firefighters daily earn their livelihood through a regular job and then use their spare time to train and upgrade their skills, answer the numerous calls for assistance from the community whether those calls be for fire, rescue, illness or accident.

Dick Fox, Ted Schultz and Jim Eline with Utility Truck

LADIES AUXILIARY TO RVFC

A BRIEF HISTORY

Ironically, the community women were at work for the fire company before the Company was established; in fact, the ladies raised the funds that established the Company.

When it was decided to have a volunteer fire company, the ladies were asked to hold a picnic supper to raise funds, which they did on May 30, 1913 in the Grove on Chatsworth Avenue, raising $412.29, a sum immediately turned over to the men to start Reisterstown Volunteer Fire Company.

Several traditions were started with that picnic supper. It continued at the Grove, held every Fourth of July, gradually growing into what is known today as the annual Carnival. And, it is still one of the major fund raisers for the Company even though the suppers were discontinued in 1965, not by the ladies but by County Health Department regulations. The reason given? Lack of sanitary conditions. However, one veteran firefighter grumbled, "Nobody ever died of those suppers that I know of; nobody even got sick."

Completely undeterred, the ladies continued to support the Company having cake, candy and lemonade stands at the carnival for many years and then diversifying into various fund raisers, always with one object to assist the Company in its growth and progress.

Officially organized July 17, 1933, the Ladies Auxiliary was formed following the annual Ladies Night held at the Grove by the firemen after the Fourth of July carnival as a way of saying thank you to the ladies for their assistance. First president was Bessie Marshall who not only organized the Reisterstown Auxiliary but in 1939 organized and was the first president of the Baltimore County Volunteer Firemen's Association Auxiliary. She didn't stop there though, becoming Maryland State Volunteer Firemen's Association Auxiliary president in 1938 and was active in all three levels of the Auxiliary for many years, years that started right here in Reisterstown.

Following the Congoleum Nairn fire at Cedarhurst in September 1947, a Relief Committee was formed for the purpose of taking sandwiches, soup and coffee to the firemen when they were fighting a fire. Whoever was in charge of the fire notified the Auxiliary president of the fire location and about how many men were working. Local stores were cooperative too, opening at all hours, day and night, for the ladies to obtain food. At one working fire, it was reported that a firemen made the comment he never thought "he would appreciate hot soup for breakfast, but it sure tasted good."

The Relief Committee was very active until the start of Box 234, better known as the Coffee Wagon, that supplanted the committee services.

First big project of the Auxiliary was equipping the kitchen in the new engine house. Two ranges, two work tables, two coffee urns and a steam table were purchased for $1,096.50. Small, but necessary, utensils and equipment were acquired by holding a kitchen shower and the kitchen was ready when the firehouse officially opened in 1949.

When the kitchen was renovated and remodeled in 1972, it became the Auxiliary's project to not only make suggestions but also help finance the project.

Throughout the years the ladies have added the amenities to the fire house such as outfitting the bunk room and making drapes for all the windows. A few of the ladies even have dual roles, being active members of the Company as well as active members of the Auxiliary.

Efforts of the group have always been to assist and support the Company; the same goal the Auxiliary had when it first started.

Hosing down the flame

THE JACKSONVILLE VOLUNTEER FIRE COMPANY

PHOENIX, MARYLAND 21131

History is a record of man in conflict with circumstance. Man never seems to be satisfied with a void or mediocrity, because someone will observe, criticize and insist that the void be filled and mediocrity be replaced.

That's how it was in Jacksonville. When the need of better service for controlling fires appeared, men started to do something about it. One particular group, namely Gene Stewared, Shelben Thompson, Harry Lindsay, Jack Askew and Charlie Dumphy got together a Community Meeting in Chestnut Grove Church in the early Spring of 1953 and discussed the vital need of a local Volunteer Fire Company. The meeting was well attended. It elected an acting Chairman and established a date for a second meeting. Officers were elected and this organization was incorporated in the Spring of 1953.

In the meantime a committee was appointed to look for a used piece of fire equipment. After a thorough search in the Civil Defense and Baltimore City Fire Department, it was decided to buy the old AMC LaFrance which Cockeysville had standing idle. This engine was bought on October 1, 1953 for $1,000 and after much repair, went into service in November 1954.

To get some money into the Treasury, a Fund Drive was started. Contributions were solicited from anybody who would stand still long enough to listen to the plea. An Oyster Roast Committee was appointed and on November 15, 1953, the Fire Company had its first affair in the American Legion Hall in Towson. We had it split the proceeds right down the middle with the Legion.

In a meeting in May 1953, Shelben Thompson was appointed chairman of the Land Committee for the purpose of finding land suitable to build a fire house. He reported in the June meeting that Mr. Murgatroyd would sell to the Fire Company a six acre tract. A deposit of $300 was made for the property and it has been the home of the Fire Company ever since. The following November, for a total of $5,800, the land was paid for and with this, the land transaction was completed. Now the Fire Company was rolling in high gear.

In September 1953, a building chairman and committee was appointed. They immediately started plans for the fire house and in March 1954 the president of the Fire Company was authorized to borrow $30,000 from the Towson National Bank for the purpose of building a Fire House. In April 1954 the first blocks were delivered for the building and October 6, 1954 the first meeting was held within the new Fire House.

In 1956 our first new piece of apparatus was purchased for $16,500. A GMC American Pumper was placed in service as engine #471.

In 1963, it was decided that our old American LaFrance be replaced. In 1964 an International American 1,000 Gallon Tanker Pumper was placed in service as engine 473 at a cost of $24,000.

A Dodge American 1 Ton Brush Unit with a 500 GPM Front Mount Pump was placed in service as brush unit 472 in 1967. This $12,700 unit was designed particularly as a drafting source of rural water and has seen extensive use at emergencies in Baltimore and Harford counties.

During the floods of 1971 and 1972, several of our members borrowed boats in order to effect the rescue of persons trapped by the rain swollen rivers. To combat the rising trend of water rescues the company had to respond to, it was decided that rescue boat be purchased. A committee was formed and a 14 foot flat bottomed aluminum boat fully equipped with water rescue and recovery equipment was purchased, partially through the generous donation of $500 from the Western Electric Company, Inc. The boat is powered by a 25 HP engine. All the men that respond on the boat are specially trained and must be qualified swimmers and proficient in boat handling. This boat covers a large area of Baltimore County and parts of Harford County, and responds to special requests wherever it may be required. The boat was dedicated to the four volunteer firemen who lost their lives during the 1971 floods.

Due to the increasing use of the Maryland State Police Helicopter for transporting accident victims to the trauma center at University Hospital, it was decided that a helicopter pad be installed at the Jacksonville Volunteer Fire Company. The helicopter pad was built by the members of the fire company through funds allocated them by the Ladies Auxiliary and a $100 donation from the Harry T. Campbell Company. On November 25, 1973, it was dedicated to the four Maryland State Policemen who have lost their lives in the line of duty since the helicopter service was initiated.

With time, the Fire Company has found the need to further expand and update its services to continue providing the best for the community. With this in mind, the early 70s found these changes: In 1971 an International Fire Engine was purchased at a cost of $38,000 to replace the 1956 GMC. It was put into service in November 1971 as Engine #471.

Also in 1971, a Jeep was purchased and outfitted for the company by the State Forester at a cost of $5,000. It was put into service in November 1971 as Jeep #474.

In 1973 a Chevrolet Ambulance equipped with the latest in ambulance equipment was purchased at a cost of 17,000 and was placed into service in May 1973 as Ambulance 475 replacing the original unit. The ambulance along with Engine #471 was dedicated to the past deceased members of the Fire Company.

Also in 1973, a 1974 Chevrolet 1/2 ton pick-up was placed into service as Utility Truck #477. This vehicle is used to transport members to meetings throughout the county and state and for other needs as required.

As our community progressed so did the Fire Company and in 1978 we replaced our ambulance with a Chevrolet Swab Medic Unit at a cost of $30,000 and was dedicated to our Ladies Auxiliary.

In 1979 we took delivery of an $89,000 Seagrave 1,000 gallon tanker pumper. This unit replaced our older International as Engine 473 and is dedicated to the past Chiefs of Jacksonville.

In 1982 a group of concerned citizens banded together with the Fire Company to enhance our service. A committee was formed to purchase a Cardiac Thumper. Mr. And Mrs. Herbert Lee came forth with 100% of the funds needed to purchase the Thumper. Due to their kind response to this critical community need a life was saved. This gave the time to put together a musical revue written especially for Jacksonville and raise the needed money to pay back the funds. We were the 2nd Volunteer Company to place a Thumper in service on our medic unit in Baltimore County.

As our community grew so did our need for sufficient water sources. In 1984 we placed in service a 1983 Dodge/Page Lambert 1 ton brush unit. The 750 GPM front mount unit was purchased at a cost of $57,000 and replaced our 1971 Jeep.

May we all hope that it will not take a catastrophe to change this trend. It would be difficult to think of another community service where so many hours are given freely and where good will represents the only financial resources.

The early to mid-80s saw many companies go to the use of the new Ford E-350 van front style ambulance. The Jacksonville Volunteer Fire Company purchased a new Ford gas powered unit in 1986. In early June 1987 the company received several safety notices from Ford regarding the gasoline fuel tanks and heat build up. The company initiated all precautions. On July 30, 1987 the fire company received a recall notice from Ford saying that the unit would have to be taken to a dealer for modifications to the gasoline fuel system. Ironically, on the same day, several hours later while leaving GBMC Hospital from an emergency call the unit burst into flames and was totally destroyed. With the support of neighboring volunteer fire companies and the career service Jacksonville was back in service with a loaner ambulance and equipment that same night. The Fire Company and county received national and international news attention. While several other similar units had been damaged due to fire it is believed that the Jacksonville unit was the first to be destroyed. Insurance coverage helped the Fire Company replace the destroyed unit with one powered by a diesel engine. Later, the insurance company recouped its pay-out from Ford.

1995 saw construction start for a much needed new facility for the Jacksonville Volunteer Fire Company. The original building constructed in 1954 had served the company well but was severely outdated and lacked much needed space. The project saw the original 40' X 100' two-story station receive a total rehab and remodel. A 120' X 80' one-story addition was added. The new station boasts eight apparatus bays each with its own overhead door as well as a state of the art maintenance bay area. The station is equipped with separate men's and women's sleeping quarters, shower and locker areas. Communications, recreation, multi-purpose rooms, kitchen, training, storage and much needed office space are included. A new 30,000 gallon underground water tank for fires in the area was also installed.

Preparing to foam

Central Alarmers, Inc., a volunteer organization, was formed on a cold winter night in 1955, when a three-alarm fire broke out at Harford Road and Taylor Avenue in Parkville. Baltimore County, at the time, did not have a coffee wagon, so one from Baltimore City was dispatched. Baltimore County Deputy Chief F. Lee Cockey was overheard by Howard Glauber, owner of Glauber's Candy, to say that Baltimore County needed a coffee wagon. It did not take Mr. Glauber and a couple of firebuff friends long to form the Central Alarmers. By May of 1955, a charter was signed by chief officers of the county fire and police departments along with 15 members of the Central Alarmers. Of course, the first coffee wagon was Glauber's Candy delivery truck and by September, thanks to a donation by the Lions Club of Towson, a Schmidt's Bread truck was purchased and converted into a canteen truck.

The name, Central Alarmers, was chosen because the group mainly covered the central section of the county, from the city line to the Pennsylvania line. The unit number 155 was chosen because our first official run was to box 155 located at Sheppard Hospital. During those first years, the group's headquarters was at the Towson Fire Station. The truck, however, was not allowed to be housed in the station itself, but rather on the back lot. Many times members had to dig the truck out of the snow in order to respond to a call.

In 1966 a custom-made truck was purchased and housed in the Hillendale Fire Station. In 1974 the unit relocated to its current location at 7856 Belair Road. This station was built in 1920 and formerly housed Baltimore County Station #8 with one engine and an ambulance. Station #8 moved into its new quarters, adding a truck company. In 1989 Central Alarmers placed in service a 1976 GMC step van donated by the Baltimore Gas & Electric Company. This unit has continued to serve the entire eastern half of Baltimore Country from Falls Road east and from the Baltimore City line north to the Maryland-Pennsylvania border, including mutual aid service to Baltimore City and Harford County,

With this 1976 truck continuing to rust and require extensive maintenance the unit decided it was about time to pursue obtaining its first brand new truck. After many years of wishing, investigation, planning, and arranging for its financing the purchase of a new truck became a reality in November 1995 when a 1996 Ford E 350 chassis with a 17 foot Grumman Olson Route Star Walk-in Van was ordered. "While awaiting its arrival the detailed planning and designing was being coordinated with the Yaissle Body Company of Pottsville, PA. On June 6, 1996 the truck arrived from Sturgis, MI and was promptly transferred to Pottsville, PA for the works! The months that followed provided a very interesting but rewarding experience, not to mention the round trips between Baltimore and Pottsville, PA. The input of the club members, particularly those of the truck committee, and the consultation with Box 234 and 414 proved to be very valuable in fine tuning the plans. On November 3, 1996 a final trip was made to Pottsville to bring the "baby" home. After some finishing touches including its lettering, the truck was placed in service on November 30th.

After a quiet beginning, with no calls for our services, on Sunday, December 8, the club's new truck was dedicated. Approximately 100 people, including many dignitaries, attended this momentous occasion at Baltimore County Station #8. While this dedication opened a new chapter in the club's history, it is with sadness we closed one chapter as Howard A Glauber Jr., one of our original founders and life member, passed away on April 1, 1995. It was through his dedication and perseverance that Unit 155, Central Alarmers, Inc. was born and to whose honor we dedicated the new truck. A plaque denoting this honor was read to Mrs. Glauber and placed on the truck. It is the club's sincere desire to continue the dedicated service that has come a long way since Mr. Glauber and his candy truck responded to our first call over 45 years ago.

The club now has approximately 45 members that responded in 1999 to 153 calls including 26 multiple alarm fires, five hazmats, two drownings, one train derailment, nine police incidents and six mutual aid calls. Through September 30 this year responses have totaled 110. Our Club continues to operate three units. In addition to our main canteen/rehab unit "old reliable 155," we respond on all "working fires" with fluids in our "quick response" utility 154. We also have available a 1979 Winnabago, designated Rehab 153, containing restrooms and seating which was renovated and placed in service last year. Our unit provides two 10x10 tents, misting fan, portable heater, auxiliary lighting, and cold towels. Just recently our utility 154, a 1986 Suburban, was replaced with a brand new 2000 Ford Super duty F-350 with crew cab, a Reading "Classic" series service body containing a special transverse through compartment behind the cab, side compartments, and a sliding top. This new unit was dedicated on September 20 in memory of a recently deceased member, James A. Evans Jr., a long time active member and retired Baltimore City Fire Fighter.

Our units continue to serve many other details including, house burnings, training exercises, funerals and various ceremonies conducted by the Baltimore County Fire and Police Departments. We are very proud to be a member of the International Fire Buff Associates and to have provided over 45 years of continuous service to the very dedicated Baltimore County Fire and Police Departments. Several notable calls over the years have resulted in participating members receiving ribbons and certificates of commendation for their service. One being the train crash in Chase, MD in 1987 and the Stealth Fighter plane crash in Middle River in 1997. Our organization has also received two unit citations for their support to the Baltimore County Fire Service. Our volunteer organization extends its sincere appreciation to the officers and members of the Baltimore County Fire and Police Departments, the Baltimore County Volunteer Firemen's Association, and the Baltimore County Council for their support

Unit 154

The Honor Guard is a group of highly motivated men and women who strive to represent the Department with pride and dignity at all official events and ceremonies. Our goal is to enhance the image of the department through public relations as well as by interdepartmental cooperation.

The Honor Guard celebrated its twentieth anniversary in 2000. Birth was given to the Honor Guard at a "B" shift activities meeting in July of 1980, held by then Deputy Chief Elwood Banister. The activities meeting was an attempt to plan events for "B" shift personnel to participate in on a county wide basis. At this meeting a decision was made to resurrect the Fire Department Memorial Service which had been discontinued. At the conclusion of the meeting Firefighter Louis Mancuso, the Station One representative, and Firefighter Richard Petry of Station One approached Chief Banister as to the possibility of a Color Team being formed to bring in flags at the beginning of the Memorial Service. Permission was granted and the formation of the Honor Guard was off and running.

There were originally nine members of the unit. Firefighters Mancuso and Petry were commanders, Firefighter Richard Brooks, III was the drill instructor, and Firefighters Norman Arbaugh, John Lloyd, Gary Wheeler, Dennis Krebs, Irvin Lowery, and Captain George Clavell were the active members. The membership is currently at twenty six personnel including buglers and bagpipers. During it's twenty year exsistence, forty-one men and women have proudly served on this prestigious team.

The first official detail for the newly formed Honor Guard was not the Memorial Church Service, but the Fire Expo held on Sunday, October 17, 1980 at Timonium Fair Grounds. Since this first detail we have performed at graduations, funerals, promotions, memorials, dedications and other details deemed necessary by the Chief of the Department.

Over the years the Honor Guard has been nationally recognized as a leader in ceremonial work. We were the Official Honor Guard of the National Fire Academy and served at all their ceremonies, greeting dignitaries from the nation and world. Our unit dedicated the National Fallen Firefighters Memorial in Emmittsburg, Md. and has served at the lead Honor Guard for the outdoor portion of the memorial since that time. We are also the Host Fire Department Honor Guard for the Annual State Fallen Heroes Day held at Dulaney Valley Memorial Gardens each May. Currently, we travel nationally for funerals of multiple life loss of Firefighters. Some of these details have been Chicago, Detroit, Orlando, Kansas City, Mo., Worcester, Pittsburgh, Philadelphia, Washington D.C. and New York. We had the honor of being the only Maryland unit invited to participate in the one hundred twenty-fifth anniversary parade for the FDNY.

The Departmental Honor Guard has had a short but fruitful life. It is the hope of its dedicated members that we continue to represent our proud membership well into the future as we endeavor to serve and protect the citizens of Baltimore County.

SPECIAL STORIES

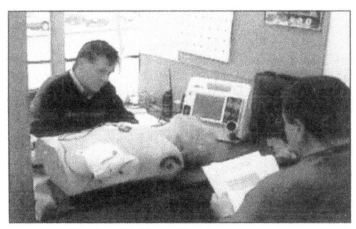

Division Chief Dave Murphy tests a student

EMT-I Class testing by PM Jim Kinard

First EMT-1 Class

Recognizing the need to update and standardize, the state of Maryland began the transaction from the Emergency Medical Technician-Ambulance certification to national standard EMT-Basic during the latter part of 1996. As of 2000, all Baltimore County affiliated EMTs took the appropriate educational upgrade sessions to become Maryland EMT-B. Consistent with transition to national standards, Maryland began to look to an upgrade of the Cardiac Rescue Technician certification. With the exception of adding skills and medications over the years, there have been no overall program re-designs since its inception in the 1970s. CRT was designed to be a basic Advanced Cardiac Life Support certification as an intermediary level of care between EMT-A and EMT-Paramedic. It concentrated primarily on cardiac related emergencies. The national standard DOT (Department of Transportation) curriculum for EMT-Intermediate seemed the appropriate replacement for CRT. Providers would be nationally registered as well as Maryland certified with a migration away from a mainly cardiac related focus to a more expansive medical, trauma and cardiac scope of study. Providers would also have a good foundation for and partial completion of the full paramedic certification program. Keeping with its history and tradition of being on the cutting edge of EMS, Baltimore County applied for and was selected as one of three counties in Maryland to conduct pilot programs for the EMT-I curriculum. The Baltimore County sponsored class is only one of two to be completed in the state thus far. The class entailed over 400 hours of evolutions, didactic sessions, clinics and ride-a-longs. The program began with an enroll-

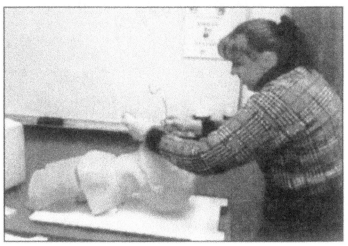

EMT-I Class

ment of 43 students with Paramedic Mark Demski taking the role of lead instructor. Closely monitoring the progress were Medical Director Ameen Ramzey, Captain Michael Robinson, and Volunteer Chairman Jim Clements. Since there was no definitive course lesson plan, many fire department and civilian medical professionals assisted in coordinating a syllabus that addressed all objectives of the DOT curriculum. After nearly a year of preparation, 15 volunteers and two career providers sat for the written exam followed by a rigorous practical evaluation. Baltimore County Fire Rescue Academy is proud to present the completion of its first Emergency Medical Technician-Intermediate program.

Station #13 Apparatus History

Station #13 opened on Monday, November 8, 1965. The original crew was:

A-shift
Captain John Ebberts
Lieutenant Lester Pague
Firefighter Nicholas Waltermeyer
Firefighter Herbert Basler
Firefighter Ronald Herion
Firefighter Gerald Bennett

Engine #13 first response was to 1305 Black Friars Road for a television on fire, on Thursday, November 11, 1965 (time unknown). The crew was:

C-shift
Captain Louis Caperoon
Lieutenant Edward Smoot
Firefighter David Bobbitt
Firefighter Kenneth Zimmerman
Firefighter Marcel Nulter
Firefighter Melvin Riddle

On February 4, 1967, extra men were assigned to Station #13 to man Truck #13 that hadn't yet arrived. In place of a truck, Reserve Engine #64 ran as a second engine out of the station. Truck #13 was received from the maintenance shop on February 20, 1967. This was Baltimore County's 4th Truck Company along with Trucks #1 (Towson), 5 (Halethorpe), and 15 (Eastview). The first truck call is not listed in the logbook.

On February 27, 1967, Civil Defense supplies were delivered to Station #13.

Ambulance #13 was placed in service in the spring of 1968; it was renamed as Medic #13 in 1978. In 1993, it would be called "Paramedic #13" if manned with an EMTP, which would now be the highest level of medical training. A High Expansion foam unit (Foam #13) would also be assigned here in 1968.

For the record: On January 1, 2000, none other than Engine #13 handled the first run of the 21st century. The call was received as an investigation of smoke in the area of 1328 Westburn Road, in a 13-6 box, Incident number 00010048. Despite the anticipation of chaos occurring on this millennium change, New-Year's Eve and Day, was relatively uneventful. The crew was from "C" shift:

Captain Edward Sipes
P.O. Michael Rehfeld
F/S Eddie Dezurn
FFEM Aaron Tapp

STATION #13'S PRIMARY EQUIPMENT

THE ENGINE COMPANIES

The first Engine #13 was a 1965 Mack, C-85, and 750 gallons per minute pumper with a 500-gallon water tank. As was all equipment it was painted red. The engine would be refurbished later on, repowered with a diesel motor, but remained red in color. The Engine would remain in service until replaced by a white over yellow 1982, Duplex/Oren pumper, with a 1250 gallons per minute pump, 500 gallon water tank and a 50' telescoping ladder/boom. This new engine was also equipped with an "around the pump" foam proportioner, and fully enclosed jumpseats. At this point, Engine #13 was one of three companies trained and on responses as a Hazardous Materials Satellite Company. This engine was totally refurbished in 1991, now painted white over red. In October of 1997, the third generation Engine #13 was placed in service. This Engine was a 1997, Freightliner chassis with a 3-D body and a Hale pump. It would be equipped with a 1250 gallons per minute pump and a 750-gallon water tank. In lieu of the foam proportioner, the engine has a 50 gallon foam tank in close proximity of the pump, for use with a "Foam Midget," foam proportioner. This Engine was also the first "conventional cab" engine assigned to Station #13.

THE TRUCK COMPANIES

The first Truck #13 was a 1965 Seagrave, 65' aerial, with a 100-gallon water tank. In November 1972, a new Truck #13 was placed in service. This was a 1972, American LaFrance Snorkel, red in color, with a 90' articulating boom. It had already had its first emergency response, before its' delivery, when it was special called to the 5 alarm fire at the Pagoda Inn restaurant, at 1010 Reisterstown Road, in Pikesville. This was the first Aerial Platform in the history of the Baltimore County Fire Department. It also served as the only snorkel in the career service. When the truck went out for refurb in 1980, it returned white over yellow with a 100' rear mounted aerial ladder. The water tank was also removed. While Truck #13 went through its refurb, a 1964 American LaFrance replaced it, 100 foot, tiller truck.

The third generation Truck #13 was placed in service by "D" shift on March 22, 1992. This was a white over red, Spartan-LTI, 106' Aerial, tiller truck. This truck is equipped with a pre-piped, bed section waterway, and a mounted deck gun, in addition to the regular flypipe. It also has a preconnected Hurst Rescue Reel system. These features were exclusive to this truck until other trucks were replaced. The first run for this unit was at 1759 hours, to a stove fire, at 1221 North Rolling Road, in box area 13-6. At 0702 hours on March 23, new Truck #13 responded on its second call, a working rescue on the Baltimore Beltway. B-shift had this call. That night, A-shift would respond with Truck #13 to a three-alarm fire on Maiden Choice Lane in Catonsville and flow all three pipes.

The current Truck 13, the 106' LTI/Spartan was placed in reserve status as Truck #95. In 1999, Truck 13 became a 100' 1995 Seagrave.

THE AMBULANCE SERVICE

The first ambulance was placed in service sometime in the spring of 1968. This was on a Ford chassis and a Swabb box. This unit was red in color and would be replaced in 1979 with a Ford "van style, walk through" unit. In 1985 a Ford Diesel, Swab box would replace the current unit. This unit was also primarily white, with yellow trimmings. In 1991 Medic #13 was once again red and white with a Chevrolet unit. This unit once again revisited the non-van front style chassis. A Ford XLT replaced this unit in 1997 with a "First Response" box. This unit is also white over red.

HAZ-MAT SATELLITE #13

Haz-mat Satellite #13 was placed in service in 1996. A former paramedic supervisor unit, this Ford F-350 diesel vehicle has compartmentation attached which carries supplies for hazardous materials responses such as Tyvec suits, duct tape, rubber boots, a wedge kit and extra absorbent and foam. It also carries the Haz-mat library of reference books. It runs with Engine #13 on all hazmat assignments.

Where Are They Now?
Former Starter J. Miller Made Transition To Fireman
Ex-Oriole helps save lives in Westview
by Doug Brown, Sun Staff writer
John Miller never has wandered far from home. He grew up in a house on the edge of Slentz Fleld in Irvington, graduated from Edmondson High and lives in Westview now.

This is a west Baltimore boy, through and through. His wife, Judy, is a Woodlawn High grad,

Miller pitched mostly as a starter for the Orioles for parts of five seasons in the 1960s, had a few good moments, then became a fireman—a real one.

When his sore right shoulder rebelled with every pitch and the Kansas City Royals released him during spring training in 1969, Miller left baseball, worked in construction for several years and then became a firefighter.

"A couple boys I grew up with in the neighborhood were in the fire department, so I took the test," Miller said. "Best thing I ever did."

Miller, 54, is in his 24th year as a driver of the ladder truck at Station 13 in Westview. In a year and a half, he plans to retire and join a friend in a home improvement business.

"This has been a good steady job, with good benefits," Miller said, "There's activity, it's helping people and I'm on a team. This is your gang of guys, same crew all the time, just like baseball."

In his senior year at Edmondson in 1960, Miller had a sore arm and a record so bad he couldn't remember it even a year later. It wasn't until August of that year, after a summer under Walter Youse, whose Leone's sandlot team was the best in the region, that the Orioles signed him.

"We figured Miller would get just as much experience pitching for Youse as he would in the minors," said Earl Weaver, then managing in the Orioles' system. "He was so impressive in the Arizona instructional league that fall that we started him in Class B in 1961.

"I remember his first game in the instructional league. We were winning 5-2, and the bases were loaded with none out when I put him in. He wasn't shaking a bit He just took the ball out of my hand and started throwing strikes."

That debut led the Orioles to elevate him to their 40-man roster which meant an additional $4,000 was tacked onto his $10,000 signing bonus. Miller spent only one full season with the Orioles, 1966, but a partial one in 1965 was his best. He started the season 6-2 at Triple-A, then was recalled and compiled a 6-4 record before hurting his shoulder with a month left in the season.

"I couldn't lift my arm for three weeks." Miller said. "The pain never left; it was like a toothache. I made the team the following year. but I don't know how, every time I pitched, it got worse."

Sold by the Orioles to the New York Mets, Miller labored in the minors for two seasons before being released by the Royals in 1969. His career record was 12-14.

"I just couldn't do it," Miller said. "My shoulder was so bad, I couldn't get the ball to the plate."

A career as a fireman beckoned.

A LITTLE HUMOR

January 24, 1992: E-6 filled in Station 9. Tom Kimbel decided to set Brian Yingling up. He called down and said that he was Donald Masonic of the county engineers and needed the footage of Station 9 that was still standing (they are building a new station). Yingling handed Dave Stuart the phone and Tom filled him in. When Yingling was finished he was supposed to call 887-7174 and tell him the footage. The number was to Councilman Donald Mason's office. Tom hung up. Twenty minutes went by and I called down. Stuart answered the phone. I asked if he (Brian) did what he was supposed to and Dave said that he is out there now. Dave said that he started toe-to-toe and I told him to take big steps and estimate. Well Yingling called the number and told him who he was and from where he was and asked for Donald Masonic, the secretary said you mean Don Mason. Yingling went silent. He asked if Donald worked there and said no but Don Mason did. Brian said that he had the wrong number and apologized and hung up. 30 minutes later Don Mason's office called Station 9. Lt. Burkhardt answered the phone. They wanted to know if anyone called from there. Fred said that he was filling in all day and didn't know if anyone did. We all laughed like crazy. Here's to you Kimbel that's a good one.

June 19, 1993: E8 received a call from BC4 about getting some ducklings out of a storm drain on Rossville Blvd. He

Crews from E-101, S-303 and E-291 preparing to attack a dwelling fire, Hillen Dale and Taylor Ave., Box 11-10, Dec. 30, 1989. (Photo by member of Providence)

Crew from E-1 preparing a line for a van fire, Bosley and Joppes Rds. (Photo by Lt. Wm. B. Allenbaugh Jr.)

also advised that the mother duck was out in the middle of the road. E8 called for T8 to assist. Upon arrival they had 10 ducklings in the storm drain and one frantic mother duck flying around. We tried the grates to lift them up but couldn't. We also tried to see if we could get through the manholes but they were to small. Some of the guys on the shift enjoy fishing and had trout nets in their cars. FS Wayne Shaw and FF Jeff Asper both had one. They were sent to the station and brought back their nets where they preceded to fish the ducklings out. While our attention was focused on them we didn't see that the mother duck was hit by a car and killed. We got all 10 out and took them to a friend of FS Blaine Kurrle who had a farm pond to release them away from roads. They became know as the Fullerton Fowls or the Rossville Renegades, but of course our friends at Station 16 made us a nice Unit Citation for the incident! On Saturday, June 26, 1993, the very next trick, we were in the middle of pass on when a woman stuck her head in the door and said, "that we were going to think she was nuts but asked if we rescued animals?" We all thought here we go again! She finished "there was a bird stuck in a tree at the Cedar Lane Driving range." Sure enough there was a mocking bird stuck by his foot upside-down. He was entangled in a kite and FS Wayne Shaw went up, untangled him and sent him on his way. Who would have thought a bird could get stuck in a tree!

June 17, 1997: I was sitting in the office when I heard someone come in and start talking to FF Jim Colliflower. Everyone else was out on a call or doing hydrants. The next thing I knew, Jim comes in and says that this guy is having suicidal tendencies. So I called dispatch to request police and they said that they would send a medic too. I went out into the watchroom to make sure, everything was okay and this guy starts telling us that he worked across the street and thought about killing himself. He hadn't taken his medication and had a pint of vodka. His eyes were bloodshot so you could tell that he had taken something. He then told us that he wanted to strangle this woman that walked in front of the building. He looked straight at Jim and said, "I am having thoughts about killing you, but I am fighting them back." I got up, went back into the office, called dispatch back again and told them to expedite police because this guy wants to kill my firefighter. Before I knew it, I had two county PD cars out front and one sheriff's car. By this time, Capt. Bragg is coming up Fredrick Rd. in E4 and sees the cops pull in and tells FADO Gary Unverzagt to pull on the apron but he pulled into the alley. Bragg comes running around to the front and asks me what is going on. I told him just some guy who did not take his medication wanted to kill my firefighter!

THE FOLLOWING STORIES ARE SERIOUS:

When you are in this business long enough you are exposed to incidents and situations that would affect anyone. Sometimes we laugh or make fun of the situation, other times we cry, it mainly depends on the individual's way of handling tragedy. It is not until we see our jobs through the eyes of a victim can we really begin to see the impact we have on people's lives.

March 28, 1998: While visiting my mother, my children and I were playing out in her back yard, when my 18-month-old daughter Jessica wandered off. After realizing that she wasn't around, we quickly searched the yard, and mom found her floating in one of her decorative fish ponds. She immediately pulled her out about the same time that I was getting to her. One look at her and I thought that I had lost my daughter. Incidents involving children are always stressful, especially severely injured children, however; most of the time we have a few minutes to size up the situation while we are en route. This time I was the call and it was developing right in front of me. I had the responsibility of caring for my daughter and controlling the scene so that my other children did not have to witness this tragedy. While mom called 911 I began CPR. I also got on the phone and real quickly requested additional equipment to the scene. Mom took my other children into the house for me. The time, which seemed like forever, only lasted about 10 minutes before Jessica took her first breath. It was about the same time that some volunteer firefighters started to arrive. Lt. Bill Ulrich had called me back from 911 to get an update and let me know that someone was there with me. Shortly after that, the rest of the crews from Hereford VFD, Hereford Ambo. M60 and EMS7 arrived. My daughter and I were flown to John's Hopkins where my wife met us as soon as she was notified. Twenty-six hours later we were headed home with a healthy and very lucky little girl.

Sometime later as I sat back to process the whole event, and I realized how it impacted so many people. The incident affected the 911 operators and fire dispatchers who had to process the call,

Crews from Towson preparing to advance a line at the 4-alarm Lucas Bros. Store fire on Pennsylvania Ave., Aug. 22, 1989. (Photo by Charles Evans)

Crew of E-41 during pumping contest at Pikesville VFD's Centennial. E-41 from Catonsville took first place. (Photo by Jim Langford Sr.)

the firefighters and paramedics who responded. It also affected friends and co-workers who prayed for a positive outcome. I realized how lucky I was to have the training to do what needed to be done as well as a healthy daughter. I also think that many people realized how close to home this was and that even though we respond as the care providers everyday, there may come a time when we may become the victim. Another positive note is that no matter what happens in the fire service, the fact remains that when something happens to one of our own, it affects us all and we are there to help. Baltimore County has the finest group of firefighters and paramedics serving their citizens and I am proud to be a part of that group.

July 6, 1998: E4 was dispatched to a seizure call at the Wal-Mart 4-14 Box at 1610 hrs. As the engine was approaching the scene, dispatch advised us that it was now a cardiac arrest. Two fellow employees were doing CPR upon our arrival. We advised them to continue while we got set up. Once set up, FF George Brooks took over ventilations, Lt. Bill Allenbaugh used the AED, FADO Reds Lewis set up an IV line and got equipment and Capt. Bill Bragg obtained information from the employees. We shocked the man twice and started an IV line when

EMS2 arrived. After two shocks the man started to breath and had good radial pulses. M355 arrived and we transferred care to them. What a save!!

However, you know you have done well, when the police are standing behind you saying, "Hell of a job guys!"

February 17, 1997: While filling in E5, E4 and M5 were dispatched to a 1050pi on I-895 between mile markers 25-35, I-695 and I-95. While en route, dispatch advised that there was as many as seven patients involved with toll-facilities police on the scene, and wanted to know if we wanted an additional medic dispatched. IV375 was dispatched as the extra unit and arrived just prior to M5 and E4. Upon arrival, units were confronted with a van rolled over down a 15 foot embankment and patients strewn about. One patient was already dead at the scene and we had 12 other victims to take care of. All of the occupants were prominent Chinese actors and actresses and did not speak English. There was one man in the other van that was traveling with them as well as the driver of the wrecked van that spoke broken English. Both of these individuals were taken from patient to patient to triage and get the extent of their injuries. A medical strike team was dispatched along with two medivacs. The total number of patients was four priority 1's, eight priority 3's and one priority 4, with two flyouts. The condition of the patients were as follows: first fly out had a fractured femur, the second fly out had a lacerated liver, fractured hip and femur. Another patient had fractures in six places and a man had his leg fractured in five places. One other patient, who refused to be boarded, suffered internal bleeding. First in units received unit citations for their actions.

July 14, 1997: Engine 4 and Engine 41 already had tow fires that night. One was at the Western Votech School and the other was an apartment fire at 1214 Westerlee Pl. E41 was still cleaning up from the previous fires that evening, when they were alerted for a fill-in to Station 5 at 2330 hrs. E5 had been dispatched to a building fire at S. Caton Ave. and the city line. The incident was actually in the city at the Joe Stein Pallet Company. E5 held the first alarm from the county and the city had already pulled a second alarm. Extra units from the county were alerted and E41 was picked up on the road. The fire was spreading quickly and more alarms were called for a total of nine alarms (six from the city and three from the county). It was one of the largest mutual aide responses in a long time and things went well. The building was totally destroyed and units cleared in the early morning hours. At one point FADO Scott Torbeck and Lt. Bill Allenbaugh asked the Captain of AT128 if they could get up in the tower. He said no problem and the two of them got a crash course on the unit and operated it for an hour or so. E41 was the last unit from the county to clear a 0550 hrs. with this transmission: "E41 to dispatch, our services are no longer needed, the cloud has finally lifted, the sun is almost up and we are finally going home." *Submitted by Lt. William B. Allenbaugh Jr., Catonsville Fire Station A-Shift.*

ESSEX FIRE STATION #7

The following information was copied from the ledger of Essex Fire Station #7. The spelling and grammar is how it was written in the ledger: November 23, 1928: Chimney Fire, Celing Rd., Rossville. While responding to fire after receiving a telephone a call that a chimney was afire on the property of Rutkowski Bros. Was proceeding to the giving destination by the rout of Eastern Ave. to Mace Ave. then to the Stemmers Run Road. After going through the culvert at the Penna. R.R. was making the said left hand turn to pass over the Stemmers Run Bridge, going at a rate of 20 to 25 miles per hour and about 75 feet more or less from the said bridge when we noticed that the boards covering the bridge were removed on half the bridge, the half removed was on the first side we would have to cross. After putting on both hand and foot brake trying to stop truck, unable to do so we turned the truck to the right into a pile of lumber and went half-way over the bank of the Stemmers Run. The back wheels on the Stemmers Run Rd. and the front wheels hanging in the air. Failure of reporting of said bridge to the fire department by Foreman Edwin F. May employed by B. Co. Highways Dept. was the cause of the accident and road not closed at such time. If a board or other device had been used to stop traffic this would not have happened. Dundalk was called to respond to this call. Mr. Wilbur Kelly arrived at 11:10 a.m. and had truck towed to quarters from Stemmers Run and worked on same till 4:16 p.m."

TALES FROM THE STREET

CASE #3: Rescue Box 54-4 was dispatched for a water rescue during a violent thunderstorm. Units arrived at location to find 20-30 windsail surfers out of control in the area from Gunpowder State Park to Miami Beach. After approximately two hours all were successfully rescued and treated for mild hypothermia. Coordination among the Baltimore County Fire and Police Departments, Department of Natural Resources, Military Police from Aberdeen Proving Ground, Maryland State Police Aviation brought this incident to a safe conclusion.

CASE #4: Medical Box 54-4 was dispatched for a drowning in the Gunpowder State Park. A swimmer at the park was walking in shallow water when he stepped on something unusual. As he reached down to investigate, he found the lifeless body of a young girl. He quickly rushed the little girl to shore and he and Park Rangers began CPR. EMS crews arrived, intubated and successfully resuscitated the victim. She was transported to Johns Hopkins Pediatric Unit.

CASE #5: Engine, Medic 11, and EMS-1 were dispatched on Medical Box 11-5 for a cardiac arrest at Pappa's Lounge at the intersection of Taylor Ave. and Oakleigh Road. On arrival a middle-aged male was found next to the bar in full arrest. CPR was initiated with difficult ventilation's. Captain Tome visualized for intubation and discovered a large piece of beef occluding the patient's airway. The obstruction was removed. PM Shifflet took over ventilation's and the patient began breathing on his own. During transport to Good Samaritan Hospital the patient regained consciousness.

PARAMEDIC 11: On January 6, 2000 at 0455 hours, Paramedic 11 was dispatched to a call at the Holiday Inn Cromwell for a subject with chest pain. The patient walked out of the lobby, met the crew outside and was ushered to the ambulance. Once inside he received a full cardiac work-up. FF/EMT Danny Kelly provided high flow oxygen to the patient and obtained baseline vital signs; as PM Bridget Poole obtained a 12 lead EKG and established an IV. As the IV was being taped down, the patient lost consciousness and began to have seizure like activity. The cardiac monitor showed V-Fib. PM Poole placed multi-function pads on the patient, confirmed the rhythm, and defibrillated the patient at 200ws. The patient subsequently converted to a sinus rhythm. The IV, which had been lost in the process, was re-established. PM Poole bolused the patient with

L-R: Capt. Paul A. Burke, County Executive C.A. Dutch Ruppersberger, Capt. Wayne L. Tome Sr., Battalion Chief David J. Murphy

Lidocaine. EMS Shift Commander Wayne Tome arrived as part of the requested medical box and accompanied the medic to the hospital. The patient was transported to a local ER and immediately underwent cardiac catherization. Shift commander Tome has maintained contact with the patient since he returned to his home in the state of Georgia. He has expressed interest in reuniting with the crew on his next trip to town. *Submitted by Capt. Wayne L. Tome Sr.*

NEW COUNTY AMBULANCE FACILITY WINS NATIONAL RECOGNITION

A new life-saving technique made possible through the "Magic" of electronics, now fully operational within two of Baltimore County's ambulance companies, will be singled out for special praise at the upcoming national convention of the National Association of Counties when that organization convenes July 22 in Dallas, Texas.

In making the announcement, County Executive Dale Anderson lauded the officers and men of the County Fire Department Ambulance Service for the award-winning achievement, noting that the award is the second consecutive NACo recognition accorded the Fire Department.

This year's prize winner is the EKG (electrocardiogram), Telemetry System, which allows heart-attack victims to be treated at the scene of attack or while en route to a hospital, rather than having to wait for arrival at a hospital. The system is installed and working in ambulances of the Dundalk and the Essex companies. Stated in its simplest terms, the system relays electrocardiogram information to coronary experts at Baltimore City Hospitals who can prescribe immediate treatment in many cases and keep patients alive until arrival at the hospital, where more sophisticated treatment is available.

Last year's NACo award was tendered for the Fire Department's Intravenous Therapy Program, begun in April 1971, for treating shock in accident victims. More than 100 fire fighters regularly assigned to ambulance duty are fully qualified in this procedure and are certified emergency medical technicians - Ambulance. Intravenous therapy is fully operational throughout the

county's 12 ambulance stations.

The NACo awards are particularly significant because they recognize only those programs that the national organization believes to be "superior accomplishments" in a particular field of government service or activity.

To insure competence in handling the EKG Telemetry System, two instructors and six ambulance attendants from the Essex and Dundalk stations have been certified by the Maryland State Board of Medical Examiners as Cardiac Rescue Technicians. Another six, now attending instructional classes, are to receive certification this month.

Commenting on the EKG System, Fire Chief J. Austin Deitz, pointed out, "We all know that no amount of money in the world can buy the most precious gift of all - that of human life, but we know we are preserving life on a daily basis through the skills of our ambulance service technicians and the enthused support, encouragement and medical technology which has been made available to us at Baltimore City Hospitals."

"We don't know exactly how many lives we're saving because we have no way of knowing how many victims would have made it to the hospital. We do know, however, that national statistics show that more than 50 per cent of heart attack victims die before arriving at hospitals or suffer deterioration to a point that little can be done for them after arrival," Dietz said.

"In the county program to date," he continued, "140 coronary cases have been handled by the Dundalk and Essex ambulances since September 1972. During that period, we can report that only one person has been dead on arrival at city hospitals, and, in that case, that victim showed no vital signs when first examined by ambulance attendants," Dietz explained.

In EKG procedures, an attendant attaches "sensors" to the suspected cardiac victim. These sensors, in turn, send the heartbeat signal via radio and leased telephone lines, into the Coronary Care Unit at City Hospitals.

There, a specialist in this field observes the heartbeat on an oscilloscope and a printed graph, and prescribes treatment, also by radio-telephone communication, directly to the ambulance crew standing by, or en route to the hospital.

If the hospital doctor advises drugs, or defibrillation, the attendant carries out these instructions. Prior to the attendants' certification, only a doctor or a physician's assistant were allowed to perform these treatments.

Six other Baltimore area hospitals and the remaining 10 ambulances are scheduled to be equipped and added to the system. It is expected to take approximately 18 months to make the program fully operational throughout the county.

In addition to city hospitals, others which will participate are St. Joseph and Greater Baltimore Medical Center in the Towson area; Franklin Square in the eastern sector; Baltimore County General in the west; Sinai, in the northwest corridor; and St. Agnes.

The large land area (610 square miles) and the unique geography of Baltimore County make this type of system not only desirable but mandatory since no one hospital can possibly be used to serve the entire area.

BALTIMORE COUNTY'S TRAINING CENTER

In October 1954, *Firemen* magazine described the diverse training facilities which were to be made available for fire fighters in Baltimore County, Maryland. This excellent fire training site was dedicated on June 18, 1955, and is now in full operation under the direction of Chief A.P. Orban, of the Baltimore County Fire Department. The training area will serve 15 fully paid and 27 volunteer fire companies in Baltimore County.

The new headquarters is about one-quarter of a mile north of Towson, and houses administration offices, a fire station, a repair shop, the Fire Prevention Bureau, civil defense headquarters for Baltimore County, a training auditorium with capacity for 300 persons, and the central fire alarm headquarters.

A few of the training facilities on the two acre site include a six story training tower, a two story attic, basement and smokehouse for fighting test fires and for training in ventilation, a building for gas mask training, drafting pits for pump operators, flammable liquid installations, high voltage electrical installations, and a driver training course. The headquarters station of the Baltimore County Fire Department has four entrances and floor space for two pumpers, an aerial ladder truck, an ambulance and two pieces of reserve apparatus. Dormitories include living space for 22 men, a guest room, recreation room, lockers, kitchen facilities and a "turnout" dressing room between the living quarters and the engine room.

Of prime importance to the operation of the fire department and the training center is the modern repair shop which features five entrances and a modern paint room installation capable of handling an aerial ladder truck. The shop also includes hydraulic equipment, facilities for hose and ladder repair, a stockroom, washroom and an office for the shop superintendent.

Good use is made of radio communications for combining activities of the Baltimore County Fire Department and the volunteer fire companies. All box and telephone alarms from the entire county are channeled through a new central alarm headquarters. Both paid and volunteer fire companies are dispatched by telephone and radio but operate independently until arrival of the fireground where all companies are under the command of the paid officer in charge.

The central alarm control room has separate facilities for radio and telephone operators. At present, two men are on duty at all times, with personnel working 8-hour shifts. Recordings are made of all radio transmissions and all emergency telephone calls. The control room features a unique mapping system where all street intersections are indexed on a rotary recorder—together with all apparatus assignments up to third alarms. Approximately 15,000 locations in the county are classified on 35mm microfilm, which can be projected quickly on a 24 by 36 in. screen.

The radio system features a 250 watt, transmitter-receiver unit with a remote controlled console. All equipment is duplicated with 3000-watt standby electric generators at both operating and transmitter ends of the line. Twenty-five sirens at volunteer fire stations are selectively controlled by push button radio operation and 109 mobile 60 watt transmitter-receiver units are operated in both the paid and volunteer fire services.

The box alarm system covers the metropolitan area of Baltimore County with two sub-centers in other sections of the county. These three alarm districts retransmit alarms into central headquarters. Each subcenter has four box circuits but the new control office has provision for expanding the box alarm system to 50 circuits.

The transmitter for the radio system is located on top of the Towson Water Tank and has an overall height of 152 feet. This is one of the highest points in the county and provides adequate radio reception throughout the area. The transmitting building is directly beneath the water tower and features two 250 watt, transmitters, alternating in operation every 24 hours, with one transmitter serving as a "standby." The "standby" generator is of 3000 watt capacity. This building is equipped with an automatic forced air ventilating system and is completely covered by a carbon dioxide extinguishing system.

At the present time, the career fire department has forty-seven 60 watt two-way mobile units while 51 pieces of apparatus in the volunteer fire companies are also equipped with these two-way radio units. Ambulances in the career and volunteer fire services also operate under radio control headquarters.

The telephone switchboard in the control room is connected by trunk lines to all telephone exchanges in the county so that fire alarms may be transmitted quickly. All fire reports pertaining to paid company response are relayed to the particular station by telephone extension lines. All fire reports requiring volunteer fire company response are transmitted through two-way radio.

The alarm and communications area in the administration building is air-conditioned. Fire department personnel include a battalion chief in charge, a fire captain, nine dispatchers having the rank of lieutenant, three linemen of the same rank, two linemen who are privates in the department, and a lieutenant in charge of radio repair. The office of the Superintendent of Fire Alarm is adjacent to the communications room.

ENDING NOTE: as this book went to publication, Baltimore County Fire was in the process of building a new facility to house the Fire-Rescue Academy, our current training facility.

THREE ALARM FIRE DESTROYS SPARKS ELEMENTARY SCHOOL

by Jerry Loiacono

Box 39-1: A three alarm fire destroyed the Sparks Elementary School, 1000 Sparks Road, the morning of January 8, 1995. Constructed in 1909, the historical school was the original home of Sparks Agricultural High School, considered to be this country's first vocational high school of agriculture. Shortly before 8:00 a.m. a school custodian opening the school for a community church service discovered a fire in room 203. Believing he successfully extinguished the fire, the fire department was summoned to investigate a fire reported out. E 391's crew gave an initial status report of nothing showing upon their arrival, but a well progressed fire was soon located in the room's ceiling. Arson investigators theorize it had burned undetected for at least and hour. Flames quickly roared through the slate roof and consumed the 86-year-old school, requiring an additional two alarms and tanker group response in a span of 10 minutes. To provide an adequate water supply, draft sites were established at nearby Piney Creek and Gunpowder Falls. Twenty one companies battled the blaze over three hours before it was declared under control at 10:18 a.m. The fire caused an estimated $4,500,000 damage with initial speculation the fire was electrical in nature, possibly a ventilation unit's electrical motor sparked the blaze. County school officials are now uncertain about the school's future and whether it will be rebuilt at the present location. Sparks Elementary School, one of only four elementary schools in the rural northern Baltimore County school district and second oldest school in the county, was previously scheduled for complete modernization in 2001. Presently, the 302 students enrollment have been reassigned to 10 classrooms at the Cockeysville Middle School, where their first day of classes were held on Friday, January 13, 1995.

Units on scene: 0750 hrs. - E 391, BCPD; 0758 (1st Alarm) - E 392, E 441, E 17, E 493, TT 399, TK 17, TK 1, BC 1, M 395; 0759 - Air 478; 0802 (2nd Alarm) - E 442, E 302, E 471, E 1, E 503, TK 404, SQ 533, CW 155, BC 5, DC 3, EMS 7; 0805 (Tanker Group) - E 451, TT 451, E 381, E 14, E 422, SU 394, SU 444; 0807 - E 301, SQ 303; 0808 (3rd Alarm) - E 473, E 501, E 403, E 291, E 11, E 412, TK 297, BR 491, SU 504, BC 4, BC 10, Car 1, EMS 1; 0812 - E 307; 0814 - M 17; 0816 - TT 488; 0852 - M 60; 0856 - SU 474, SU 781 (Harford Co.). Also: Cars 2, 3 and 9, BC 9, Academy 10, AV 1, FID 2, FID 5, FDI 15, FM 1, FM 2, MCP 1, SU 306, BR 393, BR 492, UT 304, UT 388, UT 397, UT 449, UT 486, UT 506, School Security, Board of Ed. BG & E, County Roads, State Highways.

FOUR ALARM FIRE IN COCKEYSVILLE WAREHOUSE

by Jerry Loiacono

Box 39-13: A four alarm fire, fueled by liquid polyurethane and granular rubber materials, consumed a Cockeysville warehouse on August 6, 1995. Reported at 12:36 a.m., the blaze at Alt Road and Cockeysville Road destroyed the Martin Surfacing, Inc. storage facility, a company that installs running tracks and gymnasium floors. The spectacular fire, in an industrial area west of York Road, sent flames shooting 1200 feet into the night sky and pieces of roofing material raining down on nearby residential streets and lawns. Personnel and units from 20 stations responded to the fire with additional alarms pulled at 12:40 a.m., 1:02 a.m. and 1:17 a.m. Hazmat teams were summoned, who constructed a series of toxin absorbent dikes at all water run-off points and placed containment booms on a nearby stream which feeds Lock raven Reservoir. County, state and federal environmental officials assessed the scene and determined there was no significant damage to the water supply. Approximately 125 firefighters battled the blaze, which caused damages in excess of $1,000,000, for three hours before it was contained at 3:40 a.m. However, the last remaining units were on the scene until the evening hours of August 7, 1995, extinguishing small pockets of fire among the twisted steel and cinder blocks. One firefighter, suffering heat related injuries, was treated and released from the Greater Baltimore Medical Center. Two additional firefighters were treated for smoke inhalation at Shock Trauma and released.

Units on scene: 0036 hrs. 1st Alarm: E 392, E 17, E 302, E 101, TK 17, SQ 303, BC 1, BCPD; 0040 hrs.; 2nd Alarm: E 391, E 493, E 501, E 473, E 14, TK 1, FL 293, Air 478, CW 155, BC 5, DC 2, EMS 7, M 395; 0042 hrs., TK 297; 0044 hrs., E 301, E 441, SQ 533, Car 1; 0102 hrs.; 3rd Alarm: E 494, E 503, E 291, E 11, E 10, TK 323, MCP 1, Car 2, BC 10, EMS 1; 0105 hrs. (Medical Group) - E 471, M 17, M 1, M 475, M 14, EMS 5, EMS 21; 0107 hrs. - E 403; 0117 firs. (4th Alarm) E 321, E 8, FID 1, FID 14; 0120 hrs., E 55; 0121 hrs., E 307; 0149 hrs., M 11, M 10, M 325; 0222 hrs., HM 114, HM 1; 0310 hrs., E 442; 0325 firs. - E 15, TK 15; 0430 hrs., HM 10; 1147 hrs., E 392; 1314 hrs., E 14, HM 114.

Three alarm fire

August 7, 1995, 0908 hrs., E 14, HM 114; 0938 hrs., E 17, E 18, TK 17, BC 1; 0946 hrs., E 392; 1014 hrs., CW 155.

Also on scene: DC 3, DC 5, BC 14, Car 3, Car 9, FID 5, FID 15, AV 2, FD Chaplain, TT 399, SU 394, UT 506, USCG, MDE, DEPRM, SHA, BG & E.

THE EMERGENCY RESPONSE TRAINING PROGRAM

The Emergency Response Training Program instructs students in areas of Hazardous Materials Operations, Bloodborne Pathogens, Cardiopulmonary Resuscitation, Emergency Vehicle Operations, Emergency Medical Technician-Basic, Firefighter One, and Intravenous Technician. This training is similar to that which career members of the Baltimore County Fire Department receive. The exception is that this program does not offer training as Firefighter II.

This program is creative in a number of ways. The cooperation between the Baltimore County Fire Service and Department of Social Services training and skills for the recipients that would help them become employed as firefighters, EMTs or paramedics in Baltimore County or any jurisdiction in the state of Maryland. It also provided training and skills that could be used to gain employment with any of the commercial ambulance services or EMS systems in the area. However, an even larger benefit was the diversity the training brought to the fire service. We were able to tap in to an employment resource that included individuals who had not previously considered the fire service as a profession.

In August, 1996 while attending the Bi-Annual Conference of the International Association of Black Firefighters in Chicago, Illinois, Volunteer Firefighter/EMT Kenny Younger attended a panel discussion on the use of federal and state funding under the Welfare to Work reform for emergency services.

The Baltimore County Fire Department felt the information obtained by Firefighter/EMT Younger could be used to assist the Department of Social Services (DSS) in its efforts to train welfare recipients, while also expanding the pool of professionals trained to become firefighters, Emergency Medical Technicians (EMTs) and paramedics. This was also an opportunity to provided the fire department with additional resources for educational materials that would benefit the DSS recipients as well as career and volunteer members of the fire service.

The Department of Social Services would screen applicant, and those who met the criteria for federal funding would undergo the same criminal background check given to prospective applicant of the Baltimore County Fire Service. Once the background check is complete, and the students have met other requirements set by the fire department and MIEMSS (Maryland Institute of Emergency Medical Services System), the students are placed in a six month training course.

RECEIPT OF INITIAL ALARM AND DISPATCH

On Sunday, January 4, 1987 at 13:29:47 hours, the Baltimore County Emergency Communications Center received a telephone alarm via 911 reporting "a big explosion on the railroad tracks on Eastern Avenue, on Eastern extended, at Eastern Avenue and Greenbank Road."

Another 911 telephone alarm was reported at 13:29:49 for "a train derailment, Amtrak, Eastern Avenue down by the Gunpowder State Park, Eastern Avenue down by Greenbank, a passenger train derailment, we have fire back here, you can come in by Sylvan Avenue." The two receiving 911 emergency communication technicians, realizing they were receiving duplicate calls for the same incident, forwarded the combined information on to the fire, medical and police areas for appropriate dispatching.

At 13:31:46 hours, Fire Dispatch transmitted Hazardous Materials Box #54-6 for "a train derailment, passenger train, with a fire, Eastern Avenue and Greenbank Road." (time 13:33:33 hours). See Figure 2.

The responding units on the first alarm assignment were as *follows:*

Engine #54 (First Due)
Engine #212
Engine #201
Engine #222
Truck #221
Medic #54 (First Due)
Paramedic Field Supervisor #4
EMS #2 (Emergency Medical Services Staff, Lieutenant rank)
EMS #1 (Emergency Medical Services Staff, Captain rank)
Rescue #213
Rescue #523
Haz-Mat #1 (Hazardous Materials Supervisor, Battalion Chief rank)
Haz-Mat #114
Battalion Chief #4

As the initial running assignment companies were being alerted by radio transmitted tones, dispatch personnel received additional information from 911 calls to operators reporting "at least 100 or more injured" and that "the train was on fire." Consequently, the standard running assignment was increased by sending the normally second due rescue unit and dispatch personnel began preparing for what appeared to them as the beginning of a major incident.

CONDITIONS FOUND UPON ARRIVAL

Engine #54's Captain Robert A. Hausmann gave the first report, a "Code 2," from his station, meaning "smoke showing" at 13:33:47 hours.

Job Network Training Class

At 13:36:07 hours, Dispatch reported calls being received stating heavy black smoke and at least a hundred or more injured at location. They dispatched a full medical group at that time. This was immediately increased to two medical groups at the request of Paramedic #4, EMS Supervisor Elizabeth L. Halley. (A medical group consists of four medic units, one EMS Supervisor, one Battalion Chief and one engine company.)

Engine #54 took up a position on Sylvan Avenue off Red Bird Road so as to get as close as possible to the largest body of fire. Captain Hausmann ordered the pre-connected master stream used in conjunction with the around-the-pump foam proportioner with 3% aqueous film forming foam (AFFF) to subdue the large volume of fire which was threatening two passenger cars and two private garages. This volume of fire was later determined to be Number 2 diesel fuel and covered an irregular surface area estimated in size to be approximately 50 feet by 150 feet. Engine #201 laid a 3-inch supply line in from a hydrant on Eastern Avenue to supply Engine #54.

Arriving companies were faced with a twelve (12) car, two (2) locomotive Amtrak passenger train that had been involved in a collision with three Conrail diesel locomotives. See Figure 3. The entire passenger train had derailed leaving nine (9) cars in the upright position. The remaining cars were stacked at odd angles upon one another on one of the Amtrak engines. One Amtrak locomotive and one Conrail locomotive were totally demolished. The remaining two (2) Conrail engines were upright and situated further north from the immediate incident scene. Estimates ranged that anywhere from 150 to 200 passengers had evacuated the train. Amtrak overhead 11,000 volt A.C. wires which fed the catenary system were strewn on the ground around the incident scene and it was uncertain if they were still energized. A check by Engine #54's officers revealed another body of fire under the forward passenger cars which were stacked at precarious angles.

Captain Hausmann of Engine #54 made the following requests:

•Amtrak Railroad to shut down all power and stop all train traffic.

•Next engine to lay a supply line from the hydrant on Eastern near Red Bird Road.

•Another engine stop at Station #54 and bring all reserve foam supplies.

These were acknowledged and Dispatch instructed all Emergency Medical units to switch their radios to Channel #2, with all fire and rescue apparatus to remain on Channel #3.

Arriving companies were directed to bring ground ladders to the scene, avoid the power lines and extend a handline to attack the fire threatening the trapped victims. This line also flowed AFFF. Great care had to be taken in attacking the fire in the passenger cars so as to prevent trapped or injured victims from being scalded or drowned. Firefighters from Engines 201 and 212 assisted in this attack.

Search and rescue efforts were hampered at this point by the fire re-igniting beneath the cars. Captain Hausmann set his engine up as "Amtrak Command," called for a second alarm assignment at 1342 hours to be dispatched to the Harewood Road side of the incident, and directed crews to concentrate on search and rescue efforts.

Battalion Chief #4, Donald E. Rice, arrived at location on the Eastern Avenue side at 1347 hours and assumed control of the incident. Captain Hausmann advised him that crews were laying and extending supply and hand lines, extinguishing fire, evacuating walking injured, and that search and rescue efforts were in progress. Battalion Chief Rice determined that EMS Supervisor Halley had established a medical command. Given this information, he began sectorizing the incident with Sector I being the command post area and Sector 2 being the rear nine (9) passenger cars which did not involve rescue problems.

THEY ALSO SERVE WHO WAIT...

by F. Spuziti, member Reisterstown Volunteer Fire Co.

She heard the first growl of the siren,
as it climbed painfully in pitch and
threw its three long blasts
like a knife through the cool evening
from atop the firehouse, two blocks over.
The radio on top of the refrigerator
roused itself with a series of high-pitched tones.
"ALERT BOX 70 - 2
Maysville, Centerville, Old Branch, Battalion 3, Truck 21,
Squad 74

Dispatcher sounds a little excited;
Bob's gonna be late again I know;
his favorite dinner - cold again!
Guess he heard the call
on his scanner in the car
and stopped at the firehouse
on his way home from work.
He hates his job, I know,
shame he can't get paid
for doing something he loves
like being a fireman.
He made the list last month
for the county fire department
fourteenth out of over a hundred;
They only took ten.
Maybe next year

For a dwelling fire, 411 Main Street, Maysville Cross Street, Martin Drive."

That's Mrs. Wilson's,
probably burnt up another pot on the stove.
At least it's close by,
he shouldn't be too long.
"No, Bobby, we'll eat when Daddy gets home,
it'll only be a few minutes."

"Engine 72 responding"
That's Bob, up front, officer,
and they'll be the first engine in.
Hope there's nothing to it He only made lieutenant this year
Five years in the company,
and all that training,
but in charge of a fire?
Battalion Chief's still five minutes away.
"Engine 72 at location"
That was fast,
wonder who's driving?
Some of those guys push it
a little too hard.

We have two-story frame building Code 3, first floor, front."
Damn! He'll be real late now,
"Jimmy, Bobby, c'mon, let's eat, we'll save a plate for Daddy,
he'll be home before you go to bed."

The radio's too quiet,
Second engine's there,
but the rest are slow gettin' out
"Bobby, eat your vegetables. Okay - so I haven't eaten any
   thing,
I'll eat when your father gets home;
NOW EAT!"

Radio's too damn quiet!
"Main Street Dispatch"
"Dispatch"
"Gimme an ambo, we got a firefighter hurt!"

Oh Lord! I wonder who…?
That was Jim, he must've drove - he's good.
Not just because he's my brother, either. Who's hurt?
Dammit, say something!

"No, Jimmy, Daddy's not hurt, finish your supper."
"Ambo 83, en route to County General"
They weren't there long,
least it wasn't a heart attack.
Wonder who??? What???
"Bobby and Jimmy, go take your baths now,
and put on your PJ's."
"Yes, NOW!"
"You can watch TV for a while later."

"Main Street Command, Dispatch,
Fire is under control,
Hold Engine 72, Squad 74,
Place rest of box in service,
And ask the chief to continue in."

Jim again Where's Bob?
"Boys, Hey! Stop the splashing! and get out of the tub!
You can watch TV for a while.
NO! Eight-thirty is bedtime!
Daddy'll be home before then.
What's taking them so long?

"Engine 72 out of service, returning"
Out of service?
Can't be out of water, there's a plug somewhere on Main
Didn't recognize the voice,
Where's Bob???
Must be short a crewman,
And Bob's not up front!
Where'd the ambo go?
County General, but what's the phone number?
No! I won't call, He - they'll call,
It it's anything serious.
"Engine 72, out of service, station"
Still don't recognize the voice;
Jesse, maybe?
Where's Bob?
Now the phone's too quiet;
Ring! Damn you!!

"Hi Hon, I'm home"
"Hi guys!"
"You scared me half to death -didn't hear the car,
Boy am I glad to see you.
What happened?

"Piece of cake!
My first chance at a fire on my own!
Went like clockwork, too, just like in training,
Just the kitchen,
Jim and Jesse took a two 'n' half in
and had it knocked down
before Centerville's engine could even hook up to the plug!
Paul drove, jumped out of the cab
and turned his ankle pretty bad,
He still pumped for us, but
Chief sent 'im to the hospital,
It may be broke.
Next time, I'll bet he wears his boots
like he's been taught!
I drove back.
"Anything left to eat?"

CEREMONIES AND EVENTS

Pictured L to R: Retired Fire Chief Paul Reincke, Reired Chief J. Austin Dietz, Fire Chief Elwood H. Banister and Retiring Chief Fire Surgeon Frank T. Barranco, MD.

Paramedic Michael W. Robinson promoted to EMS Field Coordinator...now Battalion Chief

Firefighter Charles E. Watkins promoted to Lieutenant...now Battalion Chief

Promotions to Paramedics

Kuruc Family...Now Division Chief Jon Kuruc

Promotion to Fire Specialists

Promotion to Lieutenants

2002 Commendations

Departmental Unit Citation

Division Chief
Captain Ronald J. Evans, Jr.
Captain George M. Knopp
Captain Charles A. Taylor, Jr.
Lieutenant Terry A. Berkereidge
Lieutenant Joseph J. Heller
Lieutenant John L. Olow, IV
Lieutenant Mike Smith
EMS Lieutenant Anthony J. Myers
Field Coordinator Mary M. Farley
FADO Dwight C. Bollinger
FADO Paul W. Faulkner
FADO Clarence J. Ludwig
FADO Gary W. Unverzagt
FADO Richard V. Yingling
Fire Specialist Michael E. Creswell
Fire Specialist Jason W. Hahn

Fire Specialist Timothy P. Harner
Fire Specialist Christopher D. Hawley
Fire Specialist Warren T. Moffitt
Fire Specialist Jeffrey Snyder
Fire Specialist Jerry L. Weckesser
Fire Specialist Harold J. Weissner, III
Firefighter/EMT James D. Carter
Firefighter/EMT Matthew D. Devers
Firefighter/EMT David C. Hohenberger
Firefighter/EMT Dianne M. Lloyd
EMT Robert A. Biggs
Harold Cohen
Firefighter Dennis C. Barnes
Firefighter Joseph P. Ryan
Firefighter Josua Schumer
Firefighter Mark Stone

Citizens Commendation Award

Michael C. Cather
Eli Etherton

Citizens Medal of Honor

William Miles
David Loughlin

Citizens CPR Award

Captain George M. Knopp
Cindy Peterson
Firefighter Dennis C. Barnes
Fire Specialist Harold J. Weissner, III

Departmental Purple Heart

Lieutenant Kyrle W. Preis, III
Paramedic Joanne R. Boyd

Citizens Certificate of Merit

John Snyder
Leila Alina
Ulysses Bellamy
Russell Green
William Hiteshew
Captain Robert D. Murray, Sr.
Lieutenant Ronald J. Huber, Jr.
Paramedic Bridget M. Poole
Paramedic Gary C. Whaley
EMT Mararet M. Smink
Fire Specialist Frank O. Spears
Fire Specialist Ronald E. Schreiber
Janet T. Johnson, Executive Officer
Battalion Chief David J. Murphy
Chief Fire Surgeon, Doctor Ameen I. Ramzy
Fire Surgeon, Doctor Eric J. Nager
Captain George C. Darr
Captain Joseph P. Griebel
Captain Michael W. Robinson
Captain Frederick N. Trentzsh
Lieutenant Vernon S. Adamson
Lieutenant Francis X. DiPaula, Jr.
Lieutenant Robert G. Perry
Lieutenant Gary F. Wheeler
EMS Lieutenant James L. Kookogey
Paramedic Mark F. Demski
Paramedic Sharon L. Jacob
Paramedic Mark W. New
Paramedic Steven M. Small

Bryan Stirn
Steven Stirn
Edward Owens, Jr.
Edward Owens, Sr.
David Ross
Dereck Forney
Fire Specialist Charles H. Tudor, III
Firefighter Warren T. Davis, III
Firefighter/EMT Todd M. Gibney
Firefighter/EMT Robert W. Lim
Firefighter/EMT Ethan T. Johnson
Firefighter/EMT Christopher M. Wilhelm
FADO Patrick S. Feeley
FADO Michael B. Fox
Fire Specialist Roland P. Bosley, Jr.
Fire Specialist Paul J. Cusic
Fire Specialist Todd M. Langeheine
Fire Specialist David M. Smith
Fire Specialist Wayne N. Weigandt
Firefighter/EMT Michael P. Eagle
Charnetta M. Holman
Rebecca A. Webb
Ganell Britton-911 Operator
Donna G. Market - 911 Operator
Roland Mangum, Bureau of Utilities
Robert Pedrick, Bureau of Utilities
John Tawes, Bureau of Utilities
James Clements, BCVFA
EMT Karen Huggins, BCVFA

56th Recruit Class

Baltimore County Fire Department, 63rd Recruit Class February 26, 1981

Paramedic Recruit Class Graduation

57th Recruit Class, December 1, 1978

First Dual-Entry Paramedic Recruit Class Graduation, February 14, 1983

Dedication of Truck Company #1 Towson Fire Station, November 1982

Dedication of Cave-In Unit #55

Dedication of Perry Hall Fire Station #55

Future Site of Memorial Shrine

Dedication Fire Station #57, August 31,1987

1st BCFD Football Team, 1982

Tug of war team at ECC

Tug of war, at old courthouse grounds, against the Police

Softball (Eastside) Team at Bowie, 1991

Eastside softball team

Softball Team Eastside

Tug of war at ECC

Softball Team at Bowie 1999

After the game

Tug of war team at ECC

Heavy Rescue Equipment

Equipment

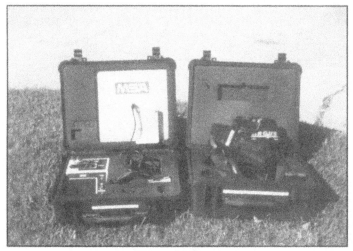

Thermal Imager

Power Fans

Salvage Tools

Ground Ladders

Ladder training at MFRI

Recruits learning auto extrication

Mopping up

Recruit House burning, Cheasapeake Village Apt.

Recruit House burning, Riverdale Apt.

PUBLIC EDUCATION

Kids Safety Day

Firehouse Expo

Fire Safety House

School visit to Company 320

Poster Contest

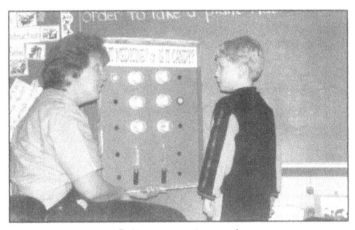

Poison prevention week

Station 16 open house

Parade line up

Parade line up

Parade preparation

Chiefo in the parade

University of Maryland Education

PERSONNEL

Abbott, John W. Jr.
Abrams, Samuel E.
Acosta, Michael D.
Adams, Donald W.
Adamson, Vernon S.

Adelsberger, Steven D.
Ailiff, Cameron M.
Akers, Jeffrey S.
Alban, John J., Jr.
Allen, Richard L., Jr.

Allenbaugh Jr., William B.
Amrhein, John P
Amole, Michael W.
Amoriello, Gregory A.
Arnold, Edward B.

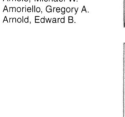      

Artis, James W., Jr.
Asper, Jeffery S.
Auld, Shawn S.
Austin, Craig, D.
Backahus, Paul G.

Badders, David L.
Badders, James A.
Badders, Nancy
Badders, Timothy A.
Baldwin, Travis J.

Balladarsch, George J., Jr.
Banister, Kevin E.
Bankard, Timothy E.
Barcikowski, Christopher H.
Bare, Timothy I.

Barnes, Dennis C.
Barranco, Frank T.
Barrow, Robert J.
Barshinger, John T.
Barton, William J.

Baublitz, Richard L.
Bauer, Harry F., III
Bauer, Steven H.
Bean, Gregory S.
Beard, Lloyd E.

Becker, Donald K., Sr.
Becker, Thomas
Bell, Calvin C.
Bell, John, Jr.
Bell, Timothy E., Sr.

Beresh, Robert M.
Berkeridge, James Kelly
Berkeridge, Terry A.
Berkeridge, Timothy P.
Berna, Michael

Berryman, John W., Jr.
Berwaldt, Paul O.
Biddison, Steven M.
Bidinger, Craig A.
Binkley, Robert

Bitzel, Steven A.
Blackmon, Keith H.
Blackwell, Glenn A.
Blades, Kenneth
Bolling, Jerry A.

Bollinger, Dwight C.
Bosley, Benjamin S.
Bosley, Raymond
Bossman, Michael B.
Bowe, Alvin S.

Bowen, Jeffrey
Boyd, Joanne
Bowman, Kathy T.
Bown, Thomas L.
Bragg, William B., Sr.

Brammer, Suzanne K.
Brehm, William E.
Breighner, Ray K., Jr.
Brewer, Walter L.
Brister, Lawrence S., Sr.

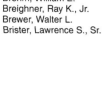

Brooks, George H.
Brooks, Lisa A.
Brothers, Curtis L.
Brothers, Dennis W.
Brown, Albert T.

Brown, Joseph, Jr.
Brown, Steven C.
Brown, Thomas F.
Browne, Carroll L.
Buckingham, David L.

Bull, Gary L.
Burnell, Harold J.
Burkhardt, Frederick L.
Burkins, Angela
Burkins, William S.

Burnett, Shelly R.
Bursey, Ronald M.
Burton, Gary N.
Bycoffe, David J.
Camak, Dana B.

Cannaday, Kevin D.
Capley, James R.
Carbaugh, Lynn W.
Carter, James D.
Carter, Robert, Jr.

Carter, William E.
Carter, William L.
Carver, Paul B.
Chamberlain, Michael G.
Chandler, Justin D.

Chaney, Robert P.
Chenoweth, Paul S.
Chilcoat, Jeffery S., Sr.
Childs, Denise A.
Chinery, David C.

Chinery III, Henry J.
Chu, Kenneth C.
Cleveland, Gregory J.
Clinton, Craig A.
Clunie, Opie F.

Cofiell, Wayne A.
Coffman, Warren H., Jr.
Cohen, Harold C.
Cole, Eric
Coleman, Glenn R., Sr.

Colleran, Thomas J.
Collifower, James E.
Combs, Virginia B.
Connally, Oscar W.
Connolly, Barbara L.

Connolly, William F., Jr.
Conrad, Bruce W.
Cook, Charles R.
Cooke, Robert F.
Cooke, Tyrone V.

Coolahan, Daniel C.
Coroneos, Nicki L.
Coulter, Mark H.
Cox, David B.
Cox, Gretchen A.

Coyle, Victoria K.
Cranston, Vern S.
Crawford, Scott E.
Creswell, Michael W.
Cromer, Jason D.

Cromwell, John E., Jr.
Crooks, Dennis L.
Crooks, J. Edward
Crooks, John R.
Crosby, Michael D.

Cruz, Edward J.
Cuffley, Wayne D.
Cullom, John H., Jr.
Curlee, Terry
Cushing, Sara

Cusic, Paul J.
D'Elia, Lawrence N., III
Dailey, Edward M.
Dales, Garth J.
Danner, William D.

Darling, Ronald W.
Darr, George C.
Davidson, Charles E.
Davidson, Scott W.
Davis, Edward S.

Davis, Warren T., III
DeFlavis, Richard A.
DeGross, Dennis G.
DeLuca, Michael E.
Dembeck, Dennis L.

Dembeck, Roland T.
Demory, Anthony A.
Demski, Mark F.
Denning, Dean A.
Devers, Donald R.

Devers, James E.
Devers, Matthew D.
DeVito, Joseph K.
DeZurn, Eddie L., Jr.
Dill, Robert G.

DiPaula, Francis X, Jr.
Dixon, Jarrett A.
Dixon, Louis A., Jr.
Drasal, Michael L.
Drees, George C.

Dryden, David K.
Dudderar, Howard K.
Duell, Kevin
Dulina, George, Jr.
Duncan, Wayne T.

Dunn, James P.
Dutterer, Allen L., Jr.
Dutterer, Ketti L.
Eagle, Mark B.
Eder, Timothy B.

Edmunds, Leroy P., III
Edwards, James J.
Efford, David R.
Elkins, Terry W.
Ellwood, Harry K.

Endryas, Eric
Endyas, M. Eileen
England-Dansicker, Danelle
Engle, LeRoy
Espinosa, Anthony S.

Essel, Andrew J., Jr.
Euler, Alvin E.
Eurice, Paul J.
Evans, Charles S.
Evans, Michael R.

Evans Jr., Ronald J.
Fabrizio, Thomas D., Jr.
Falkenhan, Mark G.
Fannon, Joseph J., Jr.
Fannon, Joshua L.

Fannon, Vincent N.
Farley, Bryan M.
Farley, Mary M.
Faulker, Paul W.
Feeley, Patrick S.

Feist, Ernest L., III
Fike, George S.
Finch, Arthur K.
Fisher, Keith W., Jr.
Flater, Thomas M., III

Fleming, Bruce D.
Fleming, Susan M.
Fogel, Robert W., III
Folio, Anthony J.
Ford, James C., Sr.

Forster, Robin J.
Fosbrink, Sarah A.
Fowble, Jeffrey Gilbert
Fox, Marvin B.
Frank, Michael J.

Fratta, Theodore M.
Freund, Glen E.
Frock, Christopher B.
Funk, Sandra
Gail, Edward W.

Gaines III, William L.
Gardner, David K.
Gardner, Mark
Gardner, Michael C.
Gardner, William E., Jr.

Garrison, Wayne
Gartside, Gregory A.
Gauss, Christopher
Gawel, Cary J.
Geho, Jeff

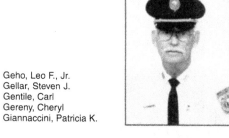

Geho, Leo F., Jr.
Gellar, Steven J.
Gentile, Carl
Gereny, Cheryl
Giannaccini, Patricia K.

Gibney, James C.
Gibney, Todd, M.
Gill, Nancy E.
Gilbert, William J.
Gilmore, Jeromek Jr.

Gisriel, Stephen T.
Gist, Michael C.
Glass, Jean M.
Godfrey, Charles K.
Goldencrown, Randy L.

Goode, Harolyn S.
Goodwin, Mark J.
Gover, Ernest W.
Grape, William M.
Greaver, John C.

Greene, Carolyn A.
Greene, Deborah L.
Griebel, Joseph P.
Griffin, Brian K.
Griffin, Christian D.

Grimes, Robert A.
Groft, Melvin D.
Groom, Vonzell J.
Grubb, Danny G., Sr.
Grubowski, Francis

Grusch, Joseph H.
Gryce, Rickey A.
Gutkoska, Joseph V.
Hahn, Jason W.
Haines, David B.

Hales, William R., Jr.
Hall, Richard H.
Halley, Ronald
Hamlett, Timothy S.
Hammond, Roger

Hannan, Timothy L.
Hardester, Robert W., Jr.
Hardesty, Bryan E.
Hare, Mark
Harker, Francis Y., Jr.

Harlee, Dora E.
Harner, Timothy P.
Harrell, David F., Jr.
Harris, Glen E.
Harrison, Hubert E., Jr.

Hart, Jonathan D.
Haughwout, Roy N.
Hawley, Christopher
Haymaker, William Richard
Hays, Michael C.

Hazelton, Damone D.
Heath, Clyde E., III
Heath, David S., Jr.
Hein, Richard W.
Heins, Gerald R.

Heinz, John M.
Heller, Joseph J.
Henderson, Patrick J.
Henry, Samuel F.
Henthorn, James E., III

Herman, Christopher W.
Hernandez, Alfonzo M.
Hess, Dale W.
Hill, Peter J.
Hill, Terri A.

Hipsley, Wayne M.
Hobbs, Steven G., III
Hoffman, Christopher M.
Hoffman, John T., Jr.
Hohenberger, David C.

Hohman, John J.
Holden, Richard L.
Holland, Joseph E.
Holloway, Dean E.
Holloway, Douglas A., Sr.

Holman, Charnetta M.
Holmes, Robert F.
Howard, Donald A.
Hubbard, Mark F.
Huber, Ronald J., Jr.

Hudnet, Frederick A.
Hudnet, Gregory B.
Hughs, Robert D.
Huppman, Paul E.
Hutchinson, Terry D..

Isaac, William G., Jr.
Jackson, Albert C.
Jacob, Sharon L.
Janowich, Steve Jr.
Jarkrewicz, Daniel J.

Jednorski, Stacey L.
Jessa, John C.
Johns, William R.
Johnson, Craig
Johnson, Damon J.

Johnson, Ethan T.
Jones, Dennis W.
Jones, Pierce H., III
Jones, Robert A.
Jones, Warren A.

Judlick, Steven J.
Kadolph, Gary O.
Kahler, Richard P.
Kane, Laura
Karcher, Robert A.

Kearney, Gregg R.
Kearney, Phil
Kearney, Tasha R.
Keller, Gary W.
Kelly, Daniel J.

Kelly, John C.
Kelly, Joseph V Jr.
Kemmer, Marc S.
Kemp, Donald B.
Kendzejeski, Francis J., Jr.

Kesting, Bruce C.
Kile, Daniel J.
Kilinski, Myer A.
Kilson, Howard E., Jr.
Kimbel, Thomas J.

Kinard, James L.
Kinsey, Lorraine M.
Kinsey, Raymond
Kluge, Daniel E.
Knazt, Scott A.

Knight, Barbara L.
Knight, William C.
Knopp, George-Michael
Kohl, John A., Sr.
Kookogey, James L.

Korn, James M.
Krause, James R.
Krebs, Gene D.
Kreimer, Jeffrey S.
Kruger, Tina J.

Kuchta, William T.
Kuhn, Keith S.
Kulisewicz, Kenneth M.
Kurrle, Blaine
Kurtz, Michael E.

Kuruc, Jonathan G.
Kyle, William A., Jr.
Lamb, Deborah L.
Lamb, Steven N.
Lamon, Lawrence E.

Lancaster, Stephen G.
Lancellotti, Harry
Lang, Christopher
Langeheine, Todd M.
Lannen, Richard A.

Latreille, Pete D.
Laurie, Hugh W.
Ledford, Barry J.
Ledford, Larry
Lee, Meril K.

Legge, Thomas E.
Lehr, Karen M.
Leidner, Mark L.
Lemmon, Daniel
Lemmon, Jennifer R.

Leonard, Charles E.
Lewis, Brent L.
Lewis, Gregory E.
Lewis, Irvin N.
Lewis, Kevin L.

Liebelt, Shawn P.
Lilley, Robert E.
Lim, Robert W.
Linker, Dennis W.
Lloyd, Dianne M.

CAREER

Lloyd, John J., Jr.
Logue, Thomas E.
Lonczynski, Deborah A.
Long, Dennis E.
Long, Richard A.

Long, Albert E. Jr.
Love, Donald W.
Lowe, Jeffrey A.
Lowman, Timothy A.
Ludwig, Brian E.

Ludwig, Clarence J., Jr.
Ludwig, Duane
Ludwig, John G., III
Lund, Robert E., II
Lurz, Paul S.

Lutostanski, Will
Lyons, Richard W.
Maas, Bernard H.
Mack, Nathaniel J.
MacLean, Pamela A.

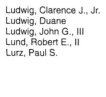

Magness, Andrew D.
Malicki, Michael E.
Malkus, David A.
Manis, Lester J.
Marino, Todd

Martucci, Jennifer
Martz, William
Maslanka, Lynda A.
Massarelli, Paul M.
Mast, Charles H.

Mastin, Julia M.
Mastin, Ronald R., Jr.
McCleary, Millard W., III
McClelland, George D.
McCluskey, Edward C.

McDonald, Diane L.
McIntyre, Michael E.
McJilton, Charles W.
McKeldin, Donald L.
McLucas, Nina A.

Meadows, Buddy E.
Means, Doreen
Merrifield, Lawrence D., Jr.
Meushaw, Margaret A.
Meyers, Corinne M.

Meyers, John B.
Meyers, Karen L.
Meyers, William E., Sr.
Mezick, Jimmie D.
Mickle, Ross W., Jr.

Milburne, Mark D.
Milby, John K.
Millender, Charles
Miller, Albert C., Jr.
Miller, David

Miller, Dawn
Miller, Jay E.
Miller, Michael A.
Miller, Stephen R.
Miller, Steven A.

Million, John B.
Mitchell, David S.
Mitchell, Marc L.
Moeller, John S.
Mooney, Steven C.

Mooney, Timothy M.
Moore, Carmen V.
Moore, Michael V.
Moses, Gary J.
Moss, Alan M.

Mudd, Patricia E.
Muddiman, Don W., Jr.
Mulder, Lynn A.
Murphy, Patrick C.
Murphy, Patrick T.

Murray, Kelly L.
Murray, Sylvia M.
Murray, Robert O. Jr.
Murray, Robert O. Sr.
Muth, Richard G.

Myers, Anthony J.
Myers, Judy W.
Myers, Richard E.
Nace, Kevin E.
Nace, Kimberly L.

Nash, Donald R.
Nelson, Randy
New, Mark W.
New, Michelle M.
Nichols, Janice M.

Nichols, Robert B.
Nickoles, Charles L., Jr.
Nickoles, Thomas M.
Nixon, Ronald L.
Noetzel, Diana L.

Noratel, Vernon E.
Nosek, Joseph J.
O'Connor, Francis D. Jr.
O'Rourke, Michael A.
Ochs, Kenneth E., Jr.

Oles, Anthony J., Jr.
Oliver, David S.
Olow, John L. IV
Oppitz, Stephen
Oursler, L. Wayne

Pack, Dana A.
Pack, Derrick E., Sr.
Pack, Millard L., Jr.
Paige, Dontay R.
Paige, Gilbert W.

Palmer, Brandee L.
Palmer, Lawrence K.
Parham, John C.
Parker, Shelton D.
Parrish, Randy G.

Patterson, Robert G.
Paugh, David D.
Paugh, Robert
Pauley, Roy I.
Peach, John

Pearce, LaVern
Pearce, Samuel, Sr.
Penn, Franklin E., Jr.
Perkins, Eugene L.
Perry, Robert G.

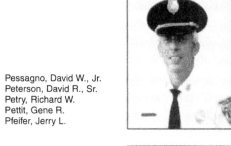    

Pessagno, David W., Jr.
Peterson, David R., Sr.
Petry, Richard W.
Pettit, Gene R.
Pfeifer, Jerry L.

Phillips, Casey
Phillips, Charles C.
Phillips, John L.
Pierson, Frank W.
Piker, Paul W.

Piker, Steven M., Sr.
Pinder, Thomas A.
Plunkert, Daniel L.
Pohlman, William A.
Polesne, Charles E., Jr.

Pollock, Charles F.
Poole, Bridget M.
Preis, Kyrle W. III
Priester, Kaaren L.
Priester, Theodore C., Jr.

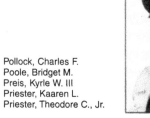     

Proffen, Evan C.
Pruitt, Donald
Pryor, Russell L., III
Punt, Mark S.
Purcell, William D.

Purkey, Gary III
Quinlan, Michael C.
Quirk, John F.
Rachinskas, Edward
Radomsky, James J.

Rafferty, Frederick C., Jr.
Rausch, Carl W.
Ray, Charles A. III
Rayner, Brian M.
Read, David A.

Real, Glen J.
Real, Wayne
Rebb, Wayne A.
Redding, Shelia L.
Reed, Kelly L.

Rehr, Frank H.
Reid, John R.
Reinecke, William H., III
Reter, Steven L.
Reter, William H., II

Reynolds, Herbert J.
Reynolds, Houston T.
Rice, Jeffrey A.
Rice, Mary F.
Rice, Thomas C.

Richards, Robert M., Jr.
Richardson, Dale E.
Rickrode, Gary L.
Riddle, Charles F.
Riley, Charles A.

Riley, Neal Stephen
Ringgold, Jay L.
Ritzmann, Charles F., Jr.
Rivers, Ellen M.
Roberts, James E., Sr.

Roberts, Michael S.
Robertson, Dennis
Robertson, Jeffrey A.
Robey, Robert R.
Robinson, Michael W.

Robinson, Timothy L.
Roche, Minta M.
Rodriguez, Jose A., Jr.
Rodriguez, Jose G., Sr.
Rogers, Charles D.

Roody, Kellie A.
Roody, L. Allen
Roos, Larry G.
Rosenberger, Jerome E.
Rosenberger, Tracey C.

Rosensteel, Paul A.
Rosier, Charles E.
Rossman, Robert C.
Rouillard, Thomas G.
Rozema, Nico A.

Rupp, Michael A.
Ruppert, Michael D.
Russell, James E., Jr.
Russell, Scott L.
Rutledge, Michael S.

Ryan, John P.
Ryan, Joseph P.
Sallahuddin, Earl
Sanders, Joseph
Sauers, Samuel E.

Saunders, William E.
Schaal, Cheryl A.
Schaefer, Fred S.
Schaeffer, Kathleen A.
Schanberger, Richard

Scheide, J. Renee
Schimpf, Stephen R.
Schenning, Richard
Schlee, Kenneth A.
Schlegel, Andrew

Schoenbrost, Paul A.
Schoenrodt, Peter E.
Schoff, Christopher C.
Schreiber, John E., Jr.
Schreiber, Ronald E.

Schultz, Bruce E.
Schultz, John R.
Schultz, Keri A.
Schwartz, Bruce E.
Schwartz, Robert M.

Schwartz, Thomas J.
Schweers, Herman N., Jr.
Schwiegerath, Gary M.
Sears, Linda J.
Sebo, Shawn M

Seidlich, William W.
Seigle, Kelvin L.
Seigle, Robert L.
Senior, Richard A.(deceased)
Serio, Robert P.

Sharpe, Wayne D.
Shaw, Wayne N.
Shelton, James G.
Shenberger, Jan. B.
Shores, James H.

Shreiber, John E., Sr.
Shultze, Philip C.
Sibiski, Douglas J.
Simmers, Mary L.
Simmons, Neal H.

Simmons, Wayne D., Jr.
Simone, John V.
Simpson, J.R., III
Sipes, Edward G.
Slezak, James L.

Small, Steven M.
Smith, Bryan T.
Smith, Burton E.
Smith, David M.
Smith, Dean G.

Smith, Lewis E., Sr.
Smith, Robert W.
Snyder, Bruce A.
Snyder, Charles E.
Snyder, Dave

Snyder, Harry C.
Snyder, Jeffrey A.
Snyder, Richard T.
Snyder, Samuel P.
Sowa, Steven

Spangler, Donald B.
Spangler, Joseph E., Jr.
Spears, Frank O.
Spilman, Richard E.
Spruell, Sherman L.

Stacharowski, Eric J.
Stause, Gerard R.
Stawski, Michael
Steinberg, Stephen S.
Stem, Colin J.

Sterner, Robert E.
Stevens, Charles
Stevens, Michelle R.
Stevens, Phillip J.
Stewart, Alvin F., Sr.

Stewart, Michael R.
Stielper, Kevin J.
Stiffler, Louis F., Jr.
Stith, Mark E.
Stith, Zachery

Stone, Mark J.
Stresewski, Sharon L.
Stump, William A.
Sturm, Charles A., Jr.
Swift, Charles R.

CAREER

Szczesniakowski, Michael L.
Szukiewicz, Richard D.
Talbott, David W.
Tankersley, Kelly L.
Tapp, Aaron V.

Tawney, Deborah A.
Taylor, Charles A., Jr.
Taylor, Herbert K.
Taylor, Patrick K.
Tephaback, Randy T.

Thamert, Dennis P.
Thayer, Barry L.
Thieman, Thomas M.
Thiergartner, Carroll W., Jr.
Thode, Pierre M.

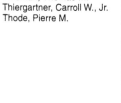

Thomas, Carlton D.
Thomas, Howard L.
Thomas, Kenneth
Thompson, Cleve J.
Thompson, Johnny E., Jr.

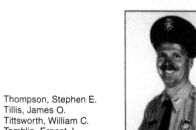

Thompson, Stephen E.
Tillis, James O.
Tittsworth, William C.
Tomblin, Ernest J.
Tome, Wayne L., Sr.

Torbeck, Lindsay S.
Tracey, Robert L.
Trenzsch, Frederick N.
Tribble, Timothy A.
Trovinger, Paul A.

128

Trump, Larry Edwin
Trump, Mark W.
Tully, James, F., III
Tudor, Charles H. Jr.
Turner, Robert W., Jr.

Ullrich, William F.
Unverzagt, Gary W.
Utz, Jennifer L.
Utzinger, Jeffrey
Valencia, Samuel A. III

Valentine, Rodney E., Jr.
Vangelder, Douglas C.
Vangelder, Kimberley C.
Van Vugt, Robert P.
Vaughan, Charles R.

Veach, John P.
Waddy, Dora
Wagenfer, Stephen A., Sr.
Wallace, Bonnie J.
Wallis, John G.

Walters, Jeffrey D.
Walters, Ronald D.
Wantz, Stephen A.
Ward, Francis P. III
Warner, James E. III

Watkins, Charles E.
Watsic, Melvin L.
Weaver, Melissa E.
Webb, Rebecca A.
Webster, James E.

Weer, Gary J.
Weigandt, Wayne M.
Weir, Christian E., Jr.
Weir, Christian E., Sr.
Weir, Mark E., Sr.

Weir, Michael H., Jr.
Weis, David T.
Weis, Donald L.
Weis, James A.
Weis, Robert A.

Weissner, Harold J., III
Welker, Byron L.
Welkie, George, Jr.
Weller, Richard L.
Welsh, Donna J.

Werry Stewart, Jennifer
Weskesser, Jerry
Wesley, Kenneth G.
West, Andrew T., Jr.
Westbrook, David R.

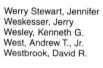

Westervelt, James R., Jr.
Wheeler, Gary F.
White, Tankia N.
White, William R.
Wiley, Mark S.

Wiley, William B. III
Wilhelm, Christopher M.
Wilkinson, Michele A.
Willats, Jeffrey J.
Willett, Cynthia S.

Williams, Alonza E.
Wilson, Timothy R.
Wingo, Louis R., Jr.
Winter, Dale R.
Wiseman, Deanna J.

Wisniewski, Gregory J.
Wolak, Charles W.
Woynovitz, Joseph R., Jr.
Wroten, Lawrence A.
Yakubowski, John A., Jr.

Yingling, Brian C.
Yingling, Richard V., Jr.
Yox, Leonard E.
Zeiler, Joseph C. III
Zimmerman, Brian W.

Bailey, Roland
Beckman Sr., Joe
Brillman, Scott
Brocato, Chris
Brown, Steven C.

Coolahan, Daniel C.
Cunningham, Dave
Goodman, Ken
Gower, Steve
Grusch, Joseph H.

Harvey III,Lew
Lynott, Gerald
Lynott, Susan
Mackey,Donald
McDowell, John

Nager, Dr. Eric
Nauman, Bob
Peacock,Glen
Preston, Edward
Robinson, Timothy L.

Shockney, Anthony
Shockney, Denny
Shockney, Pat
Simone, John V.
Simpkins Sr., Brian

Simpkins Sr., Doug
Stevens, Michelle R.
Szczesniakowski, Michael L.
Trovinger, Paul A.
Trovinger, Paul

Utzinger, Jeffrey H.
Vaughan, Charles R.
Zinkand Jr., Chuck
Zinkand Sr., James

ARCADIA

Allenbaugh Jr., William B.
Evans Jr., Ronald J.
Fleming, Susan M.
Knazt, Scott A.

   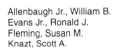

Miller, Jay E.
Ray III, Charles A.
Rice, Mary F.
Snyder, Harry C.

Trump, Mark W.
Ward III, Francis P.

Belt, Bill
Bosley, James
Bosley, Jimmy
Cowan, Bill
Crooks, John R.

Crooks, Ed
DeVilbiss Jr., Walter
Freeman, Ken
Green, Ed
Green, Val

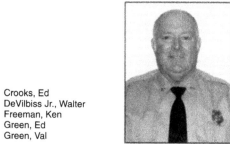    

Horner, Henry
Huffman, Chris
Schweers Jr., Herman N.
Simmers, Mary L.
Snyder, Harry C.

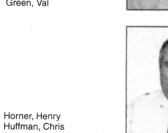

Wesley, Sam
Winans, Matt

VOLUNTEER

BOWLEYS QUARTERS

Bayne, Dennis
Cusic, Paul J.
Harker Jr., Francis Y.
Janowich Jr., Steve

Kelly, John C.
Pierson, Frank W.

BUTLER

Allendar, Casey B.
Belt, Wilbur B.
Crumbie, David L.
Curtis, Milton F.
Hackley, Wayne K.

Hann, Ronnie E.
Mann, Stewart N.
Sagal II, Joseph G.
Smith, Keith
Unglesbee, Ryan P.

Waganer, Dennis M.
Wilhelm II, Dale E.
Wilhelm Sr., Dale E.
Wilhelm, Dany R.

Wilhelm, Paul Jr.
Wilhelm, Tommy A.
Womer, Douglas

BOX 234

Batzer, Mary
Bitzel, Steven A.
Bright, Leona
Bright, William
Cox, Shirley F.

England, Anida
Hand, Bonnie
Holden, Richard C.
Jakobson, Deborah
Jakobson, Kurt

Redding, Carroll
Redding, Lillian
Waxter, Elizabeth

CENTRAL ALARMERS

Anderson, Dale
Brooks, Jim
Brown, Edith
Dorer,Frank
Ebbert,Barb

Elliott, Harry
Fales, Donald
Fox, Libby
Frederick, Jim
Freund, Ed

Geppi, Carroll
Goeb, George
Graden, John
Hayes, John
Hagen, Edith

Heathcote, Gary
Heathcote, Genett
Kemnitz, Heidi
McCrea, Barbara
Maurer, Bill

O'Connor, Charlie
Peyton, Debbie
Peyton, John
Pollock, Frank
Pollock, Leo John

VOLUNTEER

Pollock, Robert
Raborg, Marian
Reamex, Robert
Rock, Fred
Rock, Pat

Ruppersberger, Maureen
Sennett, Adam
Sennett, Cindy
Sennett, Harry
Stiegleman, Roger

Stoll, Will
Sturgill, Marge
Van-Couct, Gay
Woolery, Charlene

CHESTNUT RIDGE

Aspden, Rebecca
Cohen, Charlie
Combs, Virginia B.
Corasaniti, Frank
Corasaniti, Joey

Coroneos, Nicki L
Crystal, Jack
Foster, Vickie
Fox, Marti
Fox, Marvin B.

Volunteer

Fox, Mike
Green, Julie
Hamburger, Coos
Hand, Bonnie
Hooper, Brian

Kakel, Harry
Kopp, Valerie
Lloyd, Chastity
Lloyd, Jaime
Noetzel, Cheryl

Lubman, Dan
Lunnen, Mike
Shiller, Stacy
Strickland, Jen
Reynolds, Gene

Uddeme, Dan
Yaffe, Rick
Yaffe, Ryan

Cockeysville

Allen, John
Aung, Moe
Ball, Brian
Ball, Gary
Banister, Dawn

VOLUNTEER

Banister, Elwood
Banister, Helen
Barshinger, John T.
Barshinger, Michael
Bayne, Dennis J.

Berger, Michael
Beziat, Bridget
Bond, John
Bosley, Bernard
Brumwell, Bo

Buckwalter, Regina
Buckwalter, Scott
Carruthers, Nick
Childs, Brian
Cole, Charles

Cole, Kenneth
Cook Jr., Erin W.
Coroneos, Susan M.
Crist, Michael
Crumbie, David L.

Dana, Marc
Daughaday, Edward R.
Daughaday, Michael
Davis, Christopher
Dixon, John B.

Dold, Jim
Dooley, Richard
Dukes, Jeffrey O.
Dukes Jr., John
Fowble, Grayson E.

Frederick, Robert P.
Gribble, David B.
Gribble, Donna
Gribble Jr., Harry
Gribble, John W.

Gribble, Lawrence
Gribble, Richard
Herbert, Ann
Hoffman, Andy
Holbrook, Vicki

Holland, Debra L.
Holland, John T.
Holland, Michael K.
Howard, James
Hutton, Roger

Jeffers, Thomas J.
Kakel, Jeremy
Kamps, Lisa
Kampes, Melanie A.
Kasztejna, Paul

Kearny, Maurice
Kearny, Phillip
Kilgore, Trevor
Lambert, Michele
Lambert, Morgan

Lane, Denorah
Lemmen, Anna
Longo, Robert
Madairy, Deb
Madchrzak, Lawrence

Meinshien, Bernard
Meinschien, Beverly S.
Minick, Chris
Minton, Andrew
Murphy, David J.

Murphy, Terri
Naylor, Erin
Oehrl, Fred C.
Pagnotta, Gabriella
Passos, Deborah M.

Peacock, William
Pedrazzani, Deborah
Polich, Michele M.
Price, Catherine
Price, Paul

Reed, Michael
Roberts, Christopher P.
Roberts, Jack F.
Roberts, Jean
Roberts, Kevin W.

Roberts, Lonnie C.
Roberts, Lynda
Roberts Jr., Marvin
Roberts, Michael
Roberts, Sherry

Rubenti, Christina
Schulman, Rebecca
Scotland, Howard
Sheeler, Skip
Shephard Jr., Reggie D.

Shephard Sr., Reggie D.
Shipley, Debbie L.
Shipley, Scott L.
Simms Jr., Harry V.
Sittler, Edward A.

Smith, Charles
Smith, Douglas
Smith, Susan
Spitz, David E.
Stafford, William

Stem, Richard
Stevenson, Stanley F.
Tracey, Clarence E.
Tracey Jr., Melvin E.
Tyrie Jr., G. Walter

Urbanek, David
Wagenfuehr, Michelle
Walker, James
Walker, Katherine

Walker, Steve
Walker, William
Walker III, William J.

Zoltowski, Adam P.

143

Amrhein, John P.
Belan, Matt
Bielecki Jr., Ken
Bielecki Sr., Ken
Chilcoat, Buddy

Davidson, Scott W.
DiPaula Jr., Francis X.
DiSalvo, Christina
Engle, LeRoy
Gingell Jr., Joseph

Hayden, David
Higgins, Ryan
Jordan, Alan
Ledford, Lonnie
Lutostanski, Will

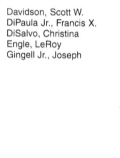     

Myers, Daniel A.
Robertson, Dennis S.
Romberger, Dennis
Schlogel, William

Schultz, Keri A.
Smith, Ryan
Thorn, Isaac M.
Trzeciah, Timothy P.

VOLUNTEER

Vaughn, Al
Weiland, Nick
Wodarczyk,Melisa

ENGLISH CONSUL

Auberzin
Batzmike
Blades, Kenneth
Branhaml
Brinkley

Burnshn
Burton
Buryrobe
Campbell
Connell

Connell
Conway
Courtney
Dimeler
Emkey

Fawley
Frye
Grewe
Hardesty
Harvey

VOLUNTEER

Hoffman
Hugle
Kaszaka
Kickmick
Kierle

Lancast
Lancast
Lucker
March
Mccarr

Mccarr
McDevit
MillerJe
MillerSa
Millersi

Moorecon
Moorevic
Oberyly
Piller Dj
Purkey, Randy

Raushcla
Sheldon
Shrorath
Stencld
St John

Trovinger, Paul A
Waldron
Weber
Wentwort

146

Whaley
Williams

GLYNDON

Abbott, Winn
Altomonte Jr., Tony
Beimschla, Carol
Brach Jr., J. Peter
Bosley, Benjamin S.

Brown, Randy
Caples, Casey
Carter, James D.
Casey, Jason
Cofiell, Wayne A.

Cole, Richard
Crooks, J. Edward
Curtis, Harry L.
Johnson, Thomas
Knife, David

Lessner, Russ
Listwan, Marty
McCracken, Justin S.
Merriken, Mary K.
Merriken, Richard C.

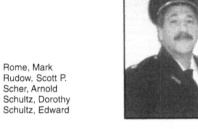

Morgenroth, Stephanie
Morris, Kenneth J.
Reitz, Kathy
Reter, Calvin
Rice, John

Rome, Mark
Rudow, Scott P.
Scher, Arnold
Schultz, Dorothy
Schultz, Edward

Schultz, John R.
Stem, Colin J.
Stem III, Richard
Stem Jr., Richard
Stem Sr., Richard

Talbert Jr., Walter
Warner, Donna
Warner, James E.
Warner III, James E.
Warner, John

Warner, Maxine
Warner, Mitchell
Warner, Scott
Wolfenden, Douglas

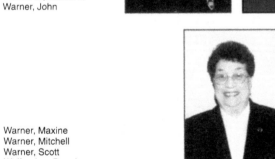   

HEREFORD AMBULANCE

Anastaiso, Judy
Banthem, Al
Bilger, Hope
Bilger, Richard
Binder, Jennifer

Blackner, Carol Ann
Ciesla, Dennis
Cole, Elizabeth
Croft, Susan
Dahl, Keith

Dell, David
Dell, Dottie
Dembeck, Dennis L.
Doub, Nancy
Fausto, John

Fink, Mary Ann
Haller, Tom
Hanavan, Tim
Hester, Jeff
Horsley, Kristen

Huggins, Jason
Humphrey, Cindy
Jednorski, Charles
Jednorski, Stacy L.
Kane, Laura

Kinsey, Justin
Kolscher, Darrell
Lang, George
Layman, Steve
Leven, Jeff

Liverette, Jim
Marshall. Jeanie
Morgan, Debbie
Novo, Sondra
O'Connell, Arthur

Rehfeld, Anne
Rico, Chris
Riley, Gail
Schwatka, Victoria
Skiba, Lisa

Spencer, Dan
Szeglia, Lou
Tice, Paul
Treaster, Cristin

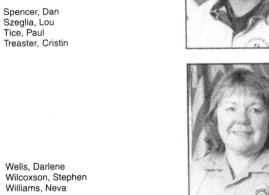

Wells, Darlene
Wilcoxson, Stephen
Williams, Neva
Woods, Joe

Adams, Jeff
Badders, David L.
Badders, Leroy
Baldwin, Teddy
Bilger, Hope

Bilger, Richard
Bollinger, Chuck
Bollinger, Danny
Bollinger, Debbie
Bollinger, Kenneth

Campanella, Pulette
Campion, Deborah
Campion, Ron
Cole, Elizabeth
Cook, Elva

Cooper, Lawrence
Croft, Ronnie
Croft, Sue
Curtis, Karie
Curtis, Shane

Ensor, Marguerite
Epps, Jen
Fleming, David
Frederick, Barb
Frederick, Charles

151

VOLUNTEER

Gardner, Mark
Garrett, Charlie
Gosnell, Betty
Gosnell, Frank
Hilgardener, Jim

Hood, Debbie
Hood, Mike
Hoshall, Mike
Hubber, Jay
Huber Jr., Ronald J.

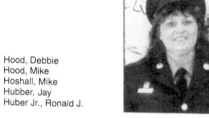

Jackson, Tim
Kapaska, Chris
Kearney, Gregg R.
Kearney, Phil
Lang, George

Lang, Jesse
Lang, Michelle
Lang, Peggy
Ledford, Larry
Leight, Abe

Miller, Robert
Montaldo, Luke
Mooney, John
Mooney, Peggy
Myers, Richard

Pearson, William "Bill"
Pruett, Joe
Pruett, Virginia
Rhine, Stewart
Rice, Kelley

Robertson, Charles
Robertson, David
Ruhl, Tom
Sagal, Joey
Sheats, Arlene

Shelley, Mark
Simmons, Roger
Simms, Jen
Simpson, Thomas
Smith, Wayne

Stiffler Jr., Louis F.
Taylor, Herbert K.
Thompson, Babbi

Thompson, Kenny
Warns, Robert

HYDE PARK

Alban Jr., John J.
Stump, William A.

VOLUNTEER

JACKSONVILLE

  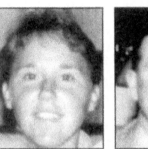 

Anderson, Keh
Auvil, Matt
Beebe, Michele
Boblits, Kathy
Brewer, Brent

Carter, Brandon
Chrusniak, Marge
Cody, Amanda
Cole, Lorraine
Dietz, Christina

Duerbeck, Jerry
Dundas, Margart
Dundas, Scott
Edwards, Jim
Essel, Andy

Fox, Matt
Fumarola, Melanie
Morgan, Barbara
Gamble, Claud
Garrison, Amy

Gavin, Laura
Gosnell, Jack
Hornbacher, Bob
Hornbacher, Eva
Hutton, Craig

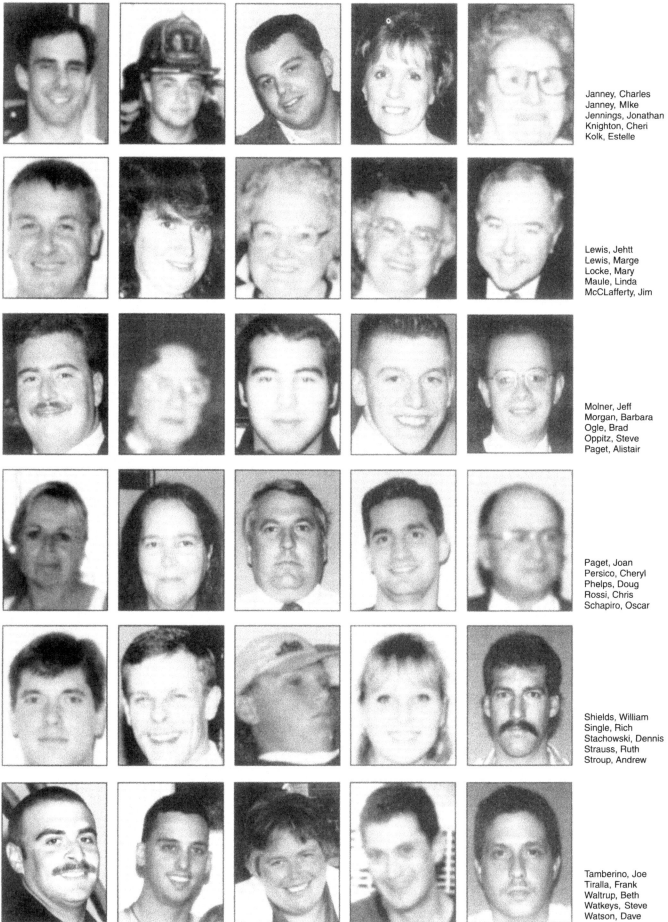

Janney, Charles
Janney, MIke
Jennings, Jonathan
Knighton, Cheri
Kolk, Estelle

Lewis, Jehtt
Lewis, Marge
Locke, Mary
Maule, Linda
McCLafferty, Jim

Molner, Jeff
Morgan, Barbara
Ogle, Brad
Oppitz, Steve
Paget, Alistair

Paget, Joan
Persico, Cheryl
Phelps, Doug
Rossi, Chris
Schapiro, Oscar

Shields, William
Single, Rich
Stachowski, Dennis
Strauss, Ruth
Stroup, Andrew

Tamberino, Joe
Tiralla, Frank
Waltrup, Beth
Watkeys, Steve
Watson, Dave

Westervelt, Jim
Wheeler, Bob
White, Bobbie
Wiedey, Chris
Wiedey, Christa

Wiedey, Howard
Wiggins, Curt
Wright, Wayne

KINGSVILLE

Berkeridge, James Kelly
Berkeridge, Terry A.
Berkeridge, Timothy P.
Berna, Michael
Boyd, Joanne

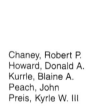      

Chaney, Robert P.
Howard, Donald A.
Kurrle, Blaine A.
Peach, John
Preis, Kyrle W. III

Berg, Robert
Blizzard, David
Burford, Jeremy
Douglas, Amanda
Douglas, Jill

Eller, Roxianna
Gill, Raymond
Hazelton, Damone D.
Keene, Luis
Mooney, James D.

Palmer, Lawrence K.
Poole, Ron
Ramzy, Ameen I.
Rayner, Brian M.
Simmons Jr., Wayne D.

Sipes, Edward G.
Spinks, Ricky

VOLUNTEER

LIBERTY ROAD

Bitzel, Nancy
Bossman, Michel B.
Chinery, David C.
Chinery III, Henry J.
Darling, Ronald W.

Dixon, Jarrett A.
Fleming, Bruce D.
Kemp, Donald B.
Love, Donald W.
Meyers, Karen L.

Miller, Stephen R.
Rosensteel, Paul A.
Van Vugt, Robert P.
Wiley III, William B.

LONG GREEN

Barkley, Howard
Barnhart, John
Brewer Jr., Barry
Delcaer, Gloria
Delcher III, William

VOLUNTEER

Eyre, Rick
Eyre, Sharon
Freidman, Brian
Gaines III, William L.
Gosnell, Wilbur

Harrison, Ron
Hayes, Lawrence "Skip"
Jackson, Earl
Jones, Donna
Maas, Bernard H.

Maas, Laurie
Martin, Craig
McCrea, Joel
Monks, Ken
Mumma, Francis

Napolillu, Lee
Peruzovic, Kirsten
Saur, Bill
Stelmack, Steve
Stolins, Gregory

Stoll, Audrey
Stoll, William
Stolins, Tracy
Rigger, Robert
Williams, Mark

Williams, Neva
Wright Jr., Ed
Yarish, Matthew

159

Bankard, Timothy E.
Barranco, Frank T.
Brewer, Walter L.
Conrad, Bruce W.
Cranston, Vern S.

Gisriel, Stephen T.
Goodwin, Mark J.
Huber Jr., Ronald J.
Oppitz, Stephen P.
O'Rourke, Michael A.

Rupp, Michael A.
Smith, David M.
Smith Sr., Lewis E.
Snyder, Dave

Tracey, Robert L.
Zeiler III, Joseph C.
Zoltowski, Adam P

MARYLAND LINE

Badders, David L.
Badders, LeRoy
Holloway, Dean E.
Weller, Richard L.

MIDDLEBOROUGH

Alemi, Craig
Benjamin, Alan
Bronson, Tony
Dranbauer Jr., Mark
Dranbauer Sr., Mark

Dranbauer, Robin
Fairley, Matt
Fairley, Tim
Filipiak, Jerry
Gellar, Steven J.

Holtz, Jan
Holtz, Rick
Horney, Matt
Horton, Josh
Iwaniw, Mike

Kinard, James L.
Kulisiewicz, Kenneth M.
Lougee, Kara
Peyton, Debbie
Peyton, John

Rayner, Brian M.
Rudasill, John
Ruppersberger, Maureen
Smith, Robert W.
Sowa, Steven

Spinelli, Neil
Stasko, Ken

= MIDDLE RIVER AMBULANCE & FIRE =

Dulina Jr., George
Falkenhan, Mark G.
Halley, Ronald
Holden, Sara
Jones, Dennis W.

Ruppert, Michael D.
Rutledge, Michael S.
Sebo, Shawn M.
Weis, James A.
Weis, Robert A.

VOLUNTEER

NORTH POINT EDGEMERE

Piker Sr., Steven M.
Proffen, Evan C.

OWINGS MILLS

Bell, Roy
Bender, Thomas J.
Brown III, Coleman P.
Burkholder, David F.
Cullands, Velda

Corones, Susan
Christian, Jere
Dews, Sarah
Fold, Michael
Gicen, River Topaz

Griffith, Jeff
Herbert, Phil
Howard, Bill
Jeroff, Marty
Johnson, Ramsey M.

Johnson III, Rudolph C.
Kraus, Scott
Lancellotti, Harry
Lippy, Christina
Meekins, Leon

Montgomery, Christopher
Nelson Jr, Craig S.
Nietubicz, Carrie Anne
Nilsen, Jenny
Pessagno, Diane

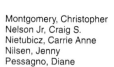

Pinkas, Macy M.
Ramsel Jr., John
Roche, Dee
Rosenberg, William
Rubenstein, Jason

Schnaw, Louise J.
Schwartz, Robert M.
Schwartz, Thomas J.
Stem III, Richard
Thode, Pierre M.

Trump, Larry Edwin
Trump, Mark W.
Trump, Wayne
Webster, Charles
Walter, James W.

Warren, Donald
Weirer, Rachael
Willett, Harry

Wallett, Kevin
Wright, Desha
Yaffie, Matthew

Pikesville

Berryman Jr., John W.
Biddison, Steven M.
Boyd, Joanne
Cohen, Harold C.
Davis, Edward S.

Dembeck, Dennis L.
England-Dansicker, Danelle
England Jr., William B.
Gaines III, William L
Gauss, Christopher

Goodwin, Mark J.
Holden, Daniel
Holden, Richard L.
Jacob, Sharon L.
Miller, Michael A.

Murray Jr., Robert D.
Murray Sr., Robert D.
Myers, Anthony J.
O'Connor Jr., Francis D.
Ray III, Charles A.

VOLUNTEER

Redding, Wayne C.
Roody, Kellie A.
Roody, L. Allen
Rossman, Robert C.
Stevens, Michelle R.

Stone, Mark J.
Thompson, Cleve J.
Turchin, Terry

PROVIDENCE

Benham, Joseph E.
Biddison, Steven M.
Bingham, Nick
Cobburn, Jeff
Coroneos, Nicki L.

Dar, Phil
Deatley, Luke
Ebbert, Scott G.
Goldberger, Dennis
Heinz, John M.

Hinton, Tony O.
Kelly, Daniel J.
Kelly Jr., Joseph V.
Kernan, Tim
Kohnle, Dan

166

Lancaster, Matthew G.
Lancaster, Stephen G.
Herweck, Matt
Kernan-Harvey, Robin
Lattanzi, Serg

Marshall, Daniel
McClean, Jack
Pearce, Ed
Pearce, Stephen
Rice, Thomas C.

Robertson Jr., George F.
Robertson Sr., George F.
Robertson, Scott A.
Ross, Ed

Smith, David M.
Steele, John
Wehrle, Tom

Zour, John

REISTERSTOWN

Bosley, Benjamin S.
Bosley, Raymond
Carter, James D.
Cofiell, Wayne A.
Crooks, Dennis L.

Evans,Michael R.
Fannon, VIncent N.
Fox, Marvin B.
Hipsley, Wayne M.
Linker, Dennis W.

Long Jr., Albert E.
Murray Jr., Robert D.
Murray Sr., Robert D.
Nickoles, Thomas M.
Patterson, Robert G.

Petry, Richard W.
Ryan, Joseph P.
Scher, Arnold L.
Schultz, John R.

Stem Jr., Richard
Stem Sr., Richard
Warner III, James E.

VOLUNTEER

ROCKAWAY BEACH

Alchimowicz, Jerome
Bromwell, Steven
Custer, David
Everly, Tammy
Julian, Jeremy

Kahler, Richard P.
Kerby, Frederick
Kerby, Steven
Ledley, Deborah
Ledley, Michael P.

Medinger, John
Ogle, Leroy
Roberts, James
Roth, Allan
Shrader, Brian

Spangler, Frank
Stuart Jr., Michael
Voyzey, Sherri
Weber, Nicholas

169

Banister, Patrice
Barnstien, Jason
Barry, Steve
Bartock, Raymond
Cioka, Justin

Cline, Karen
Cole, Eric
Cole, Robert
Endryas, Eric
Endryas, M. Eileen

Gabriele, Cody
Gabriele Jr., Rocco
Gross, Richard
Grupp, Melvin
Harding, John

Harker, Francis Y.
Howell, Christina
Hueter, Chuck
Jarkrewicz, Daniel J.
Kearney, Tasha R.

Klass, Mason
Kolego, Shawn
Lehr, Karen M.
Leiss, Chuck
Mazza, Jack

Volunteer

McDonnell, Richard
McJilton, Charles W.
Miller, Ellyse
Patterson, Crissy
Patterson, Ryan

Pearson, Bill
Pierson, Frank W.
Pizzini, Jimmy
Potts, Debbie
Rock, Red

Seeley, Steve
Stachowski, Steve
Stark, Brian
Valencia III, Samuel A.
Wilmering, Derrick

Violetville

Adcock, Mike
Bragg Sr., William B.
Cullum, Charles L.
Ficke, Wilber
Henderson, James

Huffman, Arthur
Iyams, John
Koch, Sue
Kulbe, Donald
Lucas, Norman

Melcher, Claude
Pearson, Steve
Purkey, Dorothy
Purkey, Larry
Purkey, Randy J.

Purkey Jr., John A.
Purkey III, Gary
Purkey III, John
Rausch, Laura
Rausch, Sheila A.

Rausch Jr., Robert G.
Remmell, Robert
Rositzky, Melvin

Swann, William
Turner Jr., Robert W.
Woynovitz Jr., Joseph R.

WISE AVENUE

Bowen, Jeffrey
Bruzdzinsk Jr., Michael
Copeland, Dale
Geho, Tracy
Kadolph, Gary O.

Ludwig, Tom
McLyman, Gerald
Milburne, Mark D.
Phillips, Mark
Piker, Paul W.

Ritz, John
Schaeffer, Kathleen A.
Sellers, Greg
Still, Scott
Stroh, Tyler

Tillis, James O.
Ullrich, Tim
Willinger, Will

WOODLAWN

Abiera, Pete
Artis Jr., James W.
Best, Kenny
Caldwell, Kyle
Carhart, Brian

Ceasar, Antonette
Fields, Sean
Elliott, John
Gilmore Jr., Jerome K.
Golden, Abraham

173

VOLUNTEER

Gwathney, Michael
Jones, Robert A.
Kern, William
Kinsey, Raymond A.
Lee, Antonio

Marner, Everett
Pirtle, James
Reynolds, Michelle
Robinson, Tangela
Seicke, Frank A.

Skeleton, Sam
Spicer, John
Spicer, Patti

Taylor, Mary
Weskesser, Jerry L.
Younger, Kenneth

Abbott, John W. Jr.
Abrams, Samuel E.
Acosta, Michael D.
Adams, Donald W.
Adamson, Vernon S.
Adelsberger, Steven D.
Ailiff, Cameron M.
Akers, Jeffrey S.
Alban, John J., Jr.
Allenbaugh, William B., Jr.
Allen, Richard L., Jr.
Allenbaugh, William B., Jr.
Aloysius, Connor
Altomonte, Tony, Jr.
Amereihn, Thomas R.
Amole, Michael W.
Amoriello, Gregory A.
Amrhein, John P.
Arnold, Edward B.
Artis, James W., Jr.
Asper, Jeffery S.
Auld, Shawn S.
Aung, Moe
Austin, Craig, D.
Backhaus, Paul G.
Badders, David L.
Badders, James A.
Badders, Nancy M.
Badders, LeRoy
Badders, Timothy A.
Baldwin, Travis J.
Balladarsch, George J., Jr.
Banister, Dawn M.
Banister, Kevin E.
Bankard, Timothy E.
Barcikowski, Christopher H.
Bare, Timothy I.
Barnes, Dennis C.
Barranco, Frank T., MD
Barrow, Robert J.
Barry, Steven T.
Barshinger, Bethany A.
Barshinger, John T.
Barshinger, Michael
Barton, William J.
Batzer, Mary
Baublitz, Richard L.
Bauer, Harry F., III
Bauer, Steven H.
Bayne, Dennis J.
Bean, Gregory S.
Beard, Lloyd E.
Becker, Donald K., Sr.
Becker, Thomas
Bell, Calvin C.
Bell, John, Jr.
Bell, Timothy E., Sr.
Benham, Joseph E.
Beresh, Robert M.
Berkeridge, James Kelly
Berkeridge, Terry A.
Berkeridge, Timothy P.
Berna, Michael
Berryman, John W., Jr.
Berwaldt, Paul O.
Biddison, Steven M.
Bidinger, Craig A.
Binkley, Robert
Bitters, Glenn
Bitzel, Nancy
Bitzel, Steven A.
Blackmon, Keith H.
Blackwell, Glenn A.
Blades, Kenneth L.
Boblitz, Kathy L.
Bolling, Jerry A.
Bollinger, Daniel T.
Bollinger, Debbie
Bollinger, Dwight C.
Bollinger, Kenneth C.
Bosley, Benjamin S.
Bosely, Raymond
Bossman, Michel B.
Bowe, Alvin S.
Boyd, Joanne
Bowen, Jeffrey S.

Bowman, Kathy T.
Bown, Thomas L.
Bragg, William B., Sr.
Brammer, Suzanne K.
Brehm, William E.
Breighner, Ray K., Jr.
Brewer, Walter L., III
Brister, Lawrence S., Sr.
Bright, Leona
Bright, William
Brooks, George H.
Brooks, Lisa A.
Brothers, Curtis L.
Brothers, Dennis W.
Brown, Albert T.
Brown, Joseph, Jr.
Brown, Randy
Brown, Steven C.
Brown, Thomas F.
Browne, Carroll L.
Buckingham, David L.
Bull, Gary L.
Burnell, Harold J.
Burkhardt, Frederick L.
Burkins, Angela
Burkins, William S.
Burnett, Shelly R.
Bursey, Ronald M.
Burton, Gary N.
Bycoffe, David J.
Camak, Dana B.
Cannaday, Kevin D.
Capley, James R.
Carbaugh, Lynn W.
Carter, James D.
Carter, Robert, Jr.
Carter, William E.
Carter, William L.
Carver, Paul B.
Casey, Jason
Chamberlain, Michael G.
Chandler, Justin D.
Chaney, Robert P.
Chenoweth, Paul S.
Chilcoat, Jeffery S., Sr.
Childs, Denise A.
Chinery, David C.
Chinery, Henry J., III
Chu, Kenneth C.
Cleveland, Gregory J.
Clinton, Craig A.
Clunie, Opie F.
Cobburn, Jeff
Coffman, Warren H., Jr.
Cofiell, Wayne A.
Cohen, Harold C.
Cole, Eric S.
Coleman, Glenn R., Sr.
Colleran, Thomas J.
Collifower, James E.
Combs, Virginia B.
Connally, Oscar W.
Connolly, Barbara L.
Connolly, William F., Jr.
Conrad, Bruce W.
Cook, Charles R.
Cooke, Robert F.
Cooke, Tyrone V.
Coolahan, Daniel C.
Coroneos, Nicki L.
Coulter, Mark H.
Cox, David B.
Cox, Gretchen A.
Cox, Shirley F.
Coyle, Victoria K.
Cranston, Vern S.
Crawford, Scott E.
Creswell, Michael W.
Croft, Sue
Cromer, Jason D.
Cromwell, John E., Jr.
Crooks, Dennis L.
Crooks, J. Edward
Crooks, John R.
Crosby, Michael D.
Crumbie, David L.

Cruz, Edward J.
Cuffley, Wayne D.
Cullom, John H., Jr.
Curlee, Terry
Curtis, Harry L.
Cushing, Sara
Cusic, Paul J.
D'Elia, Lawrence N., III
Dailey, Edward M.
Dales, Garth J.
Danner, William D.
Darling, Ronald W.
Darr, George C.
Darr, Philip M.
Davidson, Charles E.
Davidson, Scott W.
Davis, Amanda M.
Davis, Edward S.
Davis, Warren T., III
Deatley, Luke
DeFlavis, Richard A.
DeGross, Dennis G.
DeLuca, Michael E.
Dembeck, Dennis L.
Dembeck, Roland T.
Demory, Anthony A.
Demski, Mark F.
Denning, Dean A.
DePaula, Francis X., Jr.
Devers, Donald R.
Devers, James E.
Devers, Matthew D.
DeVito, Joseph K.
DeZurn, Eddie L., Jr.
Dill, Robert G.
Dixon, Jarrett A.
Dixon, Louis A., Jr.
Doran, James E.
Drasal, Michael L.
Drees, George C.
Dryden, David K.
Dudderar, Howard K.
Duell, Kevin
Dulina, George, Jr.
Duncan, Wayne T.
Dundas, Scott
Dunn, James P.
Dutterer, Allen L., Jr.
Dutterer, Ketti L.
Eagle, Mark B.
Ebbert, Scott G.
Eder, Timothy B.
Edmunds, Leroy P., III
Edwards, James J.
Efford, David R.
Elkins, Terry W.
Ellwood, Harry K.
England, Anida
Endryas, M. Eileen
Endryas, Eric R.
England-Dansicker, A. Danelle
England, William B., Jr.
Engle, Leroy
Epps, Jennifer
Espinosa, Anthony S.
Essel, Andrew J., Jr.
Euler, Alvin E.
Eurice, Paul J.
Evans, Charles S.
Evans, Michael R.
Evans, Ronald J.
Fabrizio, Thomas D., Jr.
Fair, Donald R., II
Falkenhan, Mark G.
Fannon, Joseph J., Jr.
Fannon, Vincent N.
Fannon, Joshua L.
Farley, Bryan M.
Farley, Mary M.
Faulkner, Paul W.
Feeley, Patrick S.
Feist, Ernest L., III
Fike, George S.
Finch, Arthur K.
Fisher, Keith W., Jr.
Flater, Thomas M., III

Fleming, Bruce D.
Fleming, David
Fleming, Susan M.
Fogel, Robert W., III
Fold, Michael A.
Folio, Anthony J.
Ford, James C., Sr.
Forster, Robin J.
Fosbrink, Sarah A.
Fowble, Jeffrey Gilbert
Fox, Marvin, B.
Fox, Matthew B.
Fox, Michael B.
Frank, Michael J.
Fratta, Theodore M.
Frederick, Charles C.
Freund, Glen E.
Frock, Christopher B.
Funk, Sandra
Gail, Edward W.
Gaines, William L., III
Gardner, David K.
Gardner, Mark E.
Gardner, Michael C.
Gardner, William E., Jr.
Garrison, Wayne
Gartside, Gregory A.
Gauss, Christopher
Gawel, Cary J.
Geho, Jeff
Geho, Leo F., Jr.
Geller, Steven J.
Gentile, Carl
Gereny, Cheryl
Giannaccini, Patricia K.
Gibney, James C.
Gibney, Todd, M.
Gill, Nancy E.
Gill, Raymond S.
Gilmore, Jerome K., Jr.
Gilbert, William J.
Gisriel, Stephen T.
Gist, Michael C.
Glass, Jean M.
Godfrey, Charles K.
Goldencrown, Randy L.
Goode, Harolyn S.
Goodwin, Mark J.
Gover, Ernest W.
Grape, William M.
Greaver, John C.
Greene, Carolyn A.
Greene, Deborah L.
Gribble, Harry W., Jr.
Gribble, Lawrence E.
Gribble, Donna L.
Griebel, Joseph P.
Griffin, Brian K.
Griffin, Christian D.
Grimes, Robert A.
Groft, Melvin D.
Groom, Vonzell J.
Grubb, Danny G., Sr.
Grubowski, Francis
Grusch, Joseph H.
Gryce, Rickey A.
Gutkoska, Joseph V.
Gwathmey, Mike
Hackley, Wayne K.
Hahn, Jason W.
Haines, David B.
Hales, William R., Jr.
Hall, Richard H.
Halley, Ronald
Hamlett, Timothy S.
Hammond, Roger
Hand, Bonnie
Hannan, Timothy L.
Hardester, Robert W., Jr.
Hardesty, Bryan E.
Hare, Mark
Harker, Francis Y., Jr.
Harlee, Dora E.
Harner, Timothy P.
Harrell, David F., Jr.
Harris, Glen E.

Harrison, Hubert E., Jr.
Hart, Jonathan D.
Haughwout, Roy N.
Hawley, Christopher
Haymaker, William Richard
Hays, Michael C.
Hazelton, Damone D.
Heath, Clyde E., III
Heath, David S., Jr.
Hebert, Phillip L.
Hein, Richard W.
Heins, Gerald R.
Heinz, John M.
Heller, Joseph J.
Henderson, Patrick J.
Henry, Samuel F.
Henthorn, James E., III
Herman, Christopher W.
Hernandez, Alfonzo M.
Hess, Dale W.
Hill, Peter J.
Hill, Terri A.
Hinton, Tony O.
Hipsley, Wayne M.
Hobbs, Steven G., III
Hoffman, Andrew T.
Hoffman, Christopher M.
Hoffman, John T., Jr.
Hohenberger, David C.
Hohman, John J.
Holden, Daniel
Holden, Richard L.
Holden, Sara
Holland, Joseph E.
Holloway, Dean E.
Holloway, Douglas A., Sr.
Holman, Charnetta M.
Holmes, Robert F.
Hood, Michael
Howard, Donald A.
Hubbard, Mark F.
Huber, Ronald J., Jr.
Hudnet, Frederick A.
Hudnet, Gregory B.
Hughes, Kenneth P.
Hughs, Robert D.
Humphrey, Cindy
Huppman, Paul E.
Hutchinson, Terry D.
Hutton, Craig L.
Hutton, Roger G.
Isaac, William G., Jr.
Jackson, Albert C.
Jacob, Sharon L.
Jakobson, Deborah
Jakobson, Kurt
Janowich, Steve, Jr.
Jarkiewicz, Daniel J.
Jednorski, Stacy L.
Jessa, John C.
Johns, William R.
Johnson, Craig
Johnson, Damon J.
Johnson, Ethan T.
Johnson, Thomas L.
Jones, Dennis W.
Jones, Pierce H., III
Jones, Robert A.
Jones, Warren A.
Judlick, Steven J.
Kadolph, Gary O.
Kahler, Richard P.
Kampes, Melanie A.
Karcher, Robert A.
Kearney, Gregg R.
Kearney, Tasha R.
Keller, Gary W.
Kelly, Daniel J.
Kelly, John C.
Kelly, Joseph V., Jr.
Kemmer, Marc S.
Kemp, Donald B.
Kendzejeski, Francis J., Jr.
Kesting, Bruce C.
Kile, Daniel J.
Kilinski, Myer A.

Kilson, Howard E., Jr.
Kimbel, Thomas J.
Kinard, James L.
Kinsey, Lorraine M.
Kinsey, Raymond A.
Kluge, Daniel E.
Knatz, Scott A.
Knight, Barbara L.
Knight, William C.
Knopp, George Michael
Kohl, John A., Sr.
Kohnle, Dan
Kookogey, James L.
Korn, James M.
Krause, James R.
Krebs, Dennis R.
Krebs, Gene D.
Kreimer, Jeffrey S.
Kruger, Tina J.
Kuchta, William T.
Kuhn, Keith S.
Kulisiewicz, Kenneth M.
Kurrle, Blaine A.
Kurtz, Michael E.
Kuruc, Jonathan G.
Kyle, William A., Jr.
Lamb, Deborah L.
Lamb, Steven N.
Lamon, Lawrence E.
Lancellotti, Harry
Lang, Christopher A.
Lang, George
Langeheine, Todd M.
Lannen, Richard A.
Latostanski, Will
Latreille, Pete D.
Laurie, Hugh W.
Ledford, Barry J.
Ledford, Larry
Lee, Meril K.
Legge, Thomas E.
Lehr, Karen M.
Leidner, Mark L.
Leight, Emory E.
Lemmon, Daniel
Lemmon, Jennifer R.
Leonard, Charles E.
Lessner, Russ
Lewis, Brent L.
Lewis, Gregory E.
Lewis, Irvin N.
Lewis, Jhett S.
Lewis, Kevin L.
Liebelt, Shawn P.
Lim, Robert W.
Linker, Dennis W.
Lilley, Robert E.
Lloyd, Dianne M.
Lloyd, John J., Jr.
Logue, Thomas E.
Lonczynski, Deborah A.
Long, Albert E., Jr.
Long, Dennis E.
Long, Richard A.
Love, Donald W.
Lowe, Jeffrey A.
Lowman, Timothy A.
Ludwig, Brian E.
Ludwig, Clarence J., Jr.
Ludwig, Duane
Ludwig, John G., III
Lund, Robert E., II
Lurz, Paul S.
Lyons, Richard W.
Maas, Bernard H.
Mack, Nathaniel J.
MacLean, Pamela A.
Magness, Andrew D.
Majchrzak, Lawrence J.
Malicki, Michael E.
Malkus, David A.
Manis, Lester J.
Marino, Todd
Marshall, Daniel
Martucci, Jennifer
Martz, William

Maslanka, Lynda A.
Massarelli, Paul M.
Mast, Charles H.
Mastin, Julia M.
Mastin, Ronald R., Jr.
McClean, John W.
McCleary, Millard W., III
McClelland, George D.
McCluskey, Edward C.
McCracken, Justin S.
McDonald, Diane L.
McIntyre, Michael E.
McJilton, Charles W.
McKeldin, Donald L.
McLucas, Nina A.
Meadows, Buddy E.
Means, Doreen
Merrifield, Lawrence D., Jr.
Merriken, Mary K.
Merriken, Richard C.
Meushaw, Margaret A.
Meyers, Corinne M.
Meyers, John B.
Meyers, Karen L.
Meyers, William E., Sr.
Mezick, Jimmie D.
Mickle, Ross W., Jr.
Milburne, Mark D.
Milby, John K.
Millender, Charles
Miller, Albert C., Jr.
Miller, Dawn
Miller, David
Miller, Jay E.
Miller, Michael A.
Miller, Stephen R.
Miller, Steven A.
Million, John B.
Mitchell, Marc L.
Mitchell, David S.
Moeller, John S.
Montaldo, Luciano D.
Mooney, Steven C.
Mooney, Timothy M.
Moore, Carmen V.
Moore, Michael V.
Morris, Kenneth J.
Moses, Gary J.
Moss, Alan M.
Mudd, Patricia E.
Muddiman, Don W., Jr.
Mulder, Lynn A.
Murphy, David J.
Murphy, Patrick C.
Murphy, Patrick T.
Murray, Kelly L.
Murray, Robert D., Jr.
Murray, Robert D., Sr.
Murray, Sylvia M.
Muth, Richard G.
Myers, Anthony J.
Myers, Judy W.
Myers, Richard E.
Nace, Kevin E.
Nace, Kimberly L.
Nash, Donald R.
Nelson, Randy
New, Mark W.
New, Michelle M.
Nichols, Janice M.
Nichols, Robert B.
Nickoles, Charles L., Jr.
Nickoles, Thomas M.
Nilsen, Jennifer B.
Nixon, Ronald L.
Noetzel, Diana L.
Noratel, Vernon E.
Nosek, Joseph J.
O'Connor, Francis D., Jr.
O'Rourke, Michael P.
Ochs, Kenneth E., Jr.
Oles, Anthony J., Jr.
Oliver, David S.
Olow, John L. IV
Oppitz, Stephen P.
Oursler, L. Wayne

Pack, Dana A.
Pack, Derrick E., Sr.
Pack, Millard L., Jr.
Paige, Dontay R.
Paige, Gilbert W.
Palmer, Brandee L.
Palmer, Lawrence K.
Parham, John C.
Parker, Shelton D.
Parrish, Randy G.
Passos, Deborah M.
Patterson, Robert G.
Paugh, David D.
Paugh, Robert
Pauley, Roy I.
Peach, John
Pearce, LaVern
Pearce, Samuel, Sr.
Penn, Franklin E., Jr.
Perkins, Eugene L.
Perry, Robert G.
Pessagno, David W., Jr.
Peterson, David R., Sr.
Petry, Richard W.
Pettit, Gene R.
Pfeifer, Jerry L.
Phillips, Casey
Phillips, Charles C.
Phillips, John L.
Pierson, Frank W.
Piker, Paul W.
Piker, Steven M., Sr.
Pinder, Thomas A.
Plunkert, Daniel L.
Pohlman, William A.
Polesne, Charles E., Jr.
Polich, Michele M.
Pollock, Charles F.
Pollock, Frank M., Sr.
Poole, Bridget M.
Preis, Kyrle W., III
Priester, Kaaren L.
Priester, Theodore C., Jr.
Proffen, Evan C.
Pruitt, Donald
Pryor, Russell L., III
Punt, Mark S.
Purcell, William D.
Purkey, Grape
Purkey, John A., III
Quinlan, Michael C.
Quirk, John F.
Rachinskas, Edward
Radomsky, James J.
Rafferty, Frederick C., Jr.
Ramzy, Ameen I., MD
Rausch, Carl W.
Ray, Charles A., III
Rayner, Brian M.
Read, David A.
Real, Glen J.
Real, Wayne
Reamex, Robert
Rebb, Wayne A.
Redding, Carroll
Redding, Lillian
Redding, Shelia L.
Redding, Wayne C.
Reed, Kelly L.
Rehr, Frank H.
Reid, John R.
Reinecke, William H., III
Reter, Calvin L.
Reter, Steven L.
Reter, William H., II
Reynolds, Herbert J.
Reynolds, Houston T.
Rice, Jeffrey A.
Rice, Mary F.
Rice, Thomas C.
Richards, Robert M., Jr.
Richardson, Dale E.
Rickrode, Gary L.
Riddle, Charles F.
Riley, Charles A.
Riley, Neal Stephen

Ringgold, Jay L.
Ritzmann, Charles F., Jr.
Rivers, Ellen M.
Roberts, Jack F.
Roberts, James E., Sr.
Roberts, Lynda C.
Roberts, Michael S.
Robertson, Dennis S.
Robertson, George F., Jr.
Robertson, George F., Sr.
Robertson, Jeffrey A.
Robertson, Scott A.
Robey, Robert R.
Robinson, Michael W.
Robinson, Timothy L.
Roche, Minta M.
Rodriguez, Jose A., Jr.
Rodriguez, Jose A., Sr.
Rogers, Charles D.
Roody, L. Allen
Roody, Kellie A.
Roos, Larry G.
Rosenberger, Tracey C.
Rosensteel, Paul A.
Rosier, Charles E.
Rossman, Robert C.
Rosenberger, Jerome E.
Rouillard, Thomas G.
Rozema, Nico A.
Rudow, Scott P.
Ruhl, Thomas E.
Rupp, Michael A.
Ruppert, Michael D.
Russell, James E., Jr.
Russell, Scott L.
Rutledge, Michael S.
Ryan, John P.
Ryan, Joseph P.
Sallahuddin, Earl
Sanders, Joseph
Sauers, Samuel E.
Saunders, William E.
Schaal, Cheryl A.
Schaefer, Fred S.
Schaeffer, Kathleen A.
Schanberger, Richard
Scheide, J. Renee
Schimpf, Stephen R.
Schenning, Richard
Scher, Arnold L.
Schlee, Kenneth A.
Schlegel, Andrew
Schlossnagle, Paul A.
Schoenbrodt, Peter E.
Schoff, Christopher C.
Shreiber, John E., Jr.
Schreiber, Ronald E.
Schultz, Bruce E.
Schultz, Dorothy C.
Schultz, Edward "Ted" C.
Schultz, John R.
Schultz, Keri A.
Schwartz, Bruce E.
Schwartz, Robert M.
Schwartz, Thomas J.
Schweers, Herman N., Jr.
Schwiegerath, Gary M.
Sears, Linda J.
Seigle, Kelvin L.
Seidlich, William W.
Sebo, Shawn M.
Seigle, Robert L.
Senior, Richard A.
Serio, Robert P.
Sharpe, Wayne D.
Shaw, Wayne N.
Shreiber, John E., Sr.
Sheene, Brenda L.
Shelton, James G.
Shenberger, Jan. B.
Shores, James H.
Shultze, Philip C.
Sibiski, Douglas J.
Silber, Pamela L.
Simmers, Mary L.
Simmons, Neal H.

Simmons, Wayne D., Jr.
Simone, John V.
Simpson, J.R., III
Sipes, Edward G.
Slezak, James L.
Small, Steven M.
Smith, Bryan T.
Smith, Burton E.
Smith, Charles A.
Smith, David M.
Smith, Dean G.
Smith, Katherine M.
Smith, Lewis E., Sr.
Smith, Robert W.
Snyder, Bruce A.
Snyder, Charles E.
Snyder, Dave
Snyder, Harry C.
Snyder, Jeffrey A.
Snyder, Richard T.
Snyder, Samuel P.
Sowa, Steven
Spangler, Donald B.
Spangler, Joseph E., Jr.
Spears, Frank O.
Spilman, Richard E.
Spitz, David E.
Spruell, Sherman L.
Stacharowski, Eric J.
Stark, Brian J.
Stause, Gerard R.
Stawski, Michael
Steele, John
Steinberg, Stephen S.
Sterner, Robert E.
Stem, Colin J.
Stem, Richard III
Stem, Richard, Jr.
Stem, Richard, Sr.
Stevens, Charles
Stevens, Michelle R.
Stevens, Phillip J.
Stewart, Alvin F., Sr.
Stewart, Michael R.
Stielper, Kevin J.
Stiffler, Louis F., Jr.
Stith, Mark E.
Stith, Zachery
Stolins, Gegory W.
Stone, Mark J.
Stresewski, Sharon L.
Stroup, Andrw G.
Stuart, Michael R., Jr.
Strump, William A.
Sturm, Charles A., Jr.
Swift, Charles R.
Szczesniakowski, Michael L.
Szukiewicz, Richard D.
Talbert, Walter, Jr.
Talbott, David W.
Tankersley, Kelly L.
Tapp, Aaron V.
Tawney, Deborah A.
Taylor, Charles A., Jr.
Taylor, Herbert K.
Taylor, Patrick K.
Tephaback, Randy T.
Thamert, Dennis P.
Thayer, Barry L.
Thieman, Thomas M.
Thiergartner, Carroll W., Jr.
Thode, Pierre M.
Thomas, Carlton D.
Thomas, Howard L.
Thomas, Kenneth
Thompson, Cleve J.
Thompson, Johnny E., Jr.
Thompson, Stephen E.
Tillis, James O.
Tittsworth, William C.
Tomblin, Ernest J.
Tome, Wayne L., Sr.
Torbeck, Lindsay S.
Tracey, Robert L.
Trenzsch, Frederick N.
Tribble, Timothy A.

Trovinger, Paul A.
Trump, Larry Edwin
Trump, Mark W.
Tully, James, F., III
Tudor, Charles H.
Turchin, Terry
Turner, Robert W., Jr.
Ullrich, William F.
Unverzagt, Gary W.
Utz, Jennifer L.
Utzinger, Jeffrey H.
Valencia, Samuel A., III
Valentine, Rodney E., Jr.
Van-Couct, Gay
Vangelder, Douglas C.
Vangelder, Kimberley C.
VanVugt, Robert P.
Vaughan, Charles R.

Veach, John P.
Waddy, Dora
Wagenfer, Stephen A., Sr.
Wallace, Bonnie J.
Wallis, John G.
Walters, Jeffrey D.
Walters, Ronald D.
Wantz, Stephen A.
Ward, Francis P., III
Warner, James E.
Warner, James E., III
Warner, Maxine
Warner, Mitchell
Warner, Scot
Watkins, Charles E.
Watsic, Melvin L.
Waxter, Elizabeth
Weaver, Melissa E.

Webb, Rebecca A.
Webster, James E.
Weckesser, Jerry L.
Weer, Gary J.
Wehrle, Tommy
Weigandt, Wayne M.
Weir, Christian E., Jr.
Weir, Christian E., Sr.
Weir, Mark E., Sr.
Weir, Michael H., Jr.
Weis, David T.
Weis, Donald L.
Weis, James A.
Weis, Robert A.
Weissner, Harold J., III
Welker, Byron L.
Welkie, George, Jr.
Weller, Richard L.

Welsh, Donna J.
Werry Stewart, Jennifer
Wesley, Kenneth G.
West, Andrew T., Jr.
Westbrook, David R.
Westervelt, James R., Jr.
Wheeler, Gary F.
White, Tankia N.
White, William R.
Wiggins, Curtis D., Sr.
Wiley, Mark S.
Wiley, William B., III
Wilhelm, Paul, Jr.
Wilhelm, Christopher M.
Wilkinson, Michele A.
Willats, Jeffrey J.
Willett, Cynthia S.
Williams, Alonza E.

Wilson, Timothy R.
Wingo, Louis R., Jr.
Winter, Dale R.
Wiseman, Deanna J.
Wisniewski, Gregory J.
Wolak, Charles W.
Woynovitz, Joseph R., Jr.
Wroten, Lawrence A.
Yakubowski, John A., Jr.
Yingling, Brian C.
Yingling, Richard V., Jr.
Yox, Leonard E.
Zeiler, Joseph C. III
Zimmerman, Brian W.
Zoltowski, Adam P.

Arbutus

Abell David B
Adolphi Michael P
Antoszewski Joseph D
Atkinson, Jr Charles W
Attumalil Alexander J
Bailey Roland N
Beckman, Jr Joseph E
Beckman, Sr Joseph E
Bees Martin L
Bellis David H
Boyce Ronald E
Brillman Scott L
Brinkley Kristie D
Brittingham James B
Brocato Chris J
Brooks Jonathan A
Brown Stephen J
Carlton Patrick A
Carpenter Shaun E
Castle Gina K
Cecere Margaret R
Choyce Lindsey M
Clark Gregory A
Clark Marie D
Cohn Eric B
Conner Aloysius A
Conrad Cory L
Coolahan Daniel C
Cullom Bonnie S
Deavers Charles A
Debock Andrew T
Depalo Philip J
Disante David J
Drayer Theresa E
Dunning Bridget A
Dyson Jeannine D
Easton Mark A
Ellenberg David
Ellzey Sarah E
Fitzpatrick Theresa S
Franklin Gloria A
Friesen Charles W
Fulkoski Donald L
Gaither John T
Glanzer Raymond H
Glover Bryan K
Glover, Jr Bryan K
Goodlin Vanessa L
Goodman Kenneth M
Gower Steven R
Grandea Mary P
Grinevicius Donald L
Grusch Ann M
Grusch Joseph H
Gutberlet Donald R
Hamilton Roy W
Hamilton, Jr Thomas B
Hammel David M
Harding Warren G
Harvey, Sr William E
Harvey, VI Lewis S
Hauenstein Calvin W
Hayakawa Takahiro
Heiland Howard
Hill Jennifer A
Hirsh Ira M
Hobbs Bradley E
Hollis Austin D
Howell Thomas J
Johnson Jessica A
Judge Gwen A
Judge James P
Kane Laura M
Kellar-Catlett Marci K
Kelly James E
Kern William F
Kirwan Patrick B
Krall Rudy R
Kuehnl Bonnie I
Kunselman Julie A
Levitt Scott P
Long Daniel C
Lookingland Brandon C
Luers Cynthia L
Lynott Susan M

Lynott, Jr Gerald T
Mackey Donald M
Malinowski Michael J
Malone, Jr James E
Malone, Sr James E
Matthiesen, Jr William W
Mc Cord Wendy L
Mccombs Robert J
Mcdowell John W
Mceldrew, Jr Patrick M
Mcneal, Sr Michael V
Mercer Mark G
Meseke, Sr Paul R
Miller Christine A
Miller Matthew D
Miller Scott D
Milota Stacy A
Moore John F
Moore Mary I
Moran Timothy G
Morris, Sr Charles R
Mueller Russell W
Munroe Barry J
Nager Eric C
Nauman Robert L
Neighoff, Jr Alfred G
Oconner Timothy M
Omelia Joseph T
Orndorff Carol A
Oshea Ryan S
Owens Stephen
Peacock Glen C
Pecor Jeffrey S
Perrera Bridget T
Pflaum Richard L
Pflug Patricia E
Phelps Ronald E
Platt, Jr Robert F
Preston Edwin F
Puppa Rebecca L
Ramey Thomas G
Ring Lawrence I
Robinson David S
Robinson Edward L
Robinson Timothy L
Rollins Mary E
Rottman, Jr Edward L
Rudowsky Asher
Rykowski Nicole L
Schley Brian K
Schoenbrodt Ewalt P
Shockney Anthony V
Shockney Dennis R
Shockney Patrick V
Silvius Kimberly A
Simister Shannon T
Simister William A
Simms John E
Simone Deborah K
Simone John V
Simpkins Melissa L
Simpkins, Jr Brian G
Simpkins, Jr Douglas R
Simpkins, Jr Norman V
Simpkins, Sr Brian G
Simpkins, Sr Keith E
Simpkins, Sr Norman V
Sipes Kenneth A
Slattery, Jr William J
Snader Richard A
Snader Sherry A
Snow Melissa A
Snyder, Jr Norman C
Speelman, Jr Clyde H
St Jean, Jr Matthew T
Stanley James E
Stevens Jennifer J
Stevens Michelle R
Sturm, Jr Norman E
Sullivan Andrew B
Summers Douglas
Szczesniakowski Michael L
Tacka Jessie E
Tacka, Sr Timothy W
Taury Angela J
Taylor Donna L

Tebo Bettina M
Tebo Joseph E
Trimper Michael L
Trovinger Paul A
Tully, Jr James L
Tyrrell George T
Utzinger Jeffrey H
Utzinger Theodore H
Vaughan Charles R
Wagner Paul E
Wagner Wayne S
Walker Kimberly A
Waters Tameka P
Watts, Jr Edwin B
Wheltle Patrick J
William, Jr Gary B
Winter Kathy A
Woodcock Mina M
Wright Adam T
Yarchin Bradley
Zinck, Jr Leonard J
Zinkand James C
Zinkand, Sr James C

Arcadia

Allenbaugh, Jr William B
Blizzard, Sr Morrell E
Boose Scott A
Boose Tammy L
Boose Jr Irvin E
Bowman Gary W
Cellin Elizabeth A
Crooks-Wisner Robin L
Davidson Roland
Dean Michael A
Dennis Charles C
Dennis Michael A
Diehel, Jr Lawerence D
Dillion Edward
Dillman George
Dooley Lonnie
Elmo Jason E
Evans, Sr Ronald J
Flannary John C
Fleming Leon M
Fleming Susan M
Freeman, Jr Kenneth A
Friedman Gary A
Furhrman Walter P
Gates Holly S
Green Edward S
Green Valeri
Hale Candice M
Hale Christopher
Hale Gail M
Hale Jeffery L
Hale Laurie A
Hale Linda S
Hale Rodney
Hale Sandra H
Hale Scott M
Hale, Jr William R
Hampt Nancy F
Hampt, III William A
Hannon Mary E
Hare Paul D
Hare William E
Hoff Sharon E
Hoffman, Jr James M
Hooper Eva D
Horner, III Henry J
Huffman Christopher M
Jackson Michelle L
Jenkins Michael W
Knatz Scott A
Krause, II John P
Krause, Jr Gerald J
Lankford Joseph E
Lankford, Jr James E
Mcginty Patrick M
Miller Jay E
Miller John F
Miller, Jr Richard E
Morganroth Lida K
Morgenroth Stephanie R
Nelson Tasha L

Oursler George A
Parry Brenda L
Parry Gregory L
Raver, Sr Herbert E
Ray, III Charles A
Rice Alfred G
Rice Mary C
Rill Douglas A
Rill John D
Rill Michael D
Rill Roger
Schapiro Ronald E
Schildhauer Clarence L
Scholtes Oliver N
Schwartz, Jr Edmund G
Shamer Eileen M
Shilke Wilfred C
Siegel Tracy B
Small Susan
Smith, Jr Richard B
Snyder Gary C
Snyder Harry C
Standiford Ernest F
Stocksdale Barry N
Stocksdale Terry L
Stocksdale, Jr Arthur E
Teal Daniel R
Thompson David C
Timberman Scott D
Tracey William M
Trawinski John B
Trump Mark W
Trump Teresa M
Trump Wayne M
Umbrell Randy E
Ward, III Francis P
Weimer Ronald J
White Robert K
Wickline Jeffrey S
Wickline, Jr Thomas P
Wilhelm Thomas A
Wirtz, Jr Kenneth W
Wirtz, Sr Kenneth W
Yarger Roger
Zumbrun, Jr William H

Boring

Arnold William H
Belt William C
Bolte Vernon
Bosley James C
Bosley James F
Bosley Marcella M
Brathuhn Thomas
Burk Dorothy M
Burk Joanne L
Burk Woodrow
Bush David G
Carter, Jr Joseph M
Cowan Delores E
Cowan William L
Cowman Mary K
Crooks John R
Crooks, Jr John E
Crooks-Wisner Robin L
Crowl Andrew J
Crowl Jerry L
Cunningham Stephan C
Devilbiss Bruce C
Devilbiss Linda G
Devilbiss, Jr Walter M
Evans, Sr Charles S
Fenker Jeffry L
Fox Charles R
Freeland Jane V
Freeland John V
Freeland, Jr Wilmer J
Freeman Matthew T
Freeman Vicki S
Freeman, Jr Kenneth A
Goodman Melissa G
Gore, Jr Howard Z
Green Edward S
Green Thomas E
Green Valerie
Grothe Edgar B

Hale Scott M
Hare William E
Harris Pascale M
Holzinger Autumm J
Holzinger, II Joseph A
Horner Kimberly A
Horner Iii Henry J
Hubbard Claudia W
Hudgins Debra L
Hudgins Martin W
Huffman Christopher M
Jones Megan T
Jones Stephen W
King Donald O
Lambert, II John W
Lankford Joseph E
Lankford, Jr James E
Lankford, Sr James E
Lauterback, II Fred W
Linthicum Benny L
Mann Marvin L
Markland, III Harry H
Martain Eric R
Merryman Granville E
Miller Jay E
Miller Thomas R
Nehls Marilyn H
Osborn Harold R
Parry Gregory L
Peltzer James H
Rill Alan L
Rill George
Schaefer Joan E
Schaefer, Jr Edgar L
Schweers, Jr Herman N
Simmers Mary L
Smith Arthur D
Smith Joyce A
Smith, Jr William A
Snyder Gary C
Snyder Harry C
Steger Kathy
Strohm Wayne P
Sullivan, III Douglas
Vangilder Alice R
Vangilder Kenneth R
Wagner Elizabeth B
Walter Linda L
Walter Robert B
Wesley Kathleena M
Wesley Laura L
Wesley, II Samuel M
Wickline, Jr Thomas P
Winans Mathew S
Wisner Kristina
Woodard Amanda C
Woodard Derek V
Woodward Logan R
Wright, III Harold B

Bowley's Quarters

Anderson, Sr Terry T
Baumgart Eric
Bayne Dennis J
Besche Christina D
Besche Joseph M
Bonadio Charles A
Bowers Harry M
Brady Kenneth W
Brown David J
Clavell George A
Clay Elizabeth
Clay, Jr Carlyle P
Clay, Sr Stephen M
Conrad, III William F
Cusic Jerome J
Cusic Paul J
Cusic, Jr Paul G
Danz Edward
Dubner, Jr Ronald R
Dufour, Jr Allen J
Eakin Brian
Eckert Tobie L
Eckert, III Bernard E
Eckert, Jr Bernard E
Eichelberger Earl

Elder Joyce F
Elder, II Roy P
Elder, Jr Roy P
Emala Walter M
Evering, Jr James L
Fairley Timothy M
Filipiak Gerald A
Fischer, III Fredrick W
Fischer, IV Fredrick
Freund Shaun M
Gent Dan
Glenn Bonny M
Glenn Joseph D
Grannas Lawerence
Hammen John E
Harker, Jr Francis X
Harker, Sr Francis
Hartmann Louis A
Hartmann, Jr Carl J
Hayden Elaine
Hayden, Jr John A
Hayden, Sr John A
Hayden ,Sr Thomas J
Hineline Michael W
Hoerner Richard E
Janowich, Jr Steve
Jenkins Lloyd L
Keil Raymond L
Keil Sonja M
Keller Douglas F
Kemp, Jr John W
Kidd, Sr Karl J
Killian Brian P
King Max K
Lacher, Jr Norman G
Leasure William A
Ledley Deborah L
Leuschel James W
Leuschel John S
Lewis Bacel R
Martin Craig C
Martin Forrest
Martin Lowell C
Martin Trudy E
Mayfield Patrick A
Mcgraw, Jr Eugene J
Miles, III John L
Newberry Joseph M
Pasko Christopher W
Pasko, Jr Richard H
Pierson Frank W
Raab William R
Reese Charles T
Rehbein, III Milton A
Ritz John E
Ritz Joseph C
Rohr William D
Schafer Francis A
Schlag Kenneth T
Shipley Lisa M
Sigrist, Jr George A
Slough John W
Smeltzer Jason M
Stanko John E
Stanko Joseph M
Stevenson Dontae D
Stewart Bradley W
Stockum William J
Sweringen Brett P
Thompson Jennifer S
Tress Edward M
Tress Mary F
Tyson Matthew N
Ving III George H
Weddle Francis H
Weinreich Henry C
Weinreich John
Welzenbach James
Widerman Bernard O
Wilhelm Mary

Box 234
Batzer Mary J
Bitzel Mary L
Bitzel Steven A
Bright Leona C

Colson Lucille C
Cox Shirley F
England Anida L
Hand Bonnie L
Holden Richard L
Holden Sara W
Holden, III Daniel L
Jakobson Deborah N
Jakobson Kurt
Kemp Sherry L
Reamer Robert I
Redding Carroll M
Redding Lillian T
Vancourt Gay L
Waxter Elizabeth L

Butler
Allender Casey B
Arbogast Brenda L
Arbogast David A
Badders Charlie L
Barclay Tod W
Belt, Jr Wilbur B
Blizzard, Jr John E
Boone John R
Bradley Donald C
Crist Michael G
Crumbie Charles L
Crumbie David L
Curtis Dorothy R
Curtis Milton E
Curtis Thomas R
Dalgarno Ryan S
Dickson Jason L
Eastwick, Jr Andrew M
Fogarty Christopher W
Fowble, III William A
Franklin Andrew C
Franklin Christopher J
Grim Richard A
Hackley Wayne K
Hann Ronald E
Henderson Joshua D
Hundermark David T
Hundertmark Gretchen K
Hundertmark Jeremy C
Kamps Elizabeth C
Kamps, Jr Jack G
Kearney Philip R
Kell Everett W
Kleinman Jessica L
Lamarr Lisa A
Mann Stewart
Markline Felicia N
Mccleary, Jr Millard W
Minton Andrew W
Norris, III William E
Pearce William M
Pearson, Jr William H
Powers James P
Redifer John P
Sagal, II Joseph G
Sagal, Sr Joseph G
Sanders Corrie A
Smith Blair T
Smith Keith W
Smith Roland E
Tegeler, Jr William V
Troxel Kristen M
Unglesbee Ryan P
Waganer Dennis M
Wilhelm Dale E
Wilhelm Danny R
Wilhelm Glen S
Wilhelm Patricia E
Wilhelm Paul E
Wilhelm Thomas A
Wilhelm, II Dale E
Wilson Robert J
Winn Elizabeth L
Womer Douglas
Wright Bradley A
Wright Stephanie

Central Alarmers
Andersen Dale A

Berni Victor W
Brooks, Jr James A
Brown Edith D
Carter Linda A
Dorer Frank W
Ebbert Barbara L
Elliott, III Harry J
Fales Joanne M
Fales, Jr Donald A
Fox Olivia C
Frederick James A
Freund Conrad E
Geppi Carroll A
Glos Mary E
Goeb George E
Graden, Jr John C
Hagen Edith
Hayes John J
Heathcote Gary M
Heathcote Genett F
Herweck Anita L
Kemnitz Heidi M
Maurer William H
Mcgrea Barbara H
O'connor Charles J
Peyton Deborah A
Peyton John J
Pollock Frank M
Pollock Robert E
Raab Mary R
Raborg Marian E
Rock Fredrick N
Rock Patricia A
Ruppersberger Maureen E
Sennett Cynthia L
Sennett, Jr Harry W
Steigleman Roger W
Stoll William A
Sturgill Margaret H
Woolery Charlene A

Chestnut Ridge
Aspden Rebecca F
Bacharach, IV Robert L
Barnstein Lee
Beck Tracey F
Beck, Jr James W
Carey Ronald E
Cohen Charles A
Combs Virginia B
Corasaniti John A
Corasaniti, II Frank J
Corasaniti, III Frank J
Coroneos Dani G
Coroneos Janice L
Coroneos Nick L
Cross, Jr George A
Crystal Jack C
Edwards Gilbert L
Edwards Jason
Edwards Ruth E
Flick Dean M
Foster Vickie L
Fox Martha M
Fox Marvin B
Fox Michael B
Glace Matthew S
Green Julie J
Hamburger Coos Z
Hand Bonnie L
Hoffstein Bart J
Hofmeister Leo C
Hooper Brian J
Hunter Jeffrey W
Kakel Joshua B
Kakel, Jr Harry R
Kemp Eugene C
Kinsey Steve F
Kopp Valerie L
Krulevitz Ann G
Larkins, Jr Charles W
Lloyd Chastity A
Lloyd Jamie D
Lloyd, Jr Frederick A
Long William E
Lubman Daniel

Lunnen Michael D
Mc Causland Albert R
Mccausland Albert R
Newberrey David W
Noetzel Cheryl L
Oberfeld Adam
Parker Scott G
Price Calvin
Reter Steven C
Reter, Jr Steven C
Reynolds Eugene O
Robinson, Jr Reginald J
Roody Louis A
Ryan, Sr Thomas E
Sereboff Aaron
Shaneybrook Gary J
Shaneybrook George W
Shiller Stacey L
Simmers Stephen G
Sindler Harvey V
Strickland Jennifer L
Uddeme Daniel
Underwood Charles F
Warner Scott A
Yaffe Richard M
Yaffe Ryan W

Cockeysville
Allen John K
Armetta Jennifer
Aung Moe
Bailone Juliet C
Baker John R
Ball Brian
Ball Gary G
Banister Dawn M
Banister Helen M
Banister, Jr Elwood H
Barshinger John T
Barshinger Michael J
Bayne Dennis J
Berger Michael
Berstock Avi W
Beziat Bridget E
Bond John K
Borum Jequetta
Bosley Bernard
Bramwell Samuel M
Buckwalter Harold S
Buckwalter Regina E
Burke John P
Carruthers Thomas N
Carter James P
Casey Jason T
Childs Brian T
Clark, Jr Frank H
Cole Charles C
Cole Kenneth M
Cook, Jr Erwin W
Cordle Jennifer
Coroneos Susan M
Crist Michael G
Crumbie David L
Dana Marc
Daughaday Edward R
Daughaday Michael E
Davis Christopher J
Davis Krista M
Dixon, III John B
Doering Karl P
Dold James P
Dooley Richard J
Dukes Jeffrey O
Dukes, Jr John R
Ellis James H
Foote Justin
Fowble Grason E
Frederick Robert P
French Tabitha L
Freund Robert A
Fundaro Janice
Gerald Gary R
Gibbons Echo L
Glace Matthew S
Gribble David B
Gribble Donna L

Gribble John W
Gribble Lawrence E
Gribble Richard A
Gribble, Jr Harry W
Hall Melissa D
Herbert Ann
Hoffman Andrew T
Holbrook Vicki L
Holland Debra L
Holland John T
Holland Michael K
Howard Donzell
Howard, Jr James H
Hutton Roger G
Jeffers Thomas J
Jensen Christer U
Kakel Jeremy W
Kampes Melanie
Kamps Elizabeth C
Kasztejna Paul J
Kearney Philip R
Kearney, Sr Maurice F
Kilgore Trevor T
Komsan Ehab
Krause Shawn
Kreller Paul J
Lambert Michelle
Lambert Morgan E
Lane Deborah E
Lecompte Annie
Lemmen Anna S
Longo Robert D
Longo Tim
Madairy Deborah A
Majchrzak Lawrence J
Mckinney Michael C
Meinschein Beverly S
Meinschein, Sr Bernard J
Minick Christopher J
Minton Andrew W
Montier Carl F
Murphy David J
Murphy Terri A
Naylor Erin A
Norris Jennifer
Oehrl Frederick C
Pagnotta Gabriella
Pappas Matthew
Passos Deborah
Patel Amar P
Peacock William
Pederazzani Deborah L
Polich Michelle M
Price M C
Price Paul H
Raivel Jennifer D
Reed Michael W
Reynolds Michael J
Roberts Christopher P
Roberts Jack F
Roberts Jean B
Roberts Kevin W
Roberts Lonnie C
Roberts Lynda C
Roberts Michael S
Roberts Sherry
Roberts, Jr Marvin L
Rosier Danielle M
Ruberti Christina
Schulman Rebecca
Scotland, III Howard V
Sheeler, Jr Raymond L
Sheggrvd Steven T
Shephard, Jr Reggie D
Shephard, Sr Reggie D
Shepherd, Sr Thomas G
Shipley Debbie L
Shipley Scott L
Simms, Jr Harry V
Sittler Angela M
Sittler Edward A
Smith Charles A
Smith Douglas B
Smith James A
Smith Robert E
Smith Susan A

VOLUNTEER ROSTER

Snyder Julie
Spitz David E
Stafford William C
Stem, Jr Richard W
Stevenson Stanley F
Tracey Clarence E
Tracey, Jr Melvin E
Tracey, Sr Melvin E
Treacy Megan M
Tyrie, Jr G W
Urbanek David
Wagenfoehr Michelle L
Walker James M
Walker Katherine I
Walker Steven
Walker, III William J
Willhite, III Paul O
Wissel Mark E

English Consul
Atkinson Robert W
Auberzinski Valerie N
Batz Michael J
Blades Kenneth L
Branham Lisa M
Brinkley Douglas A
Brinkley, Jr Edward W
Brinkley, Sr Edward W
Burns Douglas A
Burton Scott T
Burton Terry L
Burton, Sr George E
Bury Cynthia A
Bury Robert L
Calabrese, Sr Andrew J
Campbell, IV John N
Chesner Michael P
Clark-Burns Elizabeth A
Clarke William D
Connell Walter J
Conway Harry T
Courtney Charles R
Courtney Patrick R
Cudanin Kimberly L
Dimeler Jason W
Doherty Robert M
Emkey Jenifer M
Emkey John A
Emkey, Sr Edwin L
Greiser Melissa K
Gumm Guerney N
Hardesty Stephen M
Hardesty, III Sherman
Hardesty, Jr Sherman
Harmon, Jr George
Harvey, Jr Woodrow W
Hoffman Timothy N
Holcomb, Jr Martin R
Kaszak Vaughn C
Keiser Andrew P
Kick Michele P
Lancaster Chris J
Lancaster Mark E
Lancaster, Sr Burt C
Maddox William E
March Susan E
March, III Frank P
Martin Keith L
Mathison Gerald H
Mc Carren David J
Miller Savoy L
Rausch Laura N
Roach Thomas F
Rykowski Nicole L
Schorback Edwin J
Sheldon Jessica A
Sheldon Ronald W
Sheldon, Jr Ronald W
Shofroth Joshua R
Shreve, III Edward
Smith, Jr Craig M
Spence Kathleen M
St John Christopher
Thomas Bradford A
Thompson William R
Trovinger Jane P

Trovinger Paul A
Twardowicz Richard E
Ulsch Judi L
Wallace Phillip P
Weber, Jr Charles A
Wentworth, Jr Richard L
Wentworth, Sr Richard L

Glyndon
Altieri Thomas M
Altomonte, Jr Wayne A
Amole John C
Armacost Cleveland H
Battle Herbert D
Beimschla Carol J
Black Thomas H
Bosley Benjamin S
Brach, Jr J P
Brennan, III Joseph T
Brown Earl R
Brown Gary A
Brown Randy H
Caples, Jr Clarence W
Carter James D
Casey Jason T
Clagett Joshua C
Claggett Jesse G
Clark George B
Cofiell Wayne A
Cole Richard E
Cox, Jr John H
Crooks, Jr John E
Curtis Harry L
Curtis Michael S
Curtis Thomas L
Ecker Darryl
Farris Edward M
Flannary John C
Fowble, III William A
Gore Jacqueline C
Higgins Belinda A
Hoffnagle Stefan J
Jenkins, III Timothy C
Johnson, III Lorie T
King, Jr Donald W
Klauza Kevin L
Knife David H
Krause, II John P
Lessner George R
Lewis Matthew B
Listwan Martin W
Mc Cracken Justin H
Merriken Mary K
Merriken Ronnie C
Merriken, Sr Richard C
Mintz Michael S
Moorfield Donny
Morris Kenneth C
Nandara, Jr Joseph W
Pearson, Jr William H
Petry Andrew T
Reitz Katherine A
Renard Henry F
Reter Bradley
Reter Calvin L
Rice John A
Rome Mark B
Rudow Benjamin
Rudow Scott
Rutherford Timothy S
Scher Arnold L
Schultz Bruce E
Schultz Dorothy C
Schultz Edward C
Steinberg Richard W
Stem Colin J
Stem Elizabeth
Stem Rosemary B
Stem Toni R
Stem, III Richard W
Stem, Jr Richard W
Stem, Sr Richard W
Talbert, Jr Walter D
Warner John A
Warner Maxine D
Warner Mitchell

Warner Scott A
Warner, III James E
Warner, Jr James E
Warren Kristen L
Webster Charles R
Whitcomb Darryl E
White William E
Whiteside Jere
Wilhelm, Jr Paul M
Wolfenden Douglas C
Wolfenden Mary E
Wolfenden Thomas S

Hereford
Abbott Duane G
Adams Jeffery D
Allender Casey B
Anderson Robert G
Anner Michael R
Badders David L
Badders Leroy
Badders Nancy M
Baldwin Theodore C
Bilger David S
Bilger Edward W
Bilger Edwina H
Bilger Mark A
Bilger Nancy B
Bilger, Sr Richard G
Billett Christopher
Bollinger Daniel T
Bollinger Darlene E
Bollinger Deborah L
Bollinger Kenneth C
Bures David W
Burley Adam L
Burley Brian L
Campanella Paulette
Campion Deborah A
Campion Ronald S
Carey Jason S
Chilcoat Vincent T
Cole Elizabeth A
Cole, Jr Robert M
Cook Elva C
Cooper Lawrence T
Croft Michael A
Croft Ronald M
Croft Susan M
Curtis Bobby J
Curtis Karena L
Curtis Shane
Dell Dottie L
Dell, Jr David E
Dietz, Jr John C
Dunkes Catherine
Ensor Kenneth C
Epps Jennifer L
Fauer Charles E
Fleming David M
Foster Brandon P
Foster Harry B
Fowble Gilbert J
Frederick Barbara J
Frederick Charles C
Frederick Christina L
Fuhrman Adam L
Fuhrman Tricia M
Gardner Mark E
Gardner Rita M
Garrett Charles R
Gerhardt Donald E
Gosnell Elizabeth A
Gosnell Franklin C
Granger Debbie
Grim Richard A
Grubb, Jr Ernest H
Hann Timothy E
Hilgartner James H
Holbrook Mary V
Hood Debra A
Hood Michael L
Hoshall Thomas D
Huber Leeann N
Huber Patricia A
Huber, Jr Ronald J

Hughes William E
Hughes William L
Humphrey Bobbie L
Jackson Timothy N
Jednorski Stacey L
Jones Eugene M
Kearney Gregg R
Kearney Philip R
Klapaska William C
Lang Christopher A
Lang George E
Lang Jesse E
Lang Michelle L
Lang Peggy L
Ledford Larry J
Leight Barbara A
Leight Emory E
Lewis Jane G
Markline Danny R
Markline, Sr Robert A
Mcguire Ryan C
Miller Grafton B
Miller Robert R
Montaldo Luciano D
Mooney John E
Mooney Peggy Joyce M
Moskowsky Peter A
Myers Richard E
Negley Melissa M
Noel James E
Picarello Bryan A
Pontious William E
Powers Robert M
Powers Shellie A
Pruett Joseph V
Pruett Robert V
Pruett Virginia M
Pruett William E
Rambo Benjamin T
Rhine Charles S
Rice, Jr William K
Robertson Charles D
Robertson David R
Rosier James A
Ruhl Sandra L
Ruhl Thomas E
Rutledge Justin C
Sagal, II Joseph G
Schneeman Timothy L
Shaffer Carl E
Sheats Arlene G
Shelley Mark D
Simmons Brenda L
Simmons Roger L
Simms Gery E
Simms Jennifer M
Simms Marie
Simpson Linda S
Simpson Thomas C
Smith Wayne G
Sparks Jason
Squire Jeffrey R
Stiffler, Jr Louis F
Talbert W K
Taylor Herbert K
Thomas Samuel J
Thompson Bobbi A
Thompson Kenneth L
Troxel Kristen M
Valenza Kristy M
Wagner Jennifer M
Warns Joann M
Warns Robert D
Whalen John C
Wright Bradley A

Hereford Ambulance
Aiken Nancy F
Andersen Dale A
Anderson Amy J
Anderson Anne M
Balsam Sam
Banthem Alvin H
Banthem Lucinda J
Bilger Edwina H
Bilger, Sr Richard G

Bitzel Gerald D
Bond Lauren E
Brown, III Coleman P
Cain John C
Ciesla Dennis
Cole Elizabeth A
Croft Susan M
Currey Michelle D
Curtis Dorothy R
Curtis Thomas R
De Groot Tom
De Mario Mark S
Dell Dottie L
Dell, Jr David E
Demme Paul E
Depalo Philip J
Doub Nancy H
Fabiszak Paul M
Fales, Jr Donald A
Fausto John
Feeley Helen L
Foster Vickie L
Frenkil Juliana T
Granger Debbie
Green Edward S
Green Valerie
Hake Theodore J
Hanavan Timothy L
Hester Jeffrey A
Huffman Christopher M
Huggins Jason P
Huggins Karen
Humphrey Cindy L
Hums Jason
Jednorski Brian
Jednorski Charles A
Jednorski Stacey L
Jones Megan T
Kinsey Michael J
Kolscher Robert D
Krichten Christopher B
Lang George E
Lang Michelle L
Layman Russell S
Leyh Jean
Littleton David M
Lucas Melissa
Lund Saleena
Meyers Rhonda A
Meyers, Jr Walter E
Mogle Alison
Myers Jennifer K
O'connell Arthur E
Parks Katherine L
Patrick Christa L
Patterson David M
Pearce Glenn E
Perrera Bridget T
Persico Cheryl A
Pruett Virginia M
Rambo Benjamin T
Raver Laurie
Rehfeld Anne E
Rehfeld Michael R
Richardson Elizabeth W
Rosier Danielle M
Rubin Donald P
Sagal, II Joseph G
Schneeman Timothy L
Schwatka Victoria M
Simms Gery E
Tice Paul
Tippet Micheal A
Twig Rebecca
Tydings Ronald T
Wells Darlene L
Welzant Victor
Wilcoxson Stephen L
Wright Donald
Wright Laura

Hyde Park
Alban Brenda L
Alban Diana L
Alban Ruth A
Alban Thomas R

Alban, III John J
Alban, Jr John J
Alban, Sr John J
Albright Donald
Ambrose, III Walter M
Baker Jon D
Balk Rose J
Barrow Angela L
Bomberg Harry N
Bostwick Richard
Cavey Richard J
Claridge, III Harry W
Crum Carl J
Dileonardi Antonio A
Dileonardi Vincent A
Dixon Christopher L
Eck James H
Eck Louis R
Eck Robert
Ertwine Jerry K
Gove Eric J
Greifzu Wayne L
Guzman Cisco R
Hergot, Jr Milton C
Hershman Dale E
Hill Alan G
Hoffman Timothy N
Holland, Jr William T
Horton Joshua P
Huffines, Jr Carroll W
Jackson Timothy M
Johnson Steve
Kalb Mathew S
Kalb, III Matthew W
Kaszak Vaughn C
Kempisty Christopher E
Knapik Ryan M
Kneasel Benjamin W
Kulisiewicz Theodore
Lewandowski Anthony
Lewandowski Mike W
Lewandowski Thomas J
Lewandowski, Jr Joseph F
Mcgraw Patrick C
Messman Paul H
Mousdale Charles
Nigg Clint E
Oerman Robert J
Panuska Michael F
Robinson, Jr Reginald J
Rogers Richard R
Sampery Mike
Schield Anthony J
Schield James A
Schield Joseph E
Schield Mark A
Schield Michael
Schield Steve J
Sebo Shawn M
Smythers William R
Stone Ruth A
Stump John C
Stump William A
Terry Jeffrey W
Walls, III Martin O
Welty, III William H
West Edwin T
West John L
Wisniewski Paul
Ziolkowski Joe L

Jacksonville
Anderson Kenneth L
Auvil Matthew L
Ayres Dean W
Barnhardt James P
Barrows Andrew W
Berry Patricia A
Boblits Kathy L
Bosley John R
Brewer Brent K
Carter Brandon J
Cartridge Richard L
Chrusniak Margaret M
Clark Bruce T
Cody Amanda D

Cole Lorraine R
Constantino Jesse R
Dietz Christina L
Duerbeck Jerry A
Dundas Margaret J
Dundas Scott
Dundas Stephen L
Edwards James V
Ernest Rachel G
Essell, Jr Andrew J
Fields Steven B
Finke Daniel L
Fox Matthew B
Fumarola Melamie-Ann M
Gaddis Brian A
Gamble, Jr Claud C
Garrison Amy C
Gavin Laura B
Glaeser Ryan E
Golly Scott M
Gosnell John T
Gribble George M
Gugerty Robert A
Hahn Elisa K
Hansen Chris A
Hickman Evelyn M
Hornbacher Eva H
Hornbacher Robert K
Hutton Craig L
Janelsins Michelle C
Janney Michael H
Janney, Jr Charles G
Jennings Jonathan B
Kayler Norman R
Knighton Cheryl A
Kolk Estelle M
Latchaw Eliot M
Lee Robert M
Lewis Jhett S
Lewis Marjorie
Locke Mary H
Maceachern Alison L
Martin Mollie R
Maule Linda C
Mcclafferty Jim
Medinger Eric M
Molner Jeffrey A
Morgan Barbara G
Murdzak Michael J
Ogle Brad D
Oppitz Stephen P
Paget Alistair G
Paget Joan C
Persico Cheryl A
Phelps Douglas P
Piombino Dana E
Quinn Melissa M
Rauck Christina N
Reynolds Michael J
Roberts Elecia A
Romanowski Marissa J
Rossi Christopher E
Rossi, Jr Robert A
Schaefer Jay E
Schapiro Oscar
Schindhelm John W
Shields William R
Simick Jason C
Single, Jr Richard W
Stachowski Dennis J
Stack Tom W
Stafford William C
Strauss Ruth A
Stroup Andrew G
Stuart Philip M
Tamberino Joseph C
Tiralla Frank X
Tracey Charles
Waltrup Beth L
Watkeys James S
Watson David G
Wentling Jessica A
Wertz, Jr Harold O
Westervelt, Sr James R
Wheeler Robert D
White Barbara K

Wiedey Christa M
Wiedey Christopher H
Wiedey Steven M
Wiedey, Jr Howard F
Wiggins Joseph A
Wiggins, Jr Curtis D
Wiggins, Sr Curtis D
Williams Neva L
Winger Katy M
Wingler Chad E
Wright Wayne N
Yen May J
Zeman Robert M
Zour Garrett D

Kingsville
Adams Ashley L
Amereihn Thomas R
Behounek Rudolph A
Belkoff Stephen M
Berkeridge James K
Berkeridge Terry A
Berkeridge Timothy P
Berna Michael J
Bober Bernadine
Bolling Jerry A
Bowen Barbara J
Bower Brian N
Bower Thomas D
Bowman David J
Bowman John C
Boyd Joanne R
Brown Michael C
Cassett, Jr Ronald B
Cassett, Sr Ronald B
Chaney Robert P
Chapman Rosemary S
Chapman, Jr Frank E
Clayton Victoria L
Coke Peter C
Corbin Raymond J
Corbin, Jr Grayson W
Coster Lingard J
Coster Matthew B
Coster, III Donald W
Daniels Mark W
Decker Nicholas A
Deems, III Frank A
Dietrich Matthew E
Dilworth Albert C
Dodge-Hale Debra L
Dziecichowicz Francis T
Eyre Dennis L
Fifer Matthew R
Franz David G
Frye Richard R
Frye Thomas R
Garrett Scott T
Gatchalian Kasia M
Gelwicks Brittany K
Geoghegan John D
Gill, Jr Charles E
Gossman, Jr Vernon S
Graybeal Wilbert M
Griffiths Edward F
Guard Edith M
Hale Ronald W
Haut Melissa A
Heil Terry J
Henderson John E
Hopkins Evanglelin L
Howard Donald A
Huggins Jamie M
Hunt Morris T
Inouye Brooke L
King Bruce O
King Christopher P
King Katie L
Knight Robert W
Kraus Barry S
Kraus, Jr Leonard A
Krehnbrink Mary M
Kudrna Joseph E
Kuehne Bertha B
Kuklane Peter A
Kurrle Blaine A

Kurrle Elmer
Kurrle Patricia
Langrehr Donald H
Layfield Raymond
Ledzinski Helen T
List Bruce C
List Jamie R
List Joshua T
Little Shawn P
Lynch Tracey L
Mario Michael J
Martin William K
Maynard Douglas R
Mcdonald Michael A
Mcdonnell Jeremy M
Miller Harry L
Miller Irene W
Miller Stephen P
Miller Stuart D
Montley Mia W
Moorefield William C
Murray Richard J
Myers Kimberly A
New Michelle M
Ninos David M
Ninos Francis X
O'hara George R
O'laughlin Matthew W
Opdyke Mark R
Opdyke Suzanne L
Peach John C
Perrera Bridget T
Preis, III Kyrle W
Probert Harry D
Pumphrey Earl G
Pumphrey Gorman
Rebbert Patricia C
Redmer Steve J
Riesett Jean M
Riley Jason E
Riley Robert J
Ryland Kelly N
Sayler Charles E
Sayler Karen D
Sayler Rita M
Schultz Jason M
Scott Alexander C
Scott Brian D
Scott Daniel J
Scott Gerald C
Scott Gerald G
Seidel Herbert W
Sell Gregory O
Snediker, IV Edward F
Sonntag Joseph
Stevens Mark A
Stevenson, Jr Thomas B
Sweet Craig E
Taylor Scott A
Taylor, Jr Charles A
Taylor, Sr Charles A
Thorpe, Jr Michael A
Tochterman, Jr Edward S
Tochterman, Sr Edward S
Tontrup Craig B
Tripp John W
Vanik Ruth M
Vonparis John F
Wadkins, Jr Roger W
Walker Karin W
Walters Rachael N
Warfield Allen C
Weer Ella C
Weer Gary J
Weer Jeffrey A
Weer Timothy D
Westbrook, Jr David R
Willis Jennifer C
Wirtz Jennifer L
Yersin Raymond A
Young Michael M

Lansdowne
Adams James H
Adams Jan
Airey Charles F

Airey Georgette
Airey Patricia L
Airey Robert
Airey Victoria
Allen William E
Allman Steven L
Amole John C
Annis Jayme
Bailey Brian E
Bailey, Jr Brian S
Baldwin Michael
Batz Michael J
Baumgarten Douglas C
Benway Bryan E
Benway, Jr Robert L
Berg Robert A
Black Christina
Blizzard David S
Bosley Adam
Bowman, Jr Charles
Boyer Jason
Brand, Sr Thomas D
Brinkley Christine
Brinkley Douglas A
Brinkley Sean P
Brinkley, Jr John P
Bryley Jacqueline L
Buffington Louis L
Bunn Thomas P
Burford Jeremy S
Burg Laura E
Burg Michael J
Burg Patrick R
Bury Melissa L
Campbell Hope
Card Gilbert F
Card, Jr Harry E
Caudill Anthony
Cestley Timothy
Ciarpello Tina M
Clarke William D
Clevenger Andrew
Courtney Kimberly A
Cullum Charles L
Davis, Jr Harry W
Dawson Dennis E
Deitz Austin
Dell Louise E
Devoter John W
Dillow, Jr John C
Donnelly, Jr Murdock A
Douglas Casey
Douglas Danny H
Douglas Jill
Douglas Mandi
Duany Michael A
Easton Mark A
Edwards Vincent W
Eggers Patricia A
Eggers Rita T
Eller Roxianna M
Emkey John A
Fabian Krystal
Fabrizio Margie A
Fields Chad M
Fisher Cynthia R
Forrest Lakisha
Fosler Brenda M
Gerczak John
Gethmann Martha E
Gill Raymond S
Gill Valerie
Gochnauer John H
Goetz James C
Gray, III William F
Haas, Sr William C
Hall Brandon A
Hall Gordon B
Hall Jason B
Harlee Anton B
Harris Yolanda N
Harry Robert
Hawes Karl W
Hawes, Jr Eugene G
Hawe, Sr Eugene G
Hawkins Steven D

VOLUNTEER ROSTER

Hazelton Damone
Heinlein Rebecca
Hickman Sheila L
Hoback, III Giles C
Houck, Jr James A
Howell Keith
Howes Dawn R
Imbragulio Stephanie A
Imbraqulio Ronald A
Inkrote Eric V
Irvine Heather A
Jacheliski Elizabeth A
Jacobi Robert E
Jacobi Shawn
Johnson Eric C
Johnston Calvin
Kamberger Timothy M
Kaszak Ryan C
Keene Louis E
Keene Muriel M
Keene Shawn L
Kemp Jasmine D
Keppley David C
Kessler Louis I
Keys, Jr William J
Keys, Sr William J
Kiser James E
Kittle James L
Kliemisch Robert W
Klump Ellwood W
Kolb Kathryn E
Kountz Charles E
Kreveger Jennifer
Kriscumas Pete
Kropp Ronald M
Lancaster Chris J
Lands Elizabeth A
Lanham Chasity M
Lapin Ava F
Lapin Robert
Lewis Carol A
Lewis, Jr John
Lewis, Sr John A
Lucke Jennifer
Luedtke Glenn H
Lugenbeel Edward E
Lugenbeel Nimrod A
Mack Mary M
Maddox William E
Malinowski Donna
Marriott Robert
Mccabe, Jr William T
Means Dustin
Means Victoria K
Miller Jacob B
Miller Justin
Mitchell Mare B
Mooney Charles R
Mooney James D
Moucheron Paul R
Muth Jennifer A
Nelson, Jr George V
Nevins Earl
Noetzel Cheryl L
Noetzel Christina M
Noetzel, Jr William A
O'connor Wendy J
Orem Justin L
Orr Bonnie J
Painter Joshua
Palmer Lawrence K
Palmer Russel
Pearsall Steven W
Petrusik Diana Y
Pierce Virginia
Plowman Henry S
Poole, Jr Ronald W
Poole, Sr Ronald W
Potter, Jr Franklin E
Preston Donte M
Rader James M
Ramzy Ameen
Rausch Sheila L
Rausch, Jr Robert G
Rayner Brian M
Reinke, Jr Paul R

Robinette Robin D
Santmyer Ruan J
Sawyer Chris
Schmidt Patty
Schneckenburger Jon R
Seeley David
Sheldon Ronald W
Sheldon Sherry R
Shindledecker Jill
Silcox Lawrence A
Simmons Jean
Simmons Keith
Simmons Wayne
Singhas Micheal L
Singhas Michele
Sipes Edward G
Sipes Frances M
Sipes Jason T
Sipes John E
Sipes Patricia
Sipes, Sr George L
Sirbaugh Bobby
Slota Michael T
Smith Bernard J
Smith Edward C
Smith Patricia L
Smith Wanda
Smith William A
Smith, Jr Vincent J
Souza Mark A
Spinks, Jr Charles R
Suter Jason R
Suter, III Samuel P
Taylor Robert
Taylor, III Thomas T
Thomas Timothy W
Tillman Kevin
Torbeck, Jr Charles E
Torbeck, Sr Charles E
Vanaelst Joseph R
Vanaelst Robert
Wagner Audrey
Weber Jennifer L
Weber, Jr Charles A
Webster Lawerence
Welden Michael D
Williams Shane N
Wood Thomas J
Wright Donald
Yurovsky Michael V

Liberty Road
Allen William E
Antonucci Donna M
Basilier Jennifer N
Bass Leon
Berry Wilson L
Betcher Nick J
Birago Bethany A
Bolyard Kyle F
Bondroff Lauren R
Bonner James A
Bopst George J
Bossman Adele I
Bossman Martin D
Bossman Michael B
Bowersox Sam J
Bowman Justin D
Boyd, Sr William W
Chinery David C
Chinery, III Henry
Cohen Ronald E
Colliflower Clayton A
Darling Ronald W
Darling William D
Dausch Jeffrey D
Deitz John M
Dennis Charles C
Dennis Joseph A
Dennis Particia E
Dennis Sidney C
Dixon Jarrett
Donohue Jacqueline S
Donohue Joseph W
Dunn Jan C
Dunn Steve P

Engles Polly J
Engles Randi S
Evans Patrice D
Fleming Bruce D
Foelber Cathey B
Francis Travis J
Franks Teresa A
Frederick, Jr Joseph G
Freyman Brett
Fulton James R
Goldstein Ivan
Goldstein Jacquelynn
Goldstein Mark
Goldstein Michael
Goldstein Scott H
Gordon Robert
Graham Richard P
Greenfeld David N
Greenwalt Linwood H
Greenwalt Michael L
Greenwalt, Jr Charles J
Griffee Lee
Griffith Lee W
Gritz Dawn M
Hartman Dale L
Hartman Francis O
Horn David A
Iannetta Gordan A
Johnson Priscilla J
Johnson Robert A
Jones Leslie D
Jordan Rosemary
Kasser Andra D
Kemp Craig P
Kemp Donald B
Kemp Robert B
Kemp Sherry L
Kluka Kelly M
Knight Chad A
Knox Eric
Kreft Dawn M
Kreft, III John A
Kunz Jason E
Kushner David S
Lathe Melinda D
Leppert William D
Love Donald W
Love James I
Love, Jr Vernon L
Ludwig, Sr Albert L
Lurie Marsha L
Lurie Steven E
Madden, Jr Frank
Martin Lynn
Martin William B
Martin William W
May Selena M
Meeks Louis W
Meeks, Sr Roger E
Meyers Karen L
Meyers Katie L
Meyers Krista L
Miller Stephen R
Mitchell Scott T
Moore, Jr William J
Moritz Matthew S
Moses Charles A
Muser Brian
Muser Donna C
Naylor Alan J
Newton Dwight E
Newton Kathy L
Nickoles Stacey T
Parrish Randy G
Potts Derrick L
Price Thomas M
Quinn Michael
Resnick Glenn C
Roos Larry G
Rosen Edmond H
Rosensteel Paul A
Ross Jack L
Rubin Donald P
Russell Robert E
Sagel Jeffrey
Sandler Lou

Sands Douglas P
Schemm Walter A
Scherr Jeremy M
Schisler Kenneth R
Schmitt Martin A
Scott Norman A
Shipley Barry L
Shipley Lynn M
Sigler, Jr John L
Sohn Joseph J
Stakem Karen K
Stakem Patrick J
Stern Lehman C
Tinkler Ellis T
Tomlinson Jeffrey S
Upton, IV Edward
Van Vugt Robert P
Vogelsang, Jr Ronald P
Wayne Jerry A
Wayne Melody L
Wayne Scott L
Weitz Scott J
Wiley, III William B
Windsor Stephanie M
Wolf Steven R
Yarmis Derek B
Zahn Jason H
Zimmerman Karl J
Zippert Kimberly M

Long Green
Amrein Barbara A
Amrein, III Kenneth R
Amrhein John P
Armstrong David J
Barkley Mckinley H
Barnhardt John H
Breidenbaugh Ann R
Breidenbaugh Anthony N
Breidenbaugh John L
Brewer, Jr Barry N
Burton Eileen E
Butcher Frances R
Constantino Jesse R
Delcher Gloria E
Delcher, III William J
Edwards Brian A
Eyre Dennis L
Eyre Kathrine L
Eyre Richard L
Eyre Sharon A
Eyre, Jr Walter L
Fitzell David R
Frank Jacob M
Frank Joshua V
Galloway Daniel G
Gatchalian Kasia M
Gosnell Wilbur S
Harrison Ronald K
Hayes Lawrence P
Jackson, Jr Earl R
Jenkins John B
Jones Charlotte S
Jones Donna J
Maas Laurie
Maas, III Bernard H
Mcclean John W
Mccrea Joel C
Mckelvey Elizabeth N
Mester William J
Miller Carole S
Monks Kenneth E
Montague Timothy A
Mueller Stephen
Mumma David F
Napolillo Lee
Newcomb, Jr Wheeler H
O'connor Charles J
Paal, Jr Rutland B
Pearce Lawerence G
Persico Cheryl A
Peruzovic Kristen N
Raab Christopher N
Radcliffe Helen M
Rigger Robert J
Ring Barbara L

Sakers Joan M
Saur William C
Stelmack Stephen G
Stengel Melinda F
Stolins Gregory W
Stolins Tracy L
Stoll Audrey L
Stoll William A
Tolle George A
Tolle, III Howard C
Williams Mark R
Williams Neva L
Wright, Jr Edward J
Yarish Matthew C
Yoder Lewis E

Lutherville
Andrews Curtis A
Badders David L
Bankard Timothy E
Barnes, Jr James H
Baron Robert D
Barranco Frank T
Barranco Michael S
Bednar, Jr Charles A
Behles Christopher M
Best Douglas P
Beziat Bridget E
Bohlayer Kevin L
Bohlayer Marie D
Bohlayer Morris L
Bovaird Brian D
Brewer Brent K
Brewer Robert D
Brewer Scott C
Brewer, III Walter L
Brewer, Jr Walter L
Bruns Bradley J
Burns Kevin F
Burr Erica L
Cahn James D
Cameron David G
Case James H
Comotto Jeff T
Conrad Bruce W
Covell Darrell A
Cranston Vern S
Csontos Chris V
Dalsimer Kevin J
Davis Michael A
Dehoff Gregg A
Donovan Benjamin J
Donovan, Jr James J
Doran James E
Enoch Stephen W
Eppler, Jr William B
Esenwine Ronald C
Farmer Kenneth M
Flanagan Brian E
Flavin Thomas E
Ford Kevin C
Fowble Gilbert J
Fredrick Scott D
Friend James M
Fulton Dennis T
Gagliano Joseph
Gearhart William C
Gibb William L
Gisriel Stephen T
Gleitsmann Charles W
Gochnauer John H
Goeb George A
Goodwin David L
Goodwin Mark J
Gray Handy Lisa S
Handy James E
Handy Raymond T
Hartlove John A
Harvey Michael R
Hayes Christopher M
Heiler Michael J
Hendricks Jamie L
Hiebler Michael V
Hopkins Michael A
Huber Jennifer M
Huber Michael L

Huber ,Jr Ronald J
Hughes, Jr Robert L
Hunter Gregory W
Hyde Rodney T
Janney Michael H
Jobusch Michael A
Jones Milton R
Kakel Joshua B
Kane David F
Kelly Bradford A
Kilburn Lawson T
Kronen Angela C
Leber Gene P
Leverton Paul A
Lewis Todd E
Long Carroll E
Lutz Anthony J
Mahon Timothy M
Meissner Nathan P
Mullin, Jr Timothy L
Mullin, Sr Timothy L
Munoz Joseph A
Nash James C
Nash, Jr Charles W
Nayden Donald W
Niner Christopher S
Oppitz Stephen P
O'rourke Janet M
O'rourke Michael P
Owings Paul D
Patel Amar P
Pfaff Martin C
Pietziak Richard B
Pigott John W
Potts Dave W
Purkins Scott E
Riddle David B
Robinson Tangela L
Rushworth Gary T
Sawyer John P
Scanga Anthony C
Scanga Mark E
Schneidereith Kurt D
Schott David R
Schott Robert J
Schroeder Marc D
Schult Karl H
Seabolt Andrew M
Siegel, IV Gustav G
Sinton Robert S
Smart James E
Smith Bryan N
Smith David M
Smith Randall D
Smith, Sr Lewis E
Snyder David W
Spencer-Strong William H
Tracey Robert L
Tulio Anthony F
Tuma Rafid J
Underwood Charles H
Walker Michael L
Walter Meghan E
Weatherby Stephan H
Williams John E
Wilmont David P
Woolf Lewis E
Wurzbacher Gary G
Yeagle Brian L
Yeagle Dennis L
Yeagle Robert L
Yeagle, Jr Richard L
Zeiler, III Joseph C
Zoltowski Patrick A

Maryland Line
Almony James
Arbogast Brenda L
Arbogast David A
Badders David L
Badders Dennis C
Badders Leroy
Bohlayer Kevin L
Bohlayer Morris L
Brandt, II Charles W
Bull, Jr Allen B

Carlson Michael K
Carothers John D
Carter Amanda M
Casper Mandy J
Clayton Stephanie L
Coale, Jr Royston G
Copenhaver, Jr William L
Cummings Cindy B
Durman Nathan K
Fogle, III Charles
Fogle, Jr Charles
Fourhman Leroy
Fuhrman Adam L
Grim Richard A
Grim Tina M
Guethler Robert A
Heaps Chad E
Hettchen John T
Holloway Dean E
Holloway Kurt E
Humphrey Bobbie L
Jones Amanda M
Jones Brett A
Jones Darlene J
Jones Eugene M
Jones Jason E
Jones Richard A
Kenney Dean
Kenney Ellen O
Kenney Francis M
Lafferty Samuel M
Markline Danny R
Merryman Timothy H
Miller Cindy
Minton Andrew W
Neal Glen S
Ober David D
Oehrl Frederick C
Poe Noah C
Rosier Danielle M
Rosier James A
Rosier Jason A
Rosier Jeffrey A
Rutledge Justin C
Schmalzer Linda D
Schmalzer, III William J
Shaver, Jr James A
Simms Michael J
Svec Michael V
Weber Hammond E
Weller Richard L
Whipperman Byron D
Whipperman Teresa A
Wilhelm Donald L
Wright Bradley A

Middle River
Akehurst, Jr James W
Akehurst, Sr James W
Ambrose Shawn P
Ambrose, Jr Walter M
Anuszewski Vincent M
Beane James C
Bennett Edward J
Bornman John
Brewer Ronnie
Brinn Kristy L
Campbell, Sr Kenneth B
Cross David C
Dahler Robert
Diffenderfer Stewart W
Dulina John E
Dulina Stephen A
Dulina, Jr George
Freeman Raymond E
Gray, III John E
Halley Ronald J
Hardesty Keith B
Hardesty Kevin R
Harding John J
Herrick John K
Hudnet Frank A
Hug Thomas L
Hurley, Jr Louis J
Hyzer Christine L
Jagat Richard

Jaworski David A
Johnson Christopher M
Leilich Joseph A
Long, Jr Michael S
Moucheron James A
Moucheron Warren G
Moucheron William H
Mroz Daniel L
Paulus Stephen G
Peacock Michael D
Presnell David W
Pule Shane K
Rasel James P
Reynolds Katie D
Ruppert Michael D
Rutledge Michael S
Saraglou Nicholas W
Schneckenburger Jon R
Sebo Ryan P
Sinnott Timothy P
Sollenberger James E
Sopel Thomas
Sowa Robby S
Stern Raymond A
Stinchcomb George H
Stoms Glendon L
Stone Elizabeth
Stratemeyer Wayne A
Turner James F
Watson Jonathan C
Weis James A
Weis Robert A
Wigfield James
Yard Jack F
Yard Ronald S
Zuna James

Middle River Ambulance
Ambrose Nancy L
Ambrose Stacy M
Ambrose, III Walter M
Ambrose, Jr Walter M
Arndt Scott E
Arnold John F
Atherton Michelle L
Baker David L
Baker Leslie N
Baker Rita M
Bivens Jason J
Blanks Jonathan W
Bornman Connie C
Bornman George E
Bornman John
Boyce Diana E
Boyce, Sr Robert L
Breden Regina A
Brewster Christopher P
Butt Marc E
Buxenstein Michelle A
Cabezas Patricia L
Calka Deborah A
Campitelli Edward A
Casey Daniel B
Causey Fredreick A
Causey Kathleen M
Causey Sarah L
Cavey Richard J
Chason Joshua M
Conte Shirley A
Coulbourne Robin C
Cromwell, Sr John E
Daugherty Matthew D
Davis Alpha J
Davis Fred L
Dembeck Dennis L
Depalo Philip J
Dillow Danielle
Dinisio Colleen M
Dinisio, Jr Thomas
Doda Richard M
Dunkle Charles N
Emala Walter M
Ertwine Gale
Ertwine Jerry K
Ertwine Samuel L
Falkenhan Mark G

Flynn Earl
Frank Robert L
Frank Sheila J
Frank Susan
Gilbert, Jr Thomas C
Gonzalez Heather
Gwilliam Ashleigh A
Hall John T
Hayes Guy H
Heinlein Rebecca
Heins Jacob
Heins Joshua N
Hernandez Edgardo
Hewitt Kent R
Hook, III George E
Horney Matthew H
Hurd Edward P
Johnson Christopher M
Jones Dennis W
Judy Belinda J
Keener Carolyn S
Keener Michael
Kempisty Christopher E
Kohne Arthur R
Korinth Karl H
Korinth Sally A
Leadmon Harry O
Ledley Micheal
Luther Frederick M
Lynn Michael L
Mangum, Jr Roland J
Marzola Robert J
Mccarthy Jeffrey A
Mcclean Michael S
Miller Neal E
Moore Jason T
Palasik, Jr John F
Patterson Ryan M
Patton Chrystle L
Pedrick, Jr Robert S
Pickle Delores A
Pickle Lori A
Pickle, Jr Donald R
Pickle, Sr Donald R
Ratcliffe Elizabeth M
Reardon Jason A
Reichert, Jr Joseph T
Reynolds Melissa S
Schanberger Jay S
Schanberger Linda S
Sebo Christine M
Sebo Ryan P
Sebo Shawn M
Shipley Lisa M
Skidmore Rebecca A
Smith Jamie L
Spann Catherine J
Spinelli Neil A
Stern Raymond A
Sturgill, III Chester R
Sudano Lisa J
Sullivan Gwendolyn
Sykes Kenneth W
Thuerrauch Sheri L
Trzeciak Moya C
Varelli Susan D
Walker Kelly
Walter Jessica L
Watson Ernest J
Whittaker Roseann
Wilkinson Charles
Williams Jessica M
Wodarczyk Heather A
Wodarczyk Melisa L
Zannino Mark A
Zulauf, Jr George W

Middleborough
Alemi Craig R
Benjamin Alan J
Blubaugh Reynold A
Bonham Kerry R
Bronson Mark A
Brooks, Jr James A
Deckelman Jack F
Dennison, Sr James E

Dranbauer Roberta L
Dranbauer, Jr Mark R
Dranbauer, Sr Mark R
Edwards Tasha M
Emge, Jr Raymond J
Fairley Matthew S
Fairley Timothy M
Fairley Tom
Ferguson Timothy M
Filipiak Gerald A
Geaslen Erik L
Geller Steven J
Gove Eric J
Green Victoria A
Holtz Eric B
Holtz Janelle M
Horney Matthew H
Horton Joshua P
Iwaniw Michael C
Kinard James L
Lee Deryck J
Lougee Kara M
Matysek Gregory A
Morris, Jr Donald R
Olsen David D
Peyton Deborah A
Peyton John J
Rasinski Nicole L
Rayner Brian M
Redd Deangelo L
Rudasill John W
Ruppersberger Maureen E
Shipley Lisa M
Smith Robert W
Sowa Steven
Sowa, Sr Ronald W
Spinelli Neil A
Stasko Kenneth J
Taylor Scott W
Wheatley Arthur E
Woodley Stephen A

North Point-Edgemere
Aupperley Todd
Bowser-Mcelwee Stacey V
Brandenberg Tracy D
Chester Fred J
Clark Robert J
Clark Tonya M
Cooke, Sr Joseph W
Cunningham Thomas M
Davies Adam G
Davies Christopher D
Davies David L
Davies Gwilym A
Davies Melissa
Davies Shane
Davies, II Gwilym A
Dulisse David W
Eacho Edward M
Eich Frank
Elways Bernard H
Elways, Sr James H
Freeman Darrick W
Freeman David J
Graves Frank K
Harvey Brian A
Harvey James E
Harvey Susan R
Hook Erica
Jarrard Michael C
Johnston David M
Kottraba Lester E
Kottraba Robert
Kottraba, Jr Lester P
Kottraba, Sr Lester P
Lizor, Jr Joseph S
Mack Steven S
Marr Brenda J
Mcelwee Ronald G
Mcelwee, Sr William C
Mcgowan Nicholas J
Morgan Allen P
Morgan Matthew J
Morgan, Sr George E
Nicely, Jr Robert A

Pace Caroline R
Pace Garry M
Pace Matthew R
Palcher, Jr Albert L
Palmer Brian L
Palmer Percy L
Paul Matthew S
Pearson Richard J
Perkins Shane V
Peros Robert E
Pfeifer Elsyanne S
Pfeifer Raymond A
Piker Jerry B
Piker John W
Piker Melvin B
Piker Steven M
Price Lawrence D
Priester, Jr Theodore C
Priester, Sr Theodore C
Quaty Sarah
Radford Shawn L
Resavage Daniel J
Reynolds, Jr Fred B
Rice Eileen
Rice Kriston K
Rice Paul L
Rice Vincent C
Riegel, Sr James T
Rosenberger, Jr Allen A
Schultz Joseph S
Staigerwald, Jr Clarence O
Takos, Jr Steve S
Taylor Marc A
Theodoroy George
Thorn Harold C
Tormollan, Sr Robert D
Wakefield Steve
Ward, Jr Richard A
Widmeyer Norman
Zulke Jeffrey R

Owings Mills

Altieri, II Richard A
Bajkowski Thomas A
Bajkowski, Sr Frank S
Ball Roy A
Bates Kyle D
Batz John
Bauerlien Edwin L
Bender Thomas
Bosley Phillip T
Broadnax Willie J
Brown, III Coleman P
Brown, III Robert L
Burkholder David
Callands Velda H
Christian Jere N
Clagett Joshua C
Claggett Jesse G
Claggett William A
Clavell, Jr Melvin W
Cobb Melissa J
Coroneos Dani G
Coroneos Susan M
Crooks, Jr John E
Dews Sarah L
Fitzpatrick Brian M
Fold Michael A
Freyman Ethan S
Gerety Donald
Gill Keith A
Gingles Erwin R
Griffith Jeffery S
Hamburger Coos Z
Harmon, III J M
Harmon, Jr Joseph M
Hebert Phillip L
Howard, Jr William R
Isaac, Jr George W
Jenoff Martin S
Johnson Ramsey M
Johnson Rudolph C
Johnston Edward W
Katzef Shlomit S
Kellar-Catlett Marci K
Kraus David S

Kreft Dawn M
Lancellotti, Jr Harry J
Leonard, III Rudolph L
Letnaunchyn Kimberly L
Lippy Christina E
Lippy Mickey C
Love Charles
Mccoy, III Edward J
Meador Jacob J
Meekins Robert L
Miles Ronald
Miller-Paugh Veronica L
Montgomery Christoper M
Munter Charles D
Myers Jennifer K
Nelson Craig S
Nelson David
Nelson, Jr Craig S
Nicholson Christopher G
Nicholson Melissa G
Nietubicz Carrie-Ann
Nilsen Jennifer J
Nulman Seth G
Oken River T
Parker Scott G
Parker Willie S
Patchett John W
Pessagno Diane T
Pinkas Mary M
Purdham Jonathan S
Ramsel John
Rice Charles
Rice Joseph
Ritchey, Jr Wylie L
Roche Marydeanna E
Rosenberg William
Rubenstein Jason F
Schapiro Paul L
Scheinker Jeremy
Schenker Scott
Schnaier Louise J
Schwartz Edmund G
Schwartz Fred R
Schwartz Robert M
Schwartzman Phillip L
Shingleton Warner W
Silen David F
Singleton David W
Stem, III Richard W
Strack Kevin D
Thode Pierre M
Thomas Derek L
Trump Larry E
Trump Mark W
Trump Wayne M
Wallace George J
Wallett Harry L
Wallett Kevin L
Walsh Jeffrey
Walters James W
Ward George B
Ward John P
Warren Brandon E
Warren Dennis E
Warren Donald T
Warren Gary E
Warren Kristen L
Webster Charles R
Weiner Rachael A
Whitcomb Darryl E
Wilkerson Edward R
Wilson Wayne R
Wolff Jamie M
Wright Adam T
Wright Desha M
Wunder Jasen J
Yaffie Matthew R
Young Jeffrey L
Zanni Jennifer M

Pikesville

Anstine Michael J
Barrett Thomas A
Bearman Philip
Berkowitz Richard M
Berryman, Jr John W

Berryman, Sr John W
Bethea William L
Biddison Steven M
Boyd Joanne R
Braverman Jan S
Brooks Susan B
Brown Matthew W
Brown Susan L
Brown, Jr Joseph L
Brukhardt Ryan A
Bull Sharon A
Burgan Lawrence B
Burkoff Michael D
Burnham, Jr George H
Burnham, Sr George H
Bush David G
Callard Francis J
Carter Gregory S
Carter Stuart W
Cohen Harold C
Cohen Harold S
Cohen Howard S
Connors Michael A
Cosden, III William D
Cox Bradley R
Dahlem Stephen A
Dahlem, III Joseph G
Dansicker Samuel I
D'antoni Joseph P
Davis Edward S
Debaugh Wesley
Dembeck Dennis L
Dowell John S
DowellM III John L
Dryden Clifford E
EckhardtM Sr Henry W
EnglandM Jr William B
England-Dansick Anida D
Faulkner Paul W
Ferber Jonathan B
Fold Elizabeth R
Folio Anthony J
Friedel Donald M
Gauss Christopher F
Gentzel John D
Gold Matthew A
Goldberg Jerome N
Goldberg Lawrence H
Golden Avi S
Goldstein Matthais M
Goodman William R
Goodwin Mark J
Gould Robert L
Greenberg Randee S
Gutman Marc E
Hamlin, III Robert
Harmon Thomas S
Hinrichs William J
Hipsley Chad W
Hipsley Troy S
Hiteshew Michelle S
Holden Richard L
Holden, III Daniel L
Imbach Christopher L
Jacob Sharon L
Jones William B
Katz Randi A
Katz Seth A
Kearney Kevin P
Kemp Robert B
Kleeman Steven L
Klein David A
Klein Steven N
Kodeck Ari J
Korman Mark D
Krebs Dennis R
Kushner David S
Lancaster Stephen G
Leavy Emma N
Levin Norma L
Levin William B
Lewis Terrance T
Lloyd Chastity A
Lloyd Jamie D
Lubinsky Adam H
Macdonald Gregg S

Mankowitz Steven F
Mayer Clarence S
MckimM III James D
Miller Michael A
Mitchell Raymond W
Moninghoff Joseph
Morris Joseph R
Morris Richard B
Morris Sarah R
MorrisM Jr Charles F
Mullen Raymond N
Murray Benjamin S
Murray, Jr Robert D
Murray, Sr Robert D
Myers Anthony J
Needle Eric M
Needle Nicole A
Oppitz Stephen P
Paine Wesley R
Paneth Michael
Pelton John R
Perlman Reuven E
Phelps Carl J
Poist Robert R
Powell Roger N
Price Wallace D
Purcell Michael W
Purkins Everett W
Ray, III Charles A
Redding Wayne C
Resnick Glenn C
Resnick Kathleen M
Reynolds Michael J
Robinson Aaron I
Robinson Lisa R
Rodman Murray E
Roody Kellie A
Roody Louis A
Rosenbluth Marc A
Rossman Robert C
Rossman Stanley R
Sachs Lee N
Sahota Eric S
Sapp Terry L
Schaffer Jeffrey L
SchallerM Jr Louis J
Schanberger Barton T
Schapiro Barry D
Schumer Brian L
Schumer Joshua A
Schumer Justin S
Shecter Michael
Sindler Harvey V
Sindler Stephen B
Smith Edward B
Smith Michael L
Smith Patrick L
Somel Deniz S
Spencer-Strong William H
Steiner Steven R
Stevens Michelle R
Stewart Danny C
Stone Mark J
Tenenbaum Morton H
Thompson Cleve J
Turchin Terry
Udell Richard B
Warren James A
Wayne Niki L
Weikers Clark O
Weil Michael B
Williams Kathleen A
Wurzburger, III Stanley L
Wurzburger, Jr Stanley L
Yaffe Richard M
Yolken Jeremy T

Providence

Andersen Dale A
Awad Theodore V
Baker Michelle L
Bartkowiak Edward B
Beckman Sean A
Benham Joseph
Biddison Karly J
Biddison Steven M

Bingham Nicholas
Blue Craig M
Bollinger Joseph M
Cain John C
Chalthern Mark A
Clum Robert W
Coburn Jeffrey J
Coroneos Janice L
Coroneos Nick L
Darr Philip M
Davidson William J
Deatley Luke C
Denning Dean A
Diesta Roberto P
Donahue Geoffrey L
Ebbert Cory E
Ebbert Scott G
Fannon Patrick M
Fick Michael L
Gisriel Joseph A
Glos III Michael
Goldberger, Sr Dennis W
Gugel Derek A
Hanning Ernest J
Herweck Matthew K
Hinton Tony O
Hoppert III Maurice H
Hux Laurie J
Hux William R
Kemnitz Heidi M
Kernan David K
Kernan Michael S
Kernan Robin
Kernan Timothy M
King Julia L
Kohnle Daniel C
Lancaster Matthew G
Lancaster Stephen G
Laricos Matthew C
Lattanzi Sergio P
Lazowski Adam D
Lecompte Dennis L
Littleton David M
Lynn Michael L
Majchrzak Lawrence J
Manzo David M
Manzo Jennifer L
Mcclean John W
Mccloskey Edward L
Mculla Marie A
Mizansky Janis L
Murakoshi Lillian B
Murphy Joseph A
Oates Patrick J
Parr Michael F
Pearce Stephen M
Pearce, Jr Edward E
Perouty Kyle J
Rice Thomas E
Rice, Jr Robert C
Robertson Beverly E
Robertson Brian T
Robertson Scott A
Robertson, Jr George F
Robertson, Sr George F
Rook Glenn
Ross, II Edward J
Ross, III Edward J
Rung Eric M
Russo Mark H
Schneider, Jr Leonard P
Shearman Jeffrey L
Shinnick Stephen M
Skarzynski Jill E
Smith David M
Smith Wilbur H
Sprigg John L
Sprigg Todd A
Steele John W
Thomas Kevin M
Thomas Sheri L
Valentine Jennifer D
Wehrle Ann C
Wehrle Thomas
Wertz, Jr Harold O
White William K

Zour Garrett D
Zour James G
Zour John R

Reisterstown

Allen Brenton N
Almony Myron
Altieri Thomas M
Apples Glaude
Armacost Henry L
Ayers Frederick M
Barnes Alan K
Beaseman, Jr Clarence M
Belt Robert O
Blake Vincent D
Blick Gregory J
Boblits John
Bond Eugene
Boose Tammy L
Bosley Benjamin S
Bosley Cindy
Bosley, Jr Roland P
Bowers George E
Bowers Scott R
Bowser Walter C
Brach, Jr J P
Bransfield J
Brown Andrew J
Brown Nancy L
Brown, Jr Joseph L
Bucher Albert V
Burroughs Christopher
Canavan Charles E
Carrick Malcom
Carter James D
Carter Tobe S
Carter, Jr James R
Carter, Jr Joseph M
Caruso John A
Charles Jessica A
Cofiell Wayne A
Cohen Harry S
Coleman Craig E
Coleman Jeffery E
Coleman Katherine E
Crooks Dennis L
Crumbacker Michele L
Curtis Harry L
Curtis Michael S
Curtis Thomas L
Davis Cynthia A
Davis Morris W
Devilbiss, Jr Walter M
Dickson Scott A
Diefendorf Donald S
Donohue Joseph W
Eckhardt, Jr Henry W
Eline James B
Eline Joseph
Evans Michael
Fair Marion
Fannon Vincent N
Fauer Charles E
Feldman Joel E
Fields Sarah M
Forbes Charles
Fox Charles R
Fox Marvin B
Franklin Christopher J
Franklin, Jr William A
Franklin, Sr William A
Gaffney David M
Gammon Janelle
Garheart Guy R
Garman Authur L
Goldberg Jeffrey R
Gore Martha A
Grassi Theresa M
Gray Handy Lisa S
Grimes Gary
Gross Scott J
Hale Jeffery L
Hammond Southgate Y
Hann Walter B
Hannon Mary E
Harry Robert W

Harry Wilbur E
Harry, Sr Thomas R
Helm Heather G
Hennigan Mark K
Hennigan Steven
Hennigan William J
Hewitt Craig M
Higgs Robert R
Hipsley Wayne M
Holtz Robert E
Hopkins Brian
Houck Charles R
Huster Tracey
Isennock Lurlie L
Isennock, Jr Howard D
Jackson Michael L
Jackson Michelle L
Jones George E
Kafig Paul M
Katzef Shlomit S
Kaufmann Lee J
Kaufmann Monica L
Kew Brian S
Klauza Kevin L
Klinefelter Robert M
Kunkel John F
Kunkel Paul
Lavin Sol
Leaf, Sr Vernon
Lentzner William
Levin Barbara J
Linker Burford F
Linker Dennis W
Lockard Gordon
Lowe Jack
Mabry Scott
Mack Thomas D
Marquess Eric D
May Eric W
Miller Arnold C
Miller Jeanette M
Mosner Frank
Murray Benjamin S
Murray, Jr Robert D
Murray, Sr Robert D
Nickoles Thomas M
Patterson Joseph L
Patterson Robert G
Petry Andrew T
Petry Richard W
Phillips Phillip N
Piazza James A
Potts Derrick L
Quick Brian
Reeves Thomas H
Renard Henry F
Reter Bradley
Rohde Robert T
Russell Jason S
Ryan Joseph P
Ryan Lauren E
Salley Jesse N
Scher Arnold L
Scherr Stuart
Schultz Dorothy C
Schultz Edward C
Schunk John
Schweizer James L
Seohnlein Robert
Sheavly Mark T
Smith, Jr William A
Snyder James P
Snyder Michael E
Spunt Sidney M
Spurrier Leroy B
Spurrier Mark
Stem, Jr Richard W
Stem, Sr Richard W
Tawney Melvin E
Thomas William A
Trager Paul
Trager Steve
Troyer Joseph
Walter Linda L
Wang Hay-Yan J
Ward George B

Warner, Jr James E
Welsh Herbert
Whitcomb Darryl E
White William E
Whitlock Dennis A
Wilhelm Glen S
Williams David E
Williams Eugene K
Wilson Samuel Y
Wirts Bennett
Wright, Jr John R

Rockaway Beach

Alchimowicz Jerome M
Bromwell Steven G
Brown Frederick H
Custer David S
Dilegge Paul A
Everly Tammy A
French, Sr Howard V
Gove Eric J
Hewitt Kent R
Julian Jeremy P
Kahler Richard P
Kerby Frederick O
Kerby Stephen W
Kerby, Jr Steve W
Kimble David E
Ledley Deborah L
Ledley Micheal
Lewandowski Thomas J
Mcneill Howard E
Medinger John D
Ogle Leroy E
Pollack Leo J
Reynolds Christopher N
Riedel Iii Fredrick L
Robert Jr James E
Roth Allan J
Shrader Brian K
Spangler Frank J
Stuart Jr Micheal R
Voyzey Sherri L
Weber Nicholas S
Weiland Jr Jacob J

Rosedale

Adams Lakendra A
Auerweck Greg
Bandel Kimberly A
Bannister Patrice Y
Barber Michael A
Barnstein Jason P
Barry Steven T
Bartock Raymond A
Besche Christina D
Bobo Kimberly L
Boyd Kristen N
Brinn Kristy L
Bures James J
Burger, Jr Arthur H
Callahan Lena M
Carter Robert
Castle Martin C
Cioka Justin J
Cline Karen L
Cline Ray E
Cole Eric S
Cole, Jr Robert M
Davis Stephanie A
Decoursey Timothy M
Dewald Michael
Diehl, Sr Charles W
Dorer Scott W
Dranbauer Roberta L
Dranbauer, Jr Mark R
Dranbauer, Sr Mark R
Eakin Brian
Endryas Eileen M
Endryas Eric
Fairley Timothy M
Fast Iii Dorsey W
Fidler William E
Foard Amanda R
Freeman David J
Gabriele Cody T

Gabriele Mark B
Gabriele Iii Rocco J
Gabriele, Jr Rocco J
Gabriele, Sr Rocco J
Glorioso Lauren C
Goeb George E
Grannas Lawerence
Gross Richard D
Grupp Iii Melvin A
Haines Katie M
Harding John J
Harmon William B
Harmon, Jr William E
Hendricks Elise R
Henley Dartagnau H
Howell Christine L
Hueter Charles G
Hutson Chris
Ikena Brooke A
Jackson Michele
Jarkiewicz Daniel J
Jobes Diane T
Joy-Huffman Dianna L
Kearney Thomas E
Kennedy Amanda J
Kennedy Oliver J
Keyes Anthony L
Kirk Carol G
Kirkner Suzanne S
Kirkner, Jr John R
Kirts Iii William L
Klass Mason B
Kolego Shawn D
Landfeld William P
Le Hung Q
Lehr Karen
Leiss Patricia M
Leiss, Jr Charles H
Lester Jerry A
Levy, Jr Michael T
Littlefield Leah G
Lkuslka Olaheml M
Lorenzo James A
Lorenzo Lawerence D
Ludwig Iii John G
Mahoney Christopher S
Manning Tonya
Maurer William H
Mazza Jack R
Mc Greevy Patricia L
Mcdonnell Richard B
Mcgreevy Richard L
Mcjilton Charles W
Meyer Randy P
Michalski, Jr Joseph T
Miller Ellyse N
Morris Michael J
Mullahey Christopher M
Munford Jennifer L
Myers Kimberly A
Naumann Gary
Ownamana Charlene C
Patricia James K
Patterson Christina L
Patterson Ryan M
Pearson, Jr William S
Perry John P
Pierson Frank W
Pizzini James L
Polaski Jr Peter R
Porter Edward A
Potts Dave W
Potts Deborah M
Potts William M
Price Brian E
Raubaugh Maria
Ray Darwin D
Reinhardt Erik R
Resch Philip E
Rock Fredrick N
Scheuerman Gail S
Scheuerman James F
Seeley Steven A
Sennett, Jr Harry W
Shaffer Brian P
Shea Candance N

Skirvanis Gregory A
Skirvanis, Jr Albert J
Sloman Gina M
Sloman Stephanie
Small Scott A
Souza Mark A
Souza Sharon L
Stachowski Steven J
Staines John W
Stancil Tyisha L
Stark Brian J
Steinberg Sarah E
Troia Susan D
Valencia Sam
Walker Hyacinth A
Walter Joyce E
Walter Kelly L
Wareheim Blake R
Watson, Jr Donald R
Wergin Jordan T
Westbrook, Jr David R
Wiley Christopher D
Wilmering Derrick W
Wilmering Paul
Wilsynski Michael J
Winkelman Dawn M
Wolff, Jr Ray C
Young Gregory J

Violetville

Adams James H
Adcock Michael C
Bates Todd R
Bragg William B
Buffington Louis L
Burton, Sr George E
Calabrese, Jr Andrew J
Comell Carolyn A
Courtney Charles R
Cullum Charles L
Ficke Wilbur E
Green, Jr Dennis L
Gruss Joseph F
Hasson Carol L
Hasson Kenneth N
Hasson Timothy J
Henderson, Jr James W
Hershey Ronald W
Hoffman Arthur W
Hoffman Ernest J
Hughes, Jr Thomas J
Ijams John B
Keller Arthur S
Koch Susan K
Kolbe Donald J
Lancaster Chris J
Lancaster, III Raymond S
Lucas, Jr William N
Marks Russell W
Martin Keith L
Melcher Claude D
Morlok, Jr Christian F
Nash Michele M
Nash Timothy
Neville, Jr Donald F
Olson Jay R
Pearsall Steven W
Purkey Dawn M
Purkey Dorothy E
Purkey Gary W
Purkey Larry R
Purkey Randy J
Purkey, III John A
Purkey, Jr John A
Rausch Laura N
Rausch Sheila A
Rausch, Jr Robert G
Reich Robert E
Remmell Robert G
Roach Thomas F
Rositzky Melvin E
Rudasill John W
Ruff Ronald W
Smith, Jr Renford
Swann James E
Swann William J

Tolle James C
Topper Joseph M
Topper Mark P
Topper Vincent R
Trimper Michael L
Tully, Sr James L
Tully, Sr Timothy P
Turner, Jr Robert W
Uhlfelder Ronald I
Walls Joseph W
Warthen Donald
Weber Jennifer L
Weber, Jr Charles A
Winkler Charles W
Womelsdorf James
Woynovitz, Jr Joseph R

Wise Avenue
Autry Keith A
Banks Tiffany A
Basford Edgar J
Bell Eric C
Bland William B
Bowen Jeffery S
Bowen Kimberly
Brooks Sherry A
Brubach Wayne M
Bruzdzinski Charles D
Bruzdzinski Francis P
Bruzdzinski George
Bruzdzinski Joseph A
Bruzdzinski Kimberly L
Bruzdzinski Susan M
Bruzdzinski, Jr Carl
Bruzdzinski, Jr Michael O
Bruzdzinski, Sr Michael O
Carter Jason L
Cate Thomas F
Cole Christopher M
Copeland Dale A
Dennison, Sr James E
Duszynski Jeffrey J
Engler Heather N

Fisher Cynthia R
Frances Robert J
Fuscsick George G
Geho Tracy R
Gilpin, Jr Joseph E
Giorgakis Maria
Greiser Melissa K
Hobbs, Jr Samuel D
Iler Clayton E
Ingellis Frank J
Jackson Eric W
Juknelis Peter M
Kadolph Gary O
Kalwa, Sr William A
Keller Jason W
Kellner, Sr Kenneth L
Kopf Joshua M
Kosta, Jr George G
Kurant, Jr Steven S
Lary James L
Lewis Thomas E
Loiacono, Sr Gerald L
Ludwig Thomas K
Martini David C
Matthai, Jr Edwin H
Mcelwee Ronald G
Mcelwee, Sr William C
Mclyman Catherine E
Mclyman Shawn S
Mclyman, Sr Gerald N
Milburne Mark D
Morris Susan L
Morrow James W
Nickel Wayne B
Nixon Carlton W
Nodonly Douglas R
Olah Robert W
Oliver James L
Parrotta Lisa M
Parrotta, Jr Anthony M
Paulus William J
Persiani, III Angelo M
Petterson Norman R

Pfieffer Calvin F
Phillips Mark J
Piker Paul W
Polomski Adam L
Reinsfelder, Jr William J
Ritz John E
Roy Amanda L
Schaeffer Kathleen A
Schaeffer Thomas W
Schaeffer, Jr John I
Schaeffer, Sr John I
Scheufele David J
Sellers Gregory W
Singley Michael F
Smith Daniel J
Stevens Michael W
Still Scott E
Stroh James T
Sturgill, III Chester R
Sullivan Daniel E
Sykes Kenneth W
Teufer, Jr Ronald H
Tillis James O
Tormollan Brandi L
Tormollan Joan C
Ullrich Timothy W
Westbrook, Jr John A
Westbrook, Sr John A
Willinger William J
Wolff Charles W
Wood Harley T

Woodlawn
Abiera Petronilo A
Aldridge Tiba G
Allen Twana C
Artis, Jr James W
Barnes Jocelyn
Bernhart Phillip J
Best Kenneth
Bonsall, Jr Robert E
Borgmann Robert D
Brown Kevin

Burch, III Leroy M
Burch, IV Leroy
Butler Shonnie
Caldwell Kyle S
Caperoon Louis L
Carhart Brian T
Carski Michael L
Ceasar Antoingette M
Coleman Candace N
Crawford John A
East Dennis L
Ebert, Jr John I
Elliott John C
Enos Richard K
Ermatinger Robert E
Fields Sean F
Follett Barbara R
Fuchs John F
Gaddy Leenita M
Gaffney, III Theodore R
Gaither Roseann
Golden Arbaham
Goldman Dennis A
Graham Christopher A
Gwathmey Michael V
Hannon Steven C
Henson Peter E
Johnson C D
Johnson Calla R
Johnson Janet T
Johnson Keyonna C
Johnson Michele
Jones Dennis F
Jones Robert A
Jones William F
Kern Donna M
Kern William
Kinsey Raymond A
Kratochvil, Jr Michael P
Lee Antonio V
Letourneau, Jr William J
Maddox Edward L
Manning, Jr Alfay

Marner Everett D
Martinez Gerald M
Morgenstern, Jr Carl L
Morgenstern, Sr Carl L
Mullineaux Michael D
Paxton, Jr Robert I
Pirtle Jim G
Prouser Heather J
Raker Jason
Rao Mahil
Reynolds Michelle L
Reynolds Tomas R
Richarts Charles T
Richarts Colleen P
Richmond Claytawn L
Robinson Tangela L
Sacks Allen J
Schroen Arthur L
Schroen Eric L
Schroen, Jr Robert S
Seicke, III Frank A
Siff Ephram R
Sipes Robert W
Skelton Samuel J
Skinner, Jr Thomas A
Slosman Brian D
Smith Carl D
Smith Theresa L
Snyder Richard L
Spicer John R
Spicer Patti J
Talley Roseann
Taylor Mary A
Thompson Bianca L
Walukwicz, Jr Paul M
Weckessar Jerry L
White Larry D
Woodard Juron D
Younger Kenneth

FIRE STATIONS

Sta. 1, Towson

Sta. 8, Fullerton

Sta. 10, Parkville

Sta. 11, Hillendale

Sta. 14, Brooklandville

Sta. 17, Texas

Sta. 55, Perry Hall

Sta. 60, Parkton

Sta. 29, Providence

Sta. 30, Lutherville

Sta. 38, Long Green

Sta. 39, Cockeysville

Sta. 44, Hereford

Sta. 45, Maryland Line

Sta. 47, Jacksonville

Sta. 48, Kingsville

189

Sta. 49, Butler

Sta. 50, Chestnut Ridge

Sta. 53, Hereford EMS

WESTERN DIVISION

Sta. 2, Pikesville

Sta. 3, Woodlawn

Sta. 4, Catonsville

Sta. 5, Halethorpe

Sta. 13, Westview

Sta. 18, Randallstown

Sta. 19, Garrison

Sta. 56, Hannah More

Sta. 31, Owings Mills

Sta. 32, Pikesville

Sta. 33, Woodlawn

Sta. 34, Violetville

Sta. 35, Arbutus

Sta. 36, Lansdowne

Sta. 37, English Consul

Sta. 40, Glyndon

Sta. 41, Reisterstown

Sta. 42, Boring

Sta. 43, Arcadia

Sta. 46, Liberty Road

Sta. 6, Dundalk

Sta. 7, Essex

Sta. 9, Edgemere

Sta. 12, Middle River

Sta. 15, Eastview

Sta. 16, Golden Ring

Sta. 54, Chase

Sta. 57, Sparrows Point

Sta. 58, Back River Neck

Sta. 25, Hyde Park

Sta. 20, Cowenton

Sta. 22, Middle River

Sta. 23, Middleborough

Sta. 24, Rockaway Beach

Sta. 21, Bowleys Quarters

Sta. 26, North-Point Edgemere

Sta. 27, Wise Avenue

Sta. 28, Rosedale

Sta. 52, Middle River EMS

New Fire Academy Tower

Fire Academy

Jacksonville engine pump testing site

Index

Notes

Notes

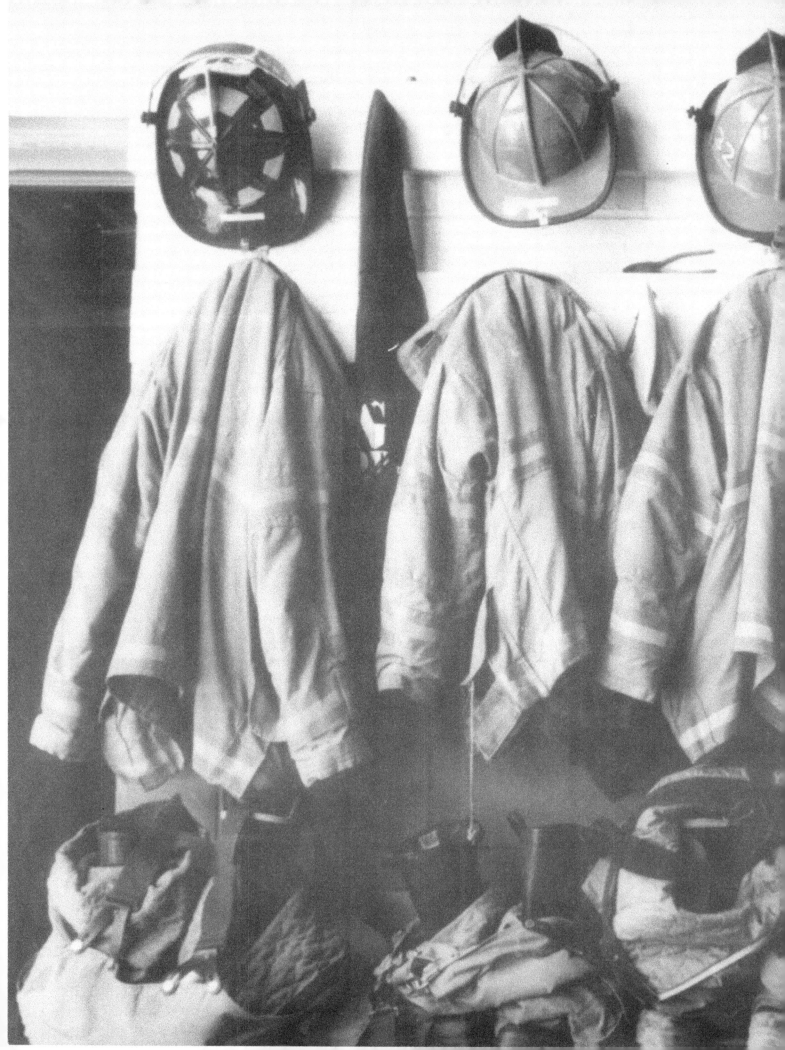

Printed in the USA
CPSIA information can be obtained
at www.ICGtesting.com
JSHW060052150824
68134JS00032B/2718